Portuguese Revolution 1974-76

Portuguese Revolution 1974-76

Edited by Lester A. Sobel

Writer: Christ Hunt

Indexer: Grace M. Ferrara

FACTS ON FILE, INC. NEW YORK, N.Y.

Portuguese Revolution 1974-76

Library of Congress Catalog Card No. 75-43353
ISBN 0-87196-223-3

9 8 7 6 5 4 3 2 1
PRINTED IN
THE UNITED STATES OF AMERICA

Contents

Introduction

THE PORTUGUESE REVOLUTION of April 25, 1974 ended a 42-year dictatorship. This long period of "benevolent" authoritarian rule had been started by Dr. Antionio de Oliveira Salazar as prime minister in 1932. It had been continued, although in a somewhat less despotic manner, by Dr. Marcello Caetano, who had succeeded Salazar in 1968 when Salazar suffered a brain hemorrhage.

The army officers who led the 1974 revolt, most of them young and all of them veterans of Portugal's unpopular thirteen-years-long colonial wars in Africa, acted from varied motives. The frustrations of fighting endlessly and inconclusively against African rebels, dissatisfactions over pay and promotion, discontent with the economic backwardness of their country, its high rate of illiteracy, the social inequities and the political rigidity of Portugal's rulers—all seemed to play a part in the organization of the officers' movement that finally overthrew the Caetano regime.

As frequently happens when a revolution takes place, the period immediately after the seizure of power was one of confusion and turmoil. During the more than four decades of one-party rule under Salazar and Caetano, nobody outside the regime had much opportunity to learn how to run a country. Even experienced political leaders without government service were relatively scarce because serious political opposition had generally been suppressed and overt dissidents had frequently been imprisoned or exiled.

The 1974 revolt, however, was seen as indicative of strong pressures that had long been building up for political change. As potential leaders surfaced and exiles began to return, competition developed among supporters of various ideologies for dominance in Portugal's evolving revolutionary government.

Although it became evident quite early that the Socialists had the greatest popular support throughout the country, the better organized Communists at first appeared to be acquiring a dominating influence in the new regime. The early Communist gains in a nation that is a member of the North Atlantic Treaty Organization were viewed with misgivings by the United States and by other Western nations.

Portugal & Its People

Mainland Portugal is a small country not quite 365 miles long and barely 130 miles in width at its widest part. Including the 1,198 square miles of the Azore and Madeira Islands, Metropolitan Portugal has an area of some 35,510 square miles.

Portugal occupies the southwest corner of the Iberian Peninsula, where it juts into the Atlantic Ocean. Its only neighbor, bordering it on the east and north, is Spain.

Despite its small size, Portugal has a varied topography, with a long coast and with lowlands, moors, plains, hills and mountains ranging in height up to 6,532-foot Serra de Estrella. The Tagus River, at whose mouth is situated Portugal's capital, Lisbon, bisects the country. North of the Tagus, the mountainous region has a moderate climate and much rain. To the south and inland, the land is drier and warmer.

Metropolitan Portugal had a population estimated at 8,782,000 as of July 1, 1974. This includes more than 550,000 inhabitants of the Azores and Madeiras. The religion of Portugal is overwhelmingly Roman Catholic, and the language is Portuguese. The early inhabitants of Portugal were Celtiberic people. The present, fairly homogeneous population evolved as a result of Roman, Suevic, Visigothic and Moorish (Arab and Berber) occupations plus Phoenician, Carthaginian, Lusitanian, German, Jewish and Negroid admixtures.

Portugal in the 11th century was a small Leonese fief that got its name from the seaport of Portus Cale (now a suburb of Oporto). Affonso Henriques (Alphonso I), a descendant of the Leonese line, founded the Portuguese kingdom in 1140 after a decade of war against Christian and Moorish claimants to the area. Further war later increased the size of the kingdom. A period of exploration and discovery in the 14th and 15th centuries added the Azores and Madeira to the kingdom as well as the overseas territories of Angola, Mozambique and Portuguese Guinea on the African continent, Sao Tome and Principe Islands in the Gulf of Guinea, the Cape Verde Islands in the Atlantic off the African coast, Macao on the Chinese coast, Portuguese Timor in the Indian Ocean, Goa, Diu and

Damao in India (India took back these three small Indian provinces in 1961) and Brazil in the New World (Brazil won its independence in the 19th century).

The early 20th century dictatorship of Joao Franco—a regime known in Portugal as the *dictadura*—ruled Portugal from May 19, 1906 until the assassination of King Carlos I and the Crown Prince Luis Feb. 1, 1908. Manoel II, Carlos' younger son, was acclaimed king by the Cortes May 6, 1908, but he was overthrown by the revolution of Oct. 3, 1910.

The revolution of 1910 ended the monarchy and established a republic. The following years were politically chaotic and marked with repeated changes of government and frequent revolts.

Dr. Antonio de Oliveira Salazar, a university professor, was brought into the government as minister of finance in 1928 with the mission of restoring financial sanity to Portugal. Salazar became prime minister in 1932, and he transformed Portugal into a "corporate republic" under a new constitution in 1933. Salazar, who assumed dictatorial powers, ruled Portugal until his brain hemorrhage, which brought Marcello Caetano to power Sept. 27, 1968. It was the less authoritarian "dictatorship" of Caetano that was overthrown by the military revolution of April 25, 1974.

Americans Fear Communist Trend

Following the overthrow of the Caetano regime, an early leftist trend and Communist political influence on Portugal's new military rulers aroused serious misgivings in Western capitals but especially in the United States.

U.S. Secretary of State Henry A. Kissinger stated a fairly widespread Western view at a press conference March 26, 1975. He said that the U.S. was "disquieted by an evolution in which there is a danger that the democratic process may become a sham, and in which parties are getting into a dominant position whose interests we would not have thought necessarily friendly to the United States. . . . What seems to be happening now in Portugal is that the Armed Forces Movement, which is substantially dominated by officers of leftist tendencies, has now appointed a new cabinet in which Communists and parties closely associated with the Communists have many of the chief portfolios. . . . [A leftist trend] will of course raise questions for the United States in relationship to its NATO policy and to its policy toward Portugal."

Mansfield Report—U.S. Senate Democratic leader Mike Mansfield of Montana visited Portugal in August 1975. In a report to the Senate Foreign Relations Committee the following month, Mansfield noted that ''fear has been expressed that a Communist-infiltrated government in Lisbon could be a conduit for vital defense secrets from NATO to the Soviet Union. It is hard to envision a nation of Portugal's size and open temperament as some sort of Trojan horse, nevertheless in November 1974 the North Atlantic Council cancelled a meeting of the NATO Nuclear Planning Group . . . apparently because of this fear. . . .'' Mansfield's report summarized his findings and impressions of Portugal within a year and a half of the 1974 coup. According to Mansfield's report:

The Portuguese officers—many of them young captains and majors—who organized the Armed Forces Movement (MFA) within the military and later carried out the revolution of April 25, 1974, were motivated at first by discontent over pay and promotion. These grievances rapidly expanded into dissatisfaction with the prosecution of the wars in Africa and into conviction of their futility and wastefulness. The political concepts adopted by the revolutionary officers ran a gamut of philosophies—some of them sophisticated and some naive and vaguely formulated. As veterans of the African wars, these professional officers saw that the Portuguese conscripts who were sent to Africa were economically and socially deprived and educationally ignorant. Portugal itself was seen by many as part of the ''Third World,'' undeveloped with an exploited and illiterate peasantry.

The revolution carried out by the MFA on April 25, 1974 . . . received virtually the universal backing of the Portuguese armed forces and much of the general population. The immediate motivation for the revolution was a desire by the MFA to end the dictatorial government as well as to terminate the costly and futile colonial wars, and the policies responsible for them. Their longer term goal was the building of a socialist and classless society. While the ultimate form of socialism has still not been defined in agreed terms by the MFA, it is thought of as something distinctly Portuguese. . . .

During the four decades of one-party dictatorship under Salazar and Caetano the Portuguese had no experience with West European-style or any other kind of representative government. President Francisco da Costa Gomes subsequently said, ''. . . we inherited political ignorance from the previous regime. . . .'' Thus the destruction of the dictatorial government left a political vacuum in which the Portuguese political parties had to organize themselves and find their constituents and the entire nation had to determine where it wanted to go, to create the government machinery to get there and to learn how to operate it. To guide the nation through this transition and learning period the MFA constituted itself the trustee of national security and governmental power. . . .

Immediately after the overthrow of the Caetano government, a number of governmental and extra-governmental organs were exercising different and overlapping responsibilities. Today the confusion has been somewhat lessened but not fully dispelled. . . .

The political choices facing the country have become more sharply defined since April 1974. Out of the welter of philosophies and viewpoints represented in the Armed Forces Movement and by the political parties which sprang into activity after the revolution, three major political currents have emerged:

(1) *The Communists*—They have had a strong foothold in the MFA and in the

government where their interests have been mainly represented by Vasco dos Santos Goncalves. The Communist Party, which has had considerable power in certain governmental ministries, especially Education and Labor, in the labor unions and in the communications media, cultivated and clung closely to the MFA. . . . It is evident that the Communist Party has recently lost ground. . . .

(2) *The Nationalist Left*—This is a loosely defined group of influential officers in the MFA. Their views are reflected in part in the "political action plan" issued by the MFA in June. This plan advocated establishment of popular organizations of direct democracy outside the parties which could be formed into local assemblies representing the people. To show its disdain of the pluralistic party process this group asked voters to cast blank ballots in the April elections as a sign of support for the MFA. Only about 7% of the voters chose to do so. The group rejects East European forms of communism with their large state bureaucracies. Some favor, in foreign policy, a nationalistic role apart from the great powers and call for Portugal's alignment with the "Third World."

Brig. Gen. Otelo de Saraiva de Carvalho, the security chief, who is prominent in this group, issued a document in August 1975 which while condemning the Communists also criticized the parties and the April elections. It advocated the idea of revolutionary neighborhood and worker councils which would eschew national elections, bypass the parties and be the base of unified political power in the country.

(3) *The Pluralist Parties*—These are the democratic political parties, principally the Socialists and the Popular Democrats, and a group of "moderates" in the MFA who advocate free elections with political parties representing the people in a parliament. They generally agree that a form of socialism should be achieved through democratic procedures. In the April elections the democratic parties received an overwhelming majority—Socialist Party, 38%; Popular Democratic Party, 26%; Center Social Democratic Party, 8%.

The principal political and ideological currents in the MFA, which is still very much in charge of the country. . . , are deeply divided and difficult to reconcile. The political parties also reflect profound conceptual differences. The Nationalist Left, the democratic parties and the moderate officer group, and the Communist-allied group all have different approaches to the political, economic and social future of Portugal. It is inevitable that any pluralistic government in Portugal will have to be based on compromise of a substantial order if it is to remain viable. . . .

Until the coup of April 25, 1974, . . . Portugal's economy was dominated by a few families (Portugal's "twenty families") and the Salazar-Caetano regime. This government-business power center promoted reasonably steady economic growth. Nevertheless, Portugal remained the least developed country in Europe. Moreover, the benefits from Portugal's economic growth which were not eaten up by Lisbon's colonial wars accrued largely to the small cluster of controlling families. Very little filtered down to the rest of the population in wages or social programs. . . .

One of the principal goals of the April revolution was to tear down the "monopolies" and to spread economic benefits more evenly throughout the population. This goal was translated initially into more power and economic benefits for workers. Although the rhetoric of the revolution became increasingly inflammatory the structure of the economy remained fundamentally unchanged until March 1975. Following . . . an attempted coup of March 11, 1975 . . . , a more radical program of socialization was inaugurated in Lisbon.

The revolution's net impact on the Portuguese economy has thus far been destabilizing, if not destructive. Old economic structures are being torn down, but effective new ones have not yet been devised to take their place. . . .

In 1973 the Portuguese GNP [gross national product] grew by 8.1%, down from 8.7% in 1972. Real growth of the Portuguese GNP in 1974 dropped to around 2 to 3 percent, and by the government's own reckoning Portugal will experience negative growth in 1975. . . .

Some of the factors which enter into this trend include the fact that there is not a skilled bureaucracy capable of running nationalized industries efficiently and many worker takeovers of businesses have resulted in loss of management skills. . . .

What economic improvements Portugal has managed in the midst of political turmoil have been severely devalued by the inflation. In 1974 Portugal's inflation rate increase was the highest in Western Europe. . . .

Portugal's economic problems are compounded further by rising unemployment. The combination of workers out of work due to the slowdown in the Portuguese economy, the flow of refugees from the former colonies, the discharged conscripts from the military forces and Portuguese workers who have lost their foreign jobs as a result of the worldwide recession, is swelling unemployment. . . .

In the past Portuguese nationals have gone in large numbers to other countries to find jobs and this practice has provided an important escape valve for unemployment. In the early 1970s the worker migration was on the increase, reaching about 45,000 a year in 1973. According to official figures, however, emigration decreased by 25% in 1974 and in 1975 is falling by another 50%. Decreasing emigration, the migration back from the colonies and other factors have caused a rise in Portugal's population from a little over 8 million in 1973 to about 9 million at present. The large number of Portuguese now pouring into the country from Angola . . . is adding seriously to the unemployment problem. . . .

One of the proclaimed goals of the revolution was to establish a Portuguese brand of socialism. The precise form of socialism has never been delineated and there is no long-range economic and social program presently guiding the Portuguese government in its socialization policy. . . .

Before that coup the number of business seizures that had taken place was very few. Afterwards, the government plunged into a series of nationalizations, starting with the banks and insurance companies. Because these were sources of credit for business and industry the government thus obtained control, indirectly at least, of a large portion of the economy. Other nationalizations that followed included railways and the national airline, oil refining and distribution companies, electric power, petrochemical, shipping and cement.

The government has also gained control or partial control over many other enterprises. Whether sought or not, government loans have become a feature of the economy, more and more necessary as businesses have been pressed or have been forced into bankruptcy by the decline in the economy. Government officials have been appointed to the management of some companies. This type of government intervention has been in addition to or sometimes parallel with seizures of businesses by workers and labor unions. One of the major consequences of the nationalizations and other types of takeovers has been decreased production and productivity.

The Portuguese government has repeatedly stressed that it would like to stimulate foreign investment and has exempted foreign firms from nationalizations and from the other government and labor "interventions." That does not change the fact, however, that foreign businesses have been affected by the depressed economic conditions in Portugal and by labor agitation. . . . For the present, new foreign investment has come to a halt.

In a military sense Portugal's contribution to NATO has been minimal. The pre-

revolutionary regime spent 40% of its budget on defense but almost all of this allo-
cation was eaten up in the wars in the African colonies. Now that decolonization is
almost complete . . . , the Portuguese armed forces are immersed in politics in the
homeland. It should be noted that as a military force, much of their equipment is of
ancient vintage or worn out, and the state of their training is uneven.

Portugal is committed to furnish one army division to NATO, but would like to
reduce even this contribution. It is expected that Portugal would also supply naval
and air forces to NATO although their equipment is outdated. Portugal now con-
tributes one destroyer-type vessel to NATO's Standing Naval Force Atlantic. The
most valuable assets Portugal brings to NATO at this time, are geography and
bases. The country serves as a host to NATO's Iberian-Atlantic Command (Iber-
lant), headquartered near Lisbon. While it is not actually a NATO installation, the
U.S. base at Lajes in the Azores is, perhaps, the most significant Portuguese contribution to Western defense.

Since the revolution, the Portuguese government has avowed its continued support of NATO. However, it is not inconceivable that some government might
emerge in Lisbon which would question continued Portuguese membership in
NATO. Such a Portuguese government might weigh whether it wished to continue
in NATO or perhaps modify the conditions of its participation. In some circumstances, too, a question could arise as to whether the United States and other
Western European governments would want to retain the Portuguese connections
within the alliance. . . .

Pell Report—U.S. Sen. Claiborne Pell (D, R.I.), who had lived
in Portugal 35 years previously when his father was U.S. minister
there, revisited Portugal Feb. 7-11, 1976. Pell reported to the Senate
Foreign Relations Committee the following month that "in my
view, the deep pessimism about the prospects for the survival of
democracy in Portugal was never justified, and recent events in that
country have borne out my earlier confidence expressed on the Senate floor on April 18, 1975 that the Portuguese people, because of
their innate common sense, conservatism and religious nature,
would find a way back from the precipice of Communist dictatorship. . . ." According to Pell's report:

. . . The culmination of this phase of Portugal's political development was the
failure of . . . a Communist inspired putsch of November 25, 1975 which marked
an important divide in Portugal's political life. While the continuing Communist
threat must not be underestimated, the Communists and the other Marxist parties of
the extreme left are clearly on the defensive and the democratic parties have the
upper hand.

In this new situation, the Portuguese people and their leaders are to be congratu-
lated on the way they have gotten themselves onto a relatively stable course after
an initial period of instability and violence. Any society or people that has been in
the darkness of dictatorship for more than two score years would understandably
wobble and zig-zag a bit as it emerged into the full light of freedom, just as a
person who had been locked in a dark room for a long time would find it difficult
to walk a straight line if he or she were suddenly thrust into bright daylight.

In fact, it is a remarkable achievement that in the short span of two years Portugal has overthrown an entrenched dictatorship, divested itself of a large colonial

empire, launched a far-reaching economic recovery program, established the framework for the re-establishment of democracy, begun the process of returning the military to the barracks, and stemmed a Communist coup—all with virtually no bloodshed. . . . Much remains to be done, however, and the achievements to date will not be secure until substance is given to the emerging democratic institutions and the health of the economy is restored.

Origins of the Revolution—The young military officers who overthrew the Caetano regime knew what they were against but had no clear idea of what they were for. They reacted against thirteen years of frustration in the African wars which they viewed as supporting a system of feudal capitalism which benefitted only a very small stratum of Portuguese society. The young captains and majors also were disturbed by the low level of education among the conscripts sent to Africa and by the attempts of the Caetano regime to undermine the integrity of the military by swelling the officer corps with reservists who received favored treatment in promotions.

With no democratic alternative to the Salazar/Caetano corporate state, the well organized Communists were the only ones prepared to talk the kind of language that the military plotters wanted to hear. In exploiting this receptivity to Marxism, a Communist party for the first time attempted to gain power by infiltrating a military establishment. When, after the overthrow of Caetano, the armed forces made it clear that they intended to become the "motor" of the revolutionary process, the Communists were well placed to wield influence out of proportion to their actual popular support.

The Decline of Communist Power—The Communists, however, overplayed their hand and were out-maneuvered by the Socialist Party. The Socialists extracted Communist agreement to holding elections on April 25, 1975 for a Constituent Assembly which would draft a new constitution. In return, the Socialists agreed to the establishment of a single labor confederation, *Intersindical,* although that involved the risk that the better organized Communists would take over the labor movement as part of a broader strategy to seize control of the country. The risk paid off, however, as the Socialists and the centrist Popular Democratic Party (PPD) scored a stunning victory in the Constituent Assembly elections of April 25, 1975, winning 64% of the vote and the Communist and small allied parties only some 19%. The Socialists, led by Mario Soares, were particularly successful in highlighting individual freedom as the principal issue dividing the Socialists and the Communists. . . .

After the election, Communist excesses, such as the takeover of the Socialist newspaper *Republica* and the Catholic radio station *Renascenca,* generated second thoughts about the Communist Party on the part of the military. Major Melo Antunes, who was principally responsible for developing the political ideology of the Armed Forces Movement (MFA) and is now foreign minister, mobilized military opposition to the Communist leanings of the then Prime Minister Vasco Goncalves. Vasco Goncalves was eventually induced to resign and was replaced last September by Admiral Pinheiro Azevedo, a political moderate. Then, on Nov. 25, 1975, the Communist Party made the fatal error of inspiring an attempted coup. Apparently foreseeing this possibility, Azevedo had quietly but effectively concentrated on restoring discipline and improving the effectiveness of one key army unit in Lisbon. That unit, aided by the lack of broad popular support for the Communists, broke the back of the coup attempt.

In all of the events culminating with the Nov. 25 coup attempt, the Communists miscalculated in assuming that they could capitalize on their influence in key power centers—the military, the media, and the labor movement—and quickly seize power. Moreover, they underestimated the strength and influence of the Catholic Church and the need to develop mass popular support. In the end, the good sense and determination of the vast majority of the Portuguese people prevailed. . . .

Since Nov. 25, Portugal has been moving back toward the center of the political spectrum. This movement has been so fast in fact that there is an increasing fear that the principal threat to Portuguese democracy may now come from the extreme right. An unstable political ping pong effect may thus be emerging. . . .

Rebuilding the Portuguese Economy—In blunt terms, the Portuguese economy is in a mess and getting worse. Almost all of the Portuguese government officials and political party leaders with whom I spoke told me that the greatest need is to stabilize the economy; otherwise there will be increasing threats from both the extreme left and the extreme right. The key to democratic development is therefore sound economic development.

Portugal's present economic problems are usually blamed on the radical policies pursued by the various governments established following the April 1974 revolution. To a large extent that is true, but it should also be borne in mind that Portugal has suffered from serious structural defects in its economy for many years and enjoyed an artificial prosperity under the Salazar/Caetano regime. During those years, Portugal ran a chronic trade deficit in its balance of payments, largely because of food imports. Food production declined in Portugal in the 1960s because some 60,000 people left the farms each year, primarily to take jobs in the booming economies of the European Economic Community. Receipts from tourism and emigrants' remittances covered the trade deficit and permitted the country to ignore its agricultural problem and the weakness of its export sector. . . .

Portugal's low level of unemployment was also artificial as approximately 100,000 workers a year left Portugal in the 1960s to work abroad. In 1974, over one million workers, or approximately one-third of Portugal's labor force, resided abroad, including in the African colonies. The swollen ranks of the civil service and the armed forces fighting in Africa further relieved pressure on the Salazar/Caetano regime to develop employment opportunities at home. . . .

When the April 1974 revolution occurred—it could not have come at a worse time economically—the international economy was deteriorating rapidly, oil prices were rising, Portuguese exports—notably textiles—were falling, and because of declining job opportunities abroad the export of Portuguese labor fell from an annual rate of 100,000 to 20,000 in 1974 thus requiring the Portuguese economy to provide jobs and housing for a larger work force. . . . Further layoffs of overseas Portuguese workers threatened to result in a large flow of Portuguese workers back to Portugal. After the revolution, the employment and housing problem was further exacerbated by the influx of some 350,000 refugees from Angola. . . . .

The revolutionary process clearly added to these economic woes. Workers felt exploited under the Salazar/Caetano regime and demanded higher wages and a shorter work week after the revolution. . . . Wages rose by 42% in 1974 and by 30% in 1975. At the same time consumption rose and output fell. The obvious result was inflation. . . . Food shortages also occurred, as the distribution system became dislocated and agrarian reform disrupted production patterns.

Most distressing of all, new fixed business investment plummeted in 1974 to less than one-third of the 1973 level. . . . Capital has fled Portugal and some plants have ceased production because of bankruptcy. Productive capacity, and therefore job opportunities, may thus actually be declining. . . .

The nationalization process also disrupted the Portuguese economy and contributed to the decline in investment. Although only Portuguese firms were to be nationalized, some foreign firms were illegally occupied by workers as were some Portuguese firms which, because of their small size, were supposed to be exempted from nationalization. The nationalization of banks had a particularly far reaching effect. Government officials discovered that because of the nature of the Portuguese economic structure, characterized by conglomerates of family fiefdoms and inter-locking corporate relationships, assuming control of one bank often resulted in taking control of some 150 other firms. I was told that the government acquired control of a half dozen or so newspapers in this manner.

For the most part, the relatively few families which controlled the Portuguese economy left Portugal. This exodus, together with the replacement of professional managers by workers committees in nationalized or occupied firms, created a large management void which the revolutionary regime has not been able adequately to fill. . . .

. . . Under an agrarian reform law, aimed at breaking up the large estates in the Alentejo region of southern Portugal, land holdings are limited to 1,250 acres of dry land or 125 acres of irrigated land. Holdings in excess of these amounts were expropriated and turned into cooperatives rather than divided among the individual tenant farmers who worked the land. As with nationalized industry, the criteria for expropriation were not always observed and many small farms were seized. The setting up of cooperative farms was done in the early days of the revolution under Communist leadership and became bases for Communist activity throughout Portugal. They became areas for storing arms and staging areas for the shock troops which the Communists dispatched to Lisbon and other urban areas. At one point the Alentejo, under the strong influence of the Communists and other extreme leftist groups, became virtually a state within a state.

Reaction set in, however, as farmers in the north, where small holdings are the rule and large estates few in number, joined with small farmers in the south and the discontented former tenant farmers who resented the cooperatives, in pressuring the authorities in Lisbon to suspend the agrarian reform law—threatening in one in-stance to cut off food supplies to Lisbon. . . .

. . . Many politicians of both the left and the right now recognize that the pro-cess of nationalization went too far. . . . Already, it is becoming increasingly common for the former owners of nationalized or illegally occupied firms to be called back—in some cases by the workers themselves—to restore efficient man-agement. . . .

The Church in Portugal—The Roman Catholic Church in Portugal made a con-scious decision not to become involved in the politics of the revolutionary process. Rather, it saw—and continues to see—its role as one of fostering reconciliation, defending human liberties, and encouraging the development of social conscious-ness and democratic values. The events of the past two years have had no apparent negative impact on the Church or on religious practices. On the contrary, the whole revolutionary process seems to have brought credibility to the Church and rein-forced its image. Even the Communists recognized the strength of the Church when they made a point of declaring prior to the Constituent Assembly election that the position of the Church would not be threatened if they won. The Church suffered from some wildcat seizures of parish residences and other property, and its *Radio Renascenca* was seized by workers; but there was never any government directed action against the Church, and all illegally seized properties have been restored.

The Role of the Military—Just over a year ago, the Armed Forces Movement created the Council of the Revolution as the supreme ruling body in Portugal and forced the political parties to sign an agreement concentrating political power in the Council's hands for the next three to five years. The armed forces seemed at that time firmly resolved to play an active and long-term role in governing Portugal. Since then, a dramatic change has occurred, particularly after the attempted coup of November 25. The Council of the Revolution, and indeed the military as a whole, is now dominated by so-called "operationals," officers who feel that politics should be left to the politicians and that the military should return to the barracks as soon as possible. The current military leadership feels that the military establishment was used by the Communist Party and that further military embroilment in politics could pose a threat to the survival of the armed forces as an instititution. . . .

THIS BOOK IS INTENDED TO SERVE as a record of the 1974 Portuguese revolution. It also records the events that preceded—and helped precipitate—the 1974 coup, and it details the happenings of the two years that followed as Portugal sought to find a way out of political chaos. The material that follows consists largely of the record compiled by FACTS ON FILE in its weekly reports on world events. As in all FACTS ON FILE works, care was taken to keep this volume free of bias and to make it a balanced and accurate reference tool.

LESTER A. SOBEL

New York, N.Y.
June, 1976

The Caetano Regime

Caetano Succeeds Salazar

Thirty-six years of "benevolent" dictatorship by Dr. Antonio de Oliveira Salazar ended in September 1968 when Salazar was felled by a brain hemorrhage. Salazar was succeeded as prime minister of Portugal by Dr. Marcello Caetano, who ruled until the revolution of April 25, 1974 overthrew the dictatorship.

Caetano in Office. Dr. Marcello Caetano, 62, was sworn in as prime minister Sept. 27, 1968 to replace Antonio de Oliveira Salazar, who had been in a coma since he suffered a brain hemorrhage Sept. 16. Salazar, 79, had governed Portugal since 1932. His successor had been named only after doctors had confirmed that he had little chance of recovering.

Caetano, a long-time associate of Salazar's, was a law professor and businessman. Since 1936, Caetano had been in and out of the government, and he had been assistant premier 1955–8. He left the government amid rumors of a growing rivalry with Salazar and served as rector of Lisbon University 1959–62.

After Salazar's hemorrhage Sept. 16, the 10-member Council of State had met several times to consider a successor. Portuguese Pres. Américo Deus Rodrigues Tomaz, 73, announced the apppointment of Caetano Sept. 26 after Salazar's 3 attending physicians had said the premier could not recuperate.

Salazar had been operated on for a blood clot on the brain (intercranial subdural hematoma) Sept. 6.

The clot had been caused Aug. 14 when Salazar fell from a collapsed deck chair at his summer home. Salazar was able to perform his normal functions for some time but later entered the hospital after experiencing headaches and loss of vision. After the operation, Salazar's condition improved steadily until the stroke.

Speaking after the swearing in ceremony, Caetano said that after being governed by a "man of genius," Portugal "must adapt itself to being governed by men like other men." He hinted that his rule would be more democratic than Salazar's strong-man regime. He said support for the government would, on occasions, "be sought through information, as frequent and complete as possible, in seeking to establish highly desirable communication between the government and the nation." He also said there was no need for "stubborn adherence to formulas or solutions that he [Salazar] at some time may have adopted. . . . Life is a constant adaptation." The government, he added, would not be prevented, "whenever timely, from carrying out necessary reforms." But Caetano also pledged to continue to maintain Portugal's African colonies and to show no tolerance towards communism. He said that in the emergency brought about by Salazar's illness, "we shall have to go on asking all to make sacrifices, including some liberties that otherwise we should like to see restored." "Public order," he

13

declared, "is the essential condition for the life of respectable people to go on normally, and so public order will be inexorably maintained."

Caetano's cabinet, sworn in Sept. 27, was the same as Salazar's except for these new appointments: Minister of State to the Premier—Alfredo Vaz Pinto; Defense—Gen. Horacio de Sa Viana Rebelo; Health—Lopo Cancela de Abreu; Public Works—Rui Alves da Silva Sanchez; Undersecretary of State—Cesar Moreira Baptista. (Salazar had named José Canto Moniz, 56, as communications minister Aug. 27 to replace Carlos Ribeiro.)

Dissent Surfaces, Some Liberalization Offered

Student Unrest. The first sign of student unrest since Caetano succeeded Salazar erupted in Lisbon Oct. 5, 1968. About 100 high school and university students carrying placards denouncing the political police and deportations and demanding liberty were chased by police and beaten. The demonstration followed a ceremony at the graves of the founders of the Portuguese republic set up in 1910 and dismantled by the Salazar regime.

A group of 50 prominent Roman Catholics petitioned Caetano Oct. 26 to investigate the death of a university student imprisoned for political reasons. The political police had reported Oct. 25 that the student, Daniel Campos de Sousa Teixeira, 23, had died of natural causes. The police said Teixeira had belonged to the outlawed League of Union and Revolutionary Action, and had been arrested for planning a terrorist campaign. Among the signers of the petition to Caetano were Jose Galvao Teles, a leader of Catholic Action, and Nuno Tetonio Pereiera, president of the Catholic Cultural Society.

Several hundred students protesting Teixeira's death were dispersed by police in Lisbon Oct. 31. The police action blocked a march on the Ministry of Interior.

About 2,000 students held a peaceful demonstration in front of Lisbon University Nov. 20, boycotting the ceremony opening the school year. The rally, organized by the student associations, was in protest against the dean's refusal to permit a student to speak at the inaugural ceremony. The demonstration started with a sit-in at the student canteen and ended with a sit-down outside the school building.

Government authorities Dec. 8 closed Lisbon University's Higher Technical Institute and suspended the school's student association leadership. The move followed a student call for "an unlimited strike" Dec. 9.

Soares Ends Exile. Mario Soares, a Socialist and leader of the political opposition to the Portuguese government was permitted to return to Portugal from exile Nov. 10, 1968. He had been banished to the West African coastal island of São Tomé Mar. 22.

The Lisbon newspaper of the ruling National Union explained Nov. 15 that Premier Marcelo Caetano had agreed to end Soares' deportation as a reaffirmation of the premier's "desire for greater coexistence . . . among Portuguese of all opinions, as long as they do not obey Moscow or Peiping."

On his arrival in Lisbon Nov. 10, Soares said he was "planning to resume now fully my professional and political activity within legality."

Soares took the leadership of a new opposition group whose formation was announced in a manifesto made public Dec. 17. The document, signed by 239 persons who described themselves as "representatives of the Socialist sector of national opinion," called on Premier Caetano to carry out political reforms to liberalize Portugal's dictatorial government. A copy of the manifesto had been sent to Caetano Dec. 16 with a request that he ease press censorship to permit its publication. Lisbon's newspapers however, did not report the manifesto in their Dec. 17 issues.

The manifesto called for: (1) an end to "the monopoly of power in the service of a single party"; (2) a press law guaranteeing freedom of thought and expression; (3) political amnesty for political prisoners, exiles and dismissed students and teachers; (4) abolition of detention laws that allowed preventive imprisonment for up to 6 months and indefinite jailing for "political delinquents"; (5) an election law incorporating "honest registration and control."

Earlier action against Soares & others— Soares had been arrested Dec. 13, 1967, then released March 1, 1968 and rearrested March 20. More than 100 lawyers had telegraphed protests to the justice ministry Jan. 13 against Soares' "arbitrary arrest," and a petition, signed by more than 1,000 persons and appealing for the release of Soares, was presented to the secretary of the presidency May 16.

Portuguese police May 11 arrested Dr. Raui Rego, 55, a newspaper editor and former seminarian, after confiscating copies of his anti-church and anti-Salazar book within 24 hours after it had been put on sale May 8. Rego's book, *In Favor of a Dialogue with the Cardinal Patriarch*, was in the form of 2 letters, addressed to Manuel Goncalves Cardinal Cerejeira, 79, the cardinal patriarch of Portugal, in which Rego accused the Catholic Church of "keeping absolute silence on numerous offenses to individual liberty" perpetrated by the Salazar regime. Rego was released May 20 after the reported intervention of Cerejeira in his behalf. Rego had been held by police Mar. 9-18 before the book was put on sale and was released after other Portuguese journalists had appealed to Cerejeira.

Portuguese police had arrested Francisco Sousa Tavares, a liberal Catholic leader, Jan. 18 and Urbano Tavares Rodrigues, a novelist and newspaper columnist, Jan. 19. No reason for the arrests was given, although the 2 had signed a petition in Nov. 1967 calling for an end to press censorship.

Liberalization Planned. Plans to liberalize Portuguese political procedures were made public before the end of 1968.

Caetano had proposed electoral reforms in a bill submitted to the National Assembly Dec. 4 in preparation for October 1969 legislative elections. The proposed law would extend the vote to all Portuguese who could read or write, including literate women (hitherto barred from voting) and would eliminate voting privileges of illiterates who paid more than a certain amount of taxes. The current law permitted adult women to vote only if they had a high school or university degree, were heads of families or paid high taxes.

The executive committee of the National Union resigned Dec. 4, paving the way for a shake-up of the government's leadership. All of the committee's members were ultraconservatives and closely connected with the previous Salazar regime.

Liberalization Slowed. People hoping for social and political liberalization in Portugal under the new Caetano government faced both encouragement and minor disappointment during early 1969. Socialists and other opponents of the regime were allowed to increase their activity, and they called for free elections in the scheduled October legislative balloting.

More than 3,000 persons attended an opposition rally Jan. 31 in Oporto. Many speakers were heckled by leftist youths who called for the "unity of all democrats" and who opposed any collaboration with the National Union, the country's only legal political movement. Mario Soares gave his pledge that the opposition "will not make secret negotiations to buy our entry into the National Assembly." He said that opponents of the regime could maintain their different factions and, "in the plurality of . . . diverse tendencies, will be able to find a common and united platform without a dispersion of votes, and thereby win." The sponsors of the rally sent Caetano a telegram urging these conditions for "a new political climate": freedom of the press; freedom of assembly and association; broad amnesty for political prisoners and exiles.

A series of meetings was held March 20 under the sponsorship of the National Center for Culture, run by liberal Roman Catholics. Once again, the main speakers were interrupted by leftwing dissidents.

A group of government opponents had announced Jan. 22 the formation of a Commission to Promote Free Elections. They appealed to Caetano to guarantee open legislative elections. The commission asked Caetano March 25 for official status and warned that violence might be unavoidable without political reform in Portugal.

Following the funeral of opposition leader Antonio Sergio de Sousa Jan. 26, demonstrators opposing the regime had marched through Lisbon streets shouting "Desert! Desert!" in front of a military hospital and "End the war in Africa!" They were dispersed by armed police.

Reacting to the demand for free elections, Interior Minister Antonio Manuel Goncalves Rapazote had said at Castelo Branco Jan. 24 that "our political structures do not admit the schemes of parties, their programs and their methods. Our basic laws do not acknowledge their existence." The New York Times reported Feb. 16 that Rapazote had said the previous week that the government would not tolerate strikes and would "intervene, with the appropriate means, to prevent the maneuvers of those persons who want to disturb the rhythms of work and jeopardize the national economy." Foreign Minister Alberto Franco Nogueira was quoted as saying: Dialogue between the government and an opposition could lead to "generalized anarchy"; "contestation destroys authority," and its final aim "is the socialization of chaos."

Increased Opposition Activity. A meeting of groups opposed to the Caetano regime, the first opposition meeting authorized by the government since 1957, was held in Aveiro May 16–18, 1969 amid Socialist calls for a "broad democratic front" to challenge the regime in the elections.

A total of 204 Socialists, including Mario Soares, had issued a manifesto May 13 appealing to anti-regime factions to join in a common platform and in common electoral committees. Criticizing the Caetano government as "Sal-

azarism without Salazar," the Socialists proposed a platform calling for guarantees of a free press and individual liberties, a progressive economic policy, and a solution to the African guerrilla wars within the principle of self-determination for Portuguese territories in Africa. The manifesto was aimed at the Liberal Catholics, Republicans, and clandestine Communists who were to be represented at the Aveiro congress.

The congress was organized by the government committee in charge of opposition electoral campaigns for the fall elections. About 1,500 intellectuals, political militants and students heard rare public denunciations of the regime in a program of 56 speakers headed by Rodrigues Lapa, a professor of literature and president of the congress, who charged that many Portuguese were "strangers in their own land." The congress ended after approving a 14-point plan for democratic action, including establishment of political parties, amnesty for political prisoners, guaranteed freedom for union representation and improved electoral laws.

Premier Caetano, however, in a New York Times interview published May 19, indicated that he would not permit opposition political parties. He said "the opposition is able to express itself in more than one way and to exert its social influence."

Interior Minister Manuel Goncalves Rapazote said June 27 that opposition candidates would be permitted access to the voting lists in the fall elections, a privilege usually reserved to the ruling National Union. Rapazote, in a television address, guaranteed equal treatment for all candidates, but warned the opposition to confine itself to local issues and not to attack the constitution or the foundations of the regime.

A group of monarchists made up of 50 leading lawyers, professors, and businessmen May 24 announced the formation of a new movement, Portuguese Renovation, aimed at restoration of the monarchy overthrown in 1910. The traditional monarchist movement, the Monarchist Cause, supported the regime.

A seven-point manifesto published May 26 and signed by 829 industrialists, pledged support for Caetano and urged a liberalization and modernization program.

Lisbon police July 6 blocked a meeting of opponents of the Caetano regime. The meeting had been called to discuss the fall elections but was interrupted before it could do so, according to AP reports.

Iberian Socialist Alliance. Leaders of Socialist movements in Spain and Portugal agreed May 30 in Lisbon to coordinate action for the restoration of democratic rule in their two countries. It marked the first formal agreement between Iberian opposition forces since the Spanish Civil War.

The agreement was announced in a communique signed by Mario Soares of Portugal and Prof. Enrique Tierno Galvan, Spanish Socialist leader.

Student Victory. Striking students at Coimbra University, after two months of protest, won a victory June 15 when the government lifted the suspension of eight student leaders.

The students had been suspended April 23 on charges of not showing proper respect to President Americo Rodrigues Tomas. Officials had refused April 17 to allow a student representative to participate at the dedication of a new building during a visit by Tomas.

More than 5,000 of the 7,200 students boycotted classes in defiance of a general ban on strikes until the university was closed May 6. Final examinations were held under police guard but were boycotted by nearly all students June 2–14.

Exiled Bishop Returns. Bishop Antonio Ferreira Gomes returned to Portugal June 19, 1969 and to his priestly duties at Oporto July 5 with the permission of Premier Caetano.

Gomes, 63, had been exiled 10 years previously for a letter critical of the regime to former Premier Salazar.

Anti-Regime Leader Captured. Herminio da Palma Inacio, leader of the clandestine League of Union and Revolutionary Action (LUAR), was captured in Madrid June 26. He had escaped from an Oporto political prison May 8. Palma had been captured in August 1968 after illegally entering Portugal from Spain.

Election Activities Curbed. The government Aug. 9 declared illegal most of the political activity planned by the opposition for the elections. The government decree, published in the Official Bulletin, banned all election campaign committees except those that had already received official recognition.

Attorney General Manuel Maria Goncalves announced the ban at the request of the Ministry of the Interior. The decree said the so-called "democratic electoral commissions" of the opposition were illegal, and it warned that leaders and members of the committees would be subject to sanctions for "subversive activities."

The government Sept. 3 loosened some restrictions on the opposition; it permitted candidates access to the lists of the 1,800,000 registered voters and allowed the establishment of electoral commissions for the presentation of lists of candidates. But democratic opposition forces discounted this action as "merely formal concessions" and called for increased freedom of press and assembly and for guarantees of equal treatment at the polls.

(The Lisbon newspaper Diario de Lisboa Aug. 15 published interviews with democratic opposition leader Mario Soares, and Jose Guilherme Melo e Castro, chairman of the National Union, the country's only legal political movement. Censors at first had suppressed Soares' statement, but the newspaper refused to publish Melo e Castro's statement without including Soares' comments. In his statement, Soares declared that "the institutionalization of freedom" was the prerequisite for solving all other problems. Melo e Castro said education was the principal problem facing Portugal. The interviews were part of a poll on Portuguese priorities being undertaken by the newspaper.)

Caetano Rival Ousted. Premier Marcello Caetano's government July 23 dismissed Dr. Adriano Jose Alves Moreira, 47, from his post as director of the Higher Institute of Social Sciences and Overseas Policy. The government announced that Moreira had been discharged for refusing to bow to an official decision to eliminate the institute's departments of social sciences and anthropology. The government said the legality of the two departments had been questioned, and it accused the 700 students in the departments of "promoting the spread of agitation" in university quarters.

Moreira, minister of overseas territory 1961–62, had been considered a leading contender, with Caetano, to succeed Premier Salazar. Moreira had been named director of the institute in 1958.

The government action was protested by the council of Lisbon University's technical school, a parents' committee and the institute's 1,200 students, who boycotted examinations.

1969 Election: Victory for Caetano Regime

Regime Retains All Seats. Premier Marcello Caetano's ruling National Union Oct. 26, 1969 won a landslide victory in the first significantly contested Portuguese election in 43 years. Opposition groups failed to win a single seat to the 130-member National Assembly.

The National Union polled approximately 89% of the vote but candidates from opposition "electoral commissions" (political parties were banned) made strong showings in the major cities. About 18% of Portugal's 9.5 million people were eligible to vote. Since the abstention rate was estimated at 40%, only a little more than 10% of Portugal's population went to the polls.

The opposition split and presented two lists of candidates from Lisbon Sept. 16. The moderate Social Democratic list was headed by Mario Soares, the Socialist leader, whereas the Radical Democratic list was led by Francisco Pereira de Moura, a progressive Catholic. A third independent list was formed Oct. 7 around the basic platform of self-determination for Portugal's African territories.

The government Sept. 23 set down specific rules of behavior for the 28-day campaign period. All street meetings and demonstrations were prohibited. Indoor meetings could be held if police permission were secured. Posters were required to carry an official stamp and could be placed only in designated locations. Twelve of the 111 opposition candidates were barred Sept. 28, including all seven members of the opposition list in Mozambique. The campaign opened officially Sept. 28 against the background of a warning from the military that it would uphold continued right-wing rule and public order.

Riot police broke up street demonstrations in honor of Republic Day Oct. 5 and arrested 17 persons.

Opposition leader Pereira de Moura told newsmen Oct. 16 that political police had made three raids on his headquarters and had seized political literature. It was reported that Urbano Tavares Rodrigues, a novelist and opposition candidate, was beaten by armed men following a rally Oct. 15. Premier Caetano condemned the actions Oct. 17 and warned that further incidents would not be tolerated. But opposition forces contended Oct. 20 they were being prevented from printing campaign literature and voting lists. The campaign ended Oct. 23.

Former Premier Antonio de Oliveira Salazar left his home to vote. In an interview Oct. 26, Salazar said he was "waiting for complete recovery in order to engage in greater activity."

(The government Oct. 23 had expelled a seven-man delegation from the London-based Socialist International Commission that had sought to observe the elections.)

(Foreign Minister Franco Nogueira resigned his post Oct. 5 to run for election to the Assembly from Lisbon.)

■The Ministry of the Interior circulated a note Nov. 9 reminding the political groupings formed during the election period that they had ceased to exist legally and must stop all political activity.

Le Monde reported Nov. 12 that two leftist political factions had merged Nov. 9 in defiance of the anti-politics order. The new Democratic Opposition Movement was made up of the Democratic Electoral Commission and the Electoral Commission of Democratic Union. The London Times reported Dec. 5 that members of the new group were negotiating through an intermediary with Caetano to obtain "minimum conditions" for the restoration of political activity.

Caetano Ends Political Police. Premier Caetano Nov. 18, 1969 announced the the abolition of Portugal's secret political police organization, the Internal and External Security Police (PIDE).

The statement said a General Office of Security had been set up in the Ministry of the Interior to assume security functions.

PIDE, set up in 1945 with the aid of German Gestapo agents, was under the command of an army officer and had served as an immigration service and secret police organization. It had functioned as the mainstay of power for former dictator Antonio de Oliveira Salazar. Caetano had said in an Oct. 23 interview with the Lisbon newspaper Diario de Noticias that he felt "the police . . . must act within legality." Official sources said the new Office of Security would not enjoy the "broad autonomy" of PIDE, but the exact nature of its structure was not disclosed.

Exile Ends. Socialist Maria Lamas, 76, ended eight years of exile with her return to Portugal from France Dec. 3. Miss Lamas' return was not made public for several days. She reportedly had received indirect assurances from government officials that she could return from Paris, where she had lived since 1962.

Caetano Visits Brazil. Prior to the election, Premier Caetano had visited Brazil July 8–13, 1969. A joint communique July 13 reported that the two na-

tions had agreed to step up commercial and cultural exchanges proposed in 1966 accords.

Caetano met with Brazilian President Arthur da Costa e Silva to discuss ways to implement the 1966 agreements. The two leaders agreed to "intensify the interchange of information and consultations" on all international events affecting the two nations. They also agreed to expand trade, to study the possibility of creating free ports in each country, and to encourage joint Brazilian-Portuguese industrial undertakings.

Caetano failed, however, to obtain a Brazilian commitment to join in the defense of Portugal's African territories, plagued by continuing guerrilla warfare. The Portuguese premier had told guests at a state dinner July 8: "Brazil's interest can only be that Portuguese holdings be conserved, defended, and benefited, because the loss of any of them will be a common loss."

(Four Portuguese Catholic organizations had urged Caetano not to make his trip because of the Brazilian government's "pitiless persecution" of Catholic priests and laymen, according to a report in Le Monde July 12.)

Troubles in Africa

Throughout the entire period in which he served as premier, Caetano was troubled by the mounting seriousness of the rebellions in the "Overseas Provinces"—Portugal's African colonies. Portugal had the basic problem of fighting a number of small but costly and unpopular wars at a distance from the homeland. These wars magnified the regime's problems at home with an increasingly vocal domestic opposition and also heightened the widespread foreign antagonism to Portugal as one of the last remaining colonial powers.

U.N. Censure. The U.N. General Assembly Nov. 29, 1968 adopted by 85–3 vote (15 abstentions) a resolution condemning Portugal's colonial policy in Africa and appealing to all states, particularly NATO members, to withhold aid that would enable Portugal to continue to fight African nationalists. The resolution, recommended Nov. 20 by the Assembly's 4th (Trust & Non-Self-Governing Territories) Committee, also called on all states to prevent the recruitment and training of mercenaries used by Portugal and requested moral and material assistance for Africans fighting to rid themselves of Portuguese control. Portugal was also scored for ignoring past UN resolutions and for violating the economic and political rights of the African population in its colonies.

The resolutions differed from past attacks on Portugal by its use of more moderate language. In what was reportedly an attempt by the African states to enlist the aid of Portugal's Western allies, the text did not refer to Portuguese policy as "a crime against humanity," and the Security Council was not asked to implement self-determination for the colonies. The resolution merely asked the Council to pay attention to the situation. The U.S. and Britain had voted against the more harshly worded resolution in 1967 but abstained in the Nov. 29 vote.

Priests Protest. A group of 150 Roman Catholic priests and laymen conducted an all-night vigil in Lisbon's Sao Domingo church Jan. 1, 1969 in protest against Portugal's African policy.

Caetano Visits Africa. Premier Marcello Caetano visited the Portuguese African territories of Portuguese Guinea, Angola and Mozambique April 14–21, 1969. With Caetano on his trip, the first made by a Portuguese premier to the Overseas Provinces, were Overseas Territories Minister Joaquim Moreira da Silva Cunha and Cesar Moreira Baptista, secretary of state for information. Caetano made his trip at a time of continued guerrilla warfare in all three of the territories; handling these troubles took nearly 40% of the national budget and about 120,000 troops (of whom 1,868 had been killed in the fighting as of April 14, according to the Portuguese Defense Ministry).

Caetano had said in a radio broadcast April 8 that he was going to Africa to assure the territories "that all Portuguese are united in the same spirit of solidarity to sustain and defend national interests." He said that the recent surrender of Lazaro Kavandame, chief of the powerful Maconde tribe in Mozambique, was a "spectacular success" for Portugal. Caetano said that Kavandame had "realized that rebellion was unjust to Portugal and detrimental to his people, and he returned to us." He invited similar action by all rebels "who wish to collaborate in the great, rewarding task of rebuilding the Portuguese multi-racial society."

Addressing the Mozambique Legislative Council in Lourenco Marques April 18, Caetano proposed increased financial and administrative autonomy for the territories in accord with their economic and social needs. Throughout his trip, however, Caetano had stressed Portugal's firm determination to hold the overseas territories.

Arriving back in Lisbon April 21, Caetano said that he had found "love for the native land and fidelity to the one and indivisible Portugal" during his travels.

(The defection of Kavandame had been announced by Portugal April 5. In a broadcast to the African territories, the government radio reported that Kavandame had left the Mozambique Liberation Front [Frelimo] after "realizing that there would be no salvation for the Maconde except integration into the Portuguese politico-administrative system." Kavandame was said to have fled from the Frelimo headquarters in Tanzania. Speaking at an April 12 news conference in Porto Amelia, Mozambique, Kavandame claimed that Frelimo had used his people as "scapegoats of the war." He said that Frelimo had acquired arms from the U.S.S.R., Red China and other Communist countries. (The Voice of Freedom radio in Mozambique reported April 8 that Kavandame had been expelled from Frelimo in January and had fled to the Portuguese with only a handful of followers. "His influence in the region is practically nil," the report added. "The population of

Mozambique considers him to be a traitor to the cause of the Mozambican people.")

Colonialism Committee in Africa. The U.N.'s Special Committee on Colonialism held meetings in the Congo (Kinshasa), Zambia and Tanzania May 2–23. The committee heard statements from 12 petitioning groups connected with liberation movements in Angola, Mozambique, Namibia (South-West Africa) and Rhodesia. The committee also heard from observers of the Organization of African Unity (OAU), UNESCO, Argentina, Czechoslovakia and Zambia.

Censure re Raids on Zambia. The U.N. Security Council July 28, 1969 approved a resolution censuring Portugal for its alleged attacks on the Zambian village of Lotte. It demanded the immediate cessation of raids against Zambia and the repatriation of Zambian nationals seized in Angola and Mozambique. The resolution warned that the Security Council would take "other measures" if Portugal did not halt the attacks.

The vote on the resolution, introduced by Pakistan and co-sponsored by Algeria, Nepal and Senegal, was 11–0, with the U.S., Britain, France and Spain abstaining.

Portugal rejected the censure July 28 and denied the raids.

The U.N. Council had met July 18 to discuss the complaint. Zambian Ambassador Vernon Mwaanga, listing alleged incidents by Portugal since 1966, charged that Portugal had used weapons obtained from NATO allies.

Bonifacio de Miranda of the Portuguese Foreign Ministry replied that the sites bombed were within the territory of Mozambique. He said Zambia had not prevented use of its territory by guerrillas fighting Portuguese rule in Mozambique.

Zambian Foreign Minister Elijah Mudenda had told the Zambian Parliament July 11 that in the period from May 18, 1966 to June 30, 1969, Portuguese forces had committed 13 border violations and 25 air raids on Zambian territory. Two civilians were said to have been killed in a raid carried out June 30 near the Mozambique border.

(The U.N. General Assembly Nov. 21, by a vote of 97–2 with 18 abstentions, called on Portugal to implement the Declaration on the Granting of Independence to Colonial Countries and Peoples. The resolution also called on all countries to end military assistance to Portugal.

(The U.N. Security Council voted 13–0 Dec. 9 to "strongly condemn" the Portuguese authorities for acts against Senegalese territory. Only Spain and the U.S. abstained in the vote. The Council also threatened stronger measures if further incidents occurred. The Portuguese were charged with shelling the village of Samine Nov. 25.)

Complaint Vs. Sweden. The Caetano regime Oct. 14, 1969 presented a formal protest against Swedish aid to nationalist movements in Angola and Portuguese Guinea. Sweden rejected the protest Oct. 17.

A message from Stockholm Oct. 1 had informed the Portuguese government that the Swedish Social Democratic Party had decided to give financial support to rebel groups fighting Portuguese control. Portugal Oct. 9 recalled its ambassador to Sweden for consultations.

Sweden's note rejecting the protest said the aid was entirely humanitarian and was given in accordance with a U.N. resolution calling on member states to give moral and material aid to the populations of Portuguese Africa.

Mondlane Killed. Dr. Eduardo Chivambo Mondlane, 48, leader of the Mozambique Liberation Front (Frelimo), was killed Feb. 3, 1969 when a time bomb exploded in a Dar es Salaam beach house where he was working. Mondlane had led the rebel organization, pledged to free Mozambique of Portuguese rule, since he had helped found it in 1964. Frelimo's headquarters were in Dar es Salaam, and its more than 3,000 guerrillas kept some 40,000 Portuguese troops active in the northern districts of Mozambique.

Mondlane was given a Tanzanian state funeral in Dar es Salaam Feb. 6. The funeral was attended by Tanzanian President Julius K. Nyerere, national and foreign dignitaries, Mondlane's white widow, the former Janet Johnson of Downer's Grove, Ill., and their three children.

Frelimo's 10-man executive committee Feb. 12 elected the front's vice president, the Rev. Uria Simango, a Methodist minister, to succeed Mondlane. Simango maintained a closer relationship with the Chinese Communists than had the Western-oriented Mondlane (who had been educated in the U.S. and was a Methodist layman). The executive committee's communique said that Simango would hold the office until a permanent president was chosen at a meeting of the 40-man Frelimo central committee.

Mondlane had said in Khartoum, Sudan Jan. 22 that his Frelimo guerrillas were disrupting work on the huge Cabora Bassa dam on the Zambezi River.

Mondlane had said that the Cabora Bassa dam was intended to provide cheap electrical power for Mozambique, Rhodesia and South Africa and to allow a large influx of Portuguese settlers into Mozambique. He said the $315 million dam would involve contracting companies from the U.S., Japan and other countries and that construction was scheduled to begin in the summer.

A Frelimo communique from Dar es Salaam Feb. 24, 1970 promised fresh guerrilla action to stop the work on the Cabora Bassa dam. It charged that the project facilitated cooperation between "Southern racist countries" by opening water transport, stimulating reciprocal labor and banking agreements and giving rise to the distribution of branches of firms, "all of which will be accompanied by arrangements for the mutual defense of such interests."

Two thousand Portuguese soldiers, the second convoy brought to Mozambique in less than a month, arrived in Beira Feb. 25. A Feb. 27 report in the French newspaper Le Monde said the Portuguese forces were planning a wide-spread offensive against guerrilla operations in the north.

The Portuguese command in Lourenco Marques announced June 22 that "the first of a series of operations" against the rebels had been started June 10.

Frelimo had been split by leadership rivalries ever since Mondlane's death. Simango had accused Marcellino Dos Santos and Samora Moise Machel, his partners in the triumvirate that led Frelimo, of attempting to assassinate him, of having executed potential rivals within Frelimo and of fostering "tribalism and regionalism."

In a defeat for Simango, Frelimo May 22, 1970 chose Machel as president and Dos Santos as vice president.

Angolan Rebellion. In 1968, the two major African rebel groups in Angola were the Angolan Popular Liberation Movement (Movimento Popular de Libertacao de Angola, or MPLA), a nationalist guerrilla movement headed by Agostinho Neto and with headquarters in Brazzaville, the Congo, and the Angolan Revolutionary Government in Exile (Governo Revolucionario de Angola no Exilo, or GRAE), headed by Holden Roberto.

Radio Brazzaville had announced March 10, 1968 that MPLA had held its first regional assembly inside Angola. The broadcast said the assembly had agreed on:

(1) The need to follow a strategy based on a prolonged struggle against the Portuguese colonial government.

(2) The reactivation of "political organization in towns by setting up clandestine cells controlled . . . by national or regional politico-military bodies."

(3) Stepped-up political mobilization efforts in Cabinda, a neighboring Portuguese colony.

(4) Studying the possibility of bringing Angolan whites into the MPLA as "sympathizer-members."

(5) Fighting tribal differences between the north and south.

(6) The need to take account of "the open counter-revolutionary and antinational activity of certain puppet organizations of a tribal nature" supported by Portugal.

(7) The development within Angola of a "war economy capable of creating conditions of self-sufficiency."

(8) The need for development of a primary education system in Angola and for transfer of the MPLA's center for "crash education programs" from Brazzaville to Angola.

MPLA accused GRAE March 27 of ordering the massacre of MPLA members held in GRAE camps. According to an Agence France-Presse report from Brazzaville, the MPLA held the Congo (Kinshasa) government responsible for all Angolans left in the control of GRAE.

Portuguese Guinea: fighting stepped up.

The military governor of Portuguese Guinea July 7, 1970 made an offer of guaranteed security for all "terrorists who wish to surrender." Five days later, a guerrilla group crossed into the territory from Senegal to launch a major attack against the Portuguese.

A Lisbon broadcast July 7 said the governor's offer had been made in reply to a radio appeal over Radio Conakry by the African Party for the Independence of Guinea and Cape Verde (PAIGC). Members of the PAIGC, according to the Lisbon report, had asked for amnesty, citing military failures and division within the movement as reasons for their desire to return. The governor, Brig. Antonio de Spinola, replied that he "absolutely guaranteed" no harm would come to those who returned.

A PAIGC spokesman July 8 denied that the guerrillas had asked for a safe return. The spokesman said it was "a propaganda maneuver." The statement was monitored by the British Broadcasting Corporation from a Radio Free Portuagal broadcast.

The Portuguese military command reported July 16 that a guerrilla force of more than 300 had crossed from Senegal July 12-13 in a surprise raid on the village of Pirada. Two other guerrilla groups attacked from Senegal at other points. Fifteen persons were killed in the raid on Pirada. Portuguese troops retaliated July 14 with artillery bombardments in the province of Casamance in Senegal.

The action prompted the Senegalese government to ask an emergency U.N. Security Council meeting to deal with the situation. In another action, Senegal ordered reinforcements into Casamance July 17. Senegalese President Leopold Senghor said in an interview July 20 that France should "intervene diplomatically" to halt Portuguese operations in Senegalese territory. Senghor cited a French-Senegalese treaty as a basis for his demand.

■ An announcement Nov. 21, 1969 said Portuguese soldiers in Portuguese Guinea had captured Capt. Pedro Rodriguez Peralta, a Cuban army officer, during a clash with nationalist guerrillas. The Cuban had reportedly admitted that he and other officers had been commissioned by the Cuban government to serve with PAIGC. A military court in Lisbon April 26, 1971 sentenced Rodriguez to 26 months in prison on charges of serving as a PAIGC instructor. The prosecution had failed to prove that Rodriguez had actually fought against Portugal or that he had acted on Cuban government orders.

■ It was reported in a Portuguese army dispatch Jan. 5, 1971 that 895 guerrillas had been killed in Portuguese Guinea during 1970. The report said that 740 had been wounded and 86 taken prisoner, including four Cuban mercenaries. Government losses were said to be fewer than 100 dead. The army said it had seized 49 tons of rebel military supplies, mainly of Soviet or Chinese origin.

■ The Portuguese military command in Bissau, capital of Portuguese Guinea, charged Jan. 23, 1971 that PAIGC was using bases in neighboring Senegal and the Republic of Guinea for attacks on Portuguese Guinea.

U.S. Policy Statement. U.S. Secretary of State William P. Rogers said in an African statement March 28, 1970 that the U.S. sought a "relationship of constructive cooperation" with African countries. "We want no military allies," he said, "no spheres of influence, no big-power competition in Africa. Our policy is a policy related to African countries and not a policy based upon our relations with non-African countries."

The statement was submitted to President Richard M. Nixon, who said in a message, that he "wholeheartedly approved" of the policy statement.

Rogers' statement declared that the U.S. would "work to bring about a change of direction in parts of Africa where racial oppression and residual colonialism still prevail." While there were "no easy solutions" in sight for "the problem of southern Africa," it said, "we take our stand on the side of those forces of fundamental human rights in southern Africa as we do at home and elsewhere."

Rogers' statement expressed support for the right of self-determination for the peoples of the Portuguese territories of Mozambique and Angola, but it said "resort to force and violence is in no one's interest." It cited the Portuguese "policy of racial toleration" as "an important factor in this equation." The U.S. intended to maintain the embargo on the shipment of arms for use in these territories.

Quarrel with Vatican. A sharp rift opened between the Portuguese regime and the Vatican July 1, 1970 when Pope Paul VI met with three leaders of liberation movements in Portugal's African territories.

The three—Agostinho Neto of MPLA, the Movement for the Freedom of Angola; Amilcar Cabral of PAIGC, the African Party for the Independence of Guinea and Cape Verde; and Marcellino Dos Santos, leader of Frelimo, the Mozambique Liberation Movement— were in Rome to attend a conference sponsored by left-wing Italian groups. The three-day conference, on "solidarity with the peoples of the Portuguese colonies," had issued a final communique June 28 denouncing Portugal and accusing the North Atlantic Treaty Organization, and in particular the U.S., West Germany and France, of supporting Portugal in "colonial wars."

The Pope's brief meeting with the three rebel leaders prompted the Portuguese government July 3 to recall its ambassador to the Vatican, Eduardo Brazao. Before returning to Lisbon, Brazao delivered a formal protest note to Vatican Secretary of State Jean Cardinal Villot.

L'Osservatore Romano, the Vatican newspaper, made no direct reference to the Portuguese protest in an article July 3. Similarly, it made no reference to Dos Santos' comments, at a July 2 press conference, that the Pope had said the church

"backed the struggle for . . . national independence" and that he would pray for the rebel leaders' cause. L'Osservatore said of the meeting: "The Holy Father greeted them [the three African leaders], and exhorted them to fidelity in the Christian principles in which they were educated." It noted that "the Pope, owing to his mission, receives all those who request the comfort of his blessing."

The Lisbon government July 5 broke its four-day public silence on the Vatican quarrel with a statement that it awaited "convincing explanations" from the Holy See. The government announcement said censorship had been imposed on the story so that the reports "should not alarm the conscience of the country."

Premier Marcello Caetano announced July 7 that an explanation had come from the Vatican and that relations between Lisbon and the Holy See had returned to their old cordiality. Caetano said the Vatican had satisfactorily explained that there was "nothing political" in the Pope's audience with the three African leaders.

Ambassador Brazao was reported Aug. 1 to be back at his post in Rome.

Churches Aid Guerrillas. The World Council of Churches announced Sept. 3, 1970 that it would grant $200,000 to groups fighting racism, including African liberation movements. The decision was made by the council's executive committee at a meeting near Frankfurt, Germany.

A "Special Fund to Combat Racism" would issue grants of $2,500 to $20,000 each to 19 groups, 14 of them associated with Africa. These included four groups fighting in Angola against the Portuguese and Frelimo in Mozambique.

Nonaligned vs. Portugal. The third world summit conference of nonaligned nations was held in Lusaka, Zambia Sept. 8–10, 1970. The 14 resolutions approved included attacks on Portuguese policy in Africa.

The conference opened Sept. 8 with Zambian President Kenneth Kaunda presiding. Ethiopian Emperor Haile Selassie set the tone for the conference with an opening speech criticizing white minority regimes and calling for specific action against South Africa and Portugal. Adopted resolutions included one submitted by Haile Selassie on decolonization. The resolution called for breaking diplomatic ties with South Africa, Portugal and Rhodesia; enforcement of trade embargoes and refusal of landing rights and shipping rights to the three countries; and contributions to a special fund for African nationalist movements;

'Invasion' of Guinea. President Sekou Toure of Guinea charged Nov. 22, 1970 that his country was being invaded by "Portuguese forces" and by "hundreds and hundreds of Portuguese and other mercenaries." Toure claimed that an attack on the capital city of Conakry had been "repulsed." He appealed to Secretary General U Thant for the immediate support of United Nations troops.

Conakry Radio quoted a prisoner, identified as Capt. Ambroise Fernando, as saying that the raiding force arrived in more than 10 heavily armed warships. The aim of the mission, Fernando reportedly said, was to seize the Guinean Defense Ministry. Another prisoner was quoted as giving the total size of the force as 350, including 50 Guinean guides. One of the Guineans, who was captured by Toure's forces, said the attackers set sail Nov. 20 in six boats from an undisclosed location and arrived off Guinea Nov. 21, according to the Conakry broadcast.

The Portuguese government formally denied Nov. 22 that Portuguese troops were involved in the reported invasion. The Foreign Ministry statement rejected the charge dealing with Portuguese forces but did not comment on the accusation that "Portuguese mercenaries" were involved.

The U.N. Security Council, meeting in special session Nov. 22, reviewed the appeal made by Toure. U.N. sources reported that Thant had received a dispatch from his representative in Conakry to the effect that an "external intervention" was taking place. The Portuguese were not named. The Council adopted a resolution Nov. 23 calling for the immediate end of all armed attacks and for the dispatch of a fact-finding team to Guinea.

In messages from Conakry Nov. 23, the deaths of several Europeans were reported. The East German Foreign Ministry announced that the deputy chief of its embassy in Guinea had been killed. One West German was also killed and two others wounded, according to West Germany's foreign office. The U.S. said one Peace Crops volunteer had been slightly wounded but the estimated 300 U.S. citizens in the country were reported safe.

In a new charge Nov. 23, Radio Conakry said that three members of the banned Guinean opposition party were directing the invasion from Abidjan, capital of the Ivory Coast. The three were identified as Nabi Youla, Ibrahim Kake and a man identified only as Diallo. But the broadcasts continued to assert that "the second day of the war that Portuguese imperialism imposed on us" had begun with a new attempt to land troops.

The Soviet Union Nov. 23 joined in denouncing Portugal, charging it had committed "a criminal act of aggression" against Guinea. In Washington, a State Department spokesman said there were "strong suggestions . . . of outside involvement." Nigeria announced it had "clear evidence of foreign involvement" and offered military assistance.

Guinea accepted the offer Nov. 24 as offers of aid came also from the other member nations of the Organization of Senegal River Riparian States—Mali, Senegal and Mauritania. A five-member U.N. fact-finding mission left New York Nov. 24 for Guinea.

A Nov. 24 London Times report said observers who had arrived in Dakar from Conakry claimed that the attackers had captured the Camayenne prison, freeing political prisoners. The observers said the raiders had also damaged the headquarters of the African Party for the Independence of Guinea and the Cape Verde Islands (PAIGC), the nationalist guerrilla movement. A Nov. 27 report said the raiders had shot their way through a Conakry residential district in search of Amilcar Cabral, leader of the PAIGC, who was out of the country at the time.

Dakar reports Nov. 28 said the invaders blew up the president's residence, Villa Bellevue, but President Sekou Toure escaped unhurt. The raiders also overran two military camps but were pushed back by Guinean reinforcements.

President Toure charged Nov. 28 that Portuguese forces had invaded his nation a scond time and called on the U.N. to investigate. Toure charged that about 200 Portuguese troops were involved in the Nov. 27 raid which occurred in the frontier region of Kouandara. Reports Nov. 29 said civilians in Conakry were being pressed into militia service and arms were being distributed. The government Nov. 30 claimed more than 50 mercenaries had been killed in the fighting and 100 captured.

Amid the virtual news blackout on the incidents, Toure Nov. 25 appealed to foreign diplomats to give evidence to the U.N. mission, which arrived that day, about the developments that they had followed "stage by stage." He coupled that appeal, broadcast over Radio Conakry, with a request for arms and planes from "friendly countries outside Africa." Meanwhile, arms and ammunition were flown from Nigeria Nov. 27 in the wake of a call by Organization of African Unity chief Diallo Telli for all OAU members to send military aid.

The U.N. team, headed by Nepalese delegate Maj. Gen. Padma Bahadur Khatri, was received coolly by Toure, who said he regretted the U.N. had not agreed to his request for troops.

Members of the mission interviewed several African prisoners in Conakry, who reportedly said they were soldiers in the Portuguese army in Portuguese Guinea. The mission saw no white prisoners; the government asserted, however, that white prisoners were taken but were too seriously wounded to be interrogated. The U.N. mission, which returned to New York Nov. 29, reportedly concluded that only a major foreign power with well-organized and well-equipped armed forces could have directed the precision landing of commando units.

OAU delegates met in Lagos, Nigeria Dec. 9-11 in a special session on the Guinea situation. In resolutions adopted Dec. 11, the OAU condemned NATO countries for complicity in Portugal's actions against Guinea and ordered steps to strengthen guerrilla organizations fighting against Portugal. But the conference failed to produce a unified African command, a proposal which had been brought up in closed session during the meeting.

The OAU's ministerial council heard speeches condemning Portuguese aggression in Guinea Dec. 9 during the only public session of the conference. Nigerian head of state Maj. Gen. Yakubu Gowon told the delegates that the invasion was "an insult...and above all, a challenge to Africa." He attributed the invasion to "Portugal, her friends and their stooges" and said "it must be dealt with, with all seriousness."

The resolution condemning NATO charged its nations with complicity in "attacks by Portugal against African territories and states." The resolution declared that "all military assistance to Portugal should cease, in any framework or form whatsoever."

Other resolutions called for the establishment of a special voluntary fund "to provide financial, military and technical assistance to Guinea;" disbursement of more funds to guerrilla organizations; encouragement of unified opposition to the use of mercenary soldiers.

The proposals for a joint military command were buried in a resolution calling on the OAU defense commission to "study ways and means of establishing adequate and speedy defense of African states." Reliable sources said that the proposals for an international African military force that could be used for emergencies had been dropped in the interests of unanimity.

More Autonomy Proposed. Premier Caetano proposed to the Portuguese parliament Dec. 2, 1970 that a new constitution provide for greater local autonomy to the African territories, particularly Angola and Mozambique.

Caetano suggested that the territories be made "autonomous regions within the Portuguese unitary state." He categorically rejected any possibility that Portugal would give up the territories.

A Dec. 14 London Times report said administrative personnel in Mozambique favored the Lisbon plan. But Marcellino Dos Santos, Frelimo leader, rejected Caetano's proposals, according to a Dec. 20 report. Dos Santos said the proposals were made in answer to Frelimo's success on the battlefield, and he added that they "in no way answer to the exigencies of the people of the Portuguese territories."

Herbicide Use Denied. The U.S. State Department Dec. 11, 1970 denied a Dec. 8 report that the department had information Portugal was using herbicides to destroy food crops in Angola.

The Dec. 8 report said information from the U.S. consulate in Luanda indicated that the Portuguese had been involved in destroying crops raised by Angolan rebels. But in a statement denying that report, a State Department official was quoted as saying "we don't know what they are doing there." The spokesman added that the U.S. was not investigating the issue.

South African Offer Rejected. The London Times, in a Dec. 22, 1970 report, disclosed that South Africa had twice offered military aid to Portugal for use in that country's wars against insurgents in Africa. Sources in Mozambique said the offers, official but secret, were rejected by Portuguese authorities.

Government Action

Cabinet changes. Premier Catano revised his cabinet Jan. 14, 1970, reducing its size from 15 ministers to 10 and merging several portfolios. The ministry of state, virtually a vice-premiership, was eliminated.

Rui Manuel de Medeiros d'Espiney Patricio was appointed foreign minister, a post held by Caetano himself since the resignation in October 1969 of Alberto Franco Nogueira. The education post was taken over by Jose Veiga Simao, former rector of Lourenco Marques University in Mozambique. The ministries of national defense and army were merged, as were those of public works and communications and corporations and public health.

(Foreign Minister Patricio said July 23 that Portugal would seek to improve ties with countries adjacent to Angola, Mozambique and Portuguese Guinea. In his first news conference since taking office, Patricio said Portugal had a "constant policy" to improve ties with all African nations, but "particularly with those territories that have frontiers with our overseas provinces.")

The first woman was appointed to a post in the Portuguese government Aug. 20. Maria Teresa Lobo, an Angola-born lawyer of Goan ancestry, was named undersecretary of health.

Accord with Spain. Portugal and Spain May 23, 1970 signed an agreement extending the Iberian pact for 10 years and expanding its provisions. The agreement came at the end of a four-day state visit to Spain by Portuguese Premier Marcello Caetano. It was the first visit to Madrid by a Portuguese head of state since the Spanish Civil War.

Caetano arrived May 20 with his ministers of foreign affairs, defense and finances. Generalissimo Francisco Franco scheduled two meetings with the Portuguese premier—an indication by observers of a desire by the two countries for more significant and friendlier relations; Franco usually saw official visitors only once.

The Iberian pact, a friendship treaty reached in 1939 and extended in 1940, provided for mutual assistance in case of aggression or serious internal threats. The widening of the pact called for annual meetings of both nations' foreign ministers to discuss matters of mutual interest.

Caetano returned to Portugal May 23.

U.S. bases. U.S. Secretary of State William P. Rogers visited Portugal May 29–30, 1970 and conferred with Caetano and Foreign Minister Patricio. They agreed to resume negotiations later on U.S. bases in the Azores.

Brazilian-Portuguese agreement. Brazilian Foreign Minister Mario Gibson Barbosa and Portuguese Foreign Minister Rui Patricio signed a treaty which would grant equal rights to the nationals of each country (reported Sept. 14, 1971).

The treaty aimed at "the harmonious development of the Luso-Brazilian community" and gave Brazilian citizens in Portugal full political rights including the rights to vote and hold office, and vice versa.

Other matters included in the treaty were Portugal's approval of Brazil's claim to a 200-mile territorial water limit, a concerted effort at an international level to combat acts of terrorism, the abolition of dual taxes and the signing of a protocol on cultural exchanges.

Proposals for religious reform. The government of Premier Caetano presented a proposed law on religious liberty to the parliament Oct. 5, 1970.

The Portuguese council of bishops, in a resolution passed Nov. 14, expressed reservations about the new bill, which would reinforce the separation of church and state and strip the Catholic Church of some of its privileges. The bishops' conference particularly opposed a provision eliminating obligatory religious training in schools and obligatory attendance at religious services by members of the armed forces. Claiming that "the state cannot be neutral in the religious domain," the bishops expressed their fear that the Catholic Church would be "on the same footing" as other religions in Portugal if the bill were passed.

Caetano, answering the bishops in a Nov. 16 statement, said the proposed bill should not be a "motive of alarm" for the Catholic Church. He asserted that the provisions calling for elimination of mandatory religious education were not contrary to the Concordat of 1940 with the Vatican, which gave the Catholic Church authority over spiritual matters in the country. "The families are the natural judges of the Christian education of their children," Caetano said.

Economic growth low. A survey of Portugal's economy by the Organization for Economic Cooperation and Development, reported Oct. 16, 1970, showed that economic growth fell short of the 7% target rate set in the Third Plan. The report cited a sharp setback in agricultural harvest as well as a balance of payments surplus. The cost of living rose 10% for Lisbon and Oporto, while wages also continued to rise.

Reform group authorized. The Caetano government, after about nine months of consideration of the matter, authorized the organization of an Association for Economic & Social Development (reported Nov. 7, 1970). The group said its purpose was to promote a "profound transformation" of Portuguese society. It planned courses and also information centers and seminars, information centers and documented reports on economic and social issues. In a manifesto released by censors Nov. 4, it urged political change without revolution.

The 147 founders of the new group included Miguel de Barros Alves Caetano, son of the premier, and two government members—Commerce Minister Xavier Pintado and Deputy Planning Minister Joao Salgueiro. Prominent opposition figures in the group were: lawyer Antonio Alcada Baptista, journalist Rogerio Fernandes and architect Mario Bruxelas.

Politics & Dissent

New political movement. The fifth congress of the National Union, Portugal's only legal political organization, opened in Estoril Feb. 20, 1970. Delegates to the congress approved the formation of a new organization, the National Popular Action (ANP), as a replacement for the National Union. Members of the National Union would automatically become members of the ANP.

The congress, the first in 14 years, was opened by Albino Soares Pinto dos Reis, leader of the National Union since the illness of former Prime Minister Antonio Salazar. Dos Reis called for new life and vigor in the 40-year-old movement "to galvanize our organization."

Prime Minister Marcello Caetano was elected president of the ANP Feb. 21. Caetano characterized the new organization as a "civic association" which would seek "to bring to the conscience of the Portuguese their duties as citizens" and would "establish permanent contacts at all levels among government, the administration and the masses." While attacking socialism, the prime minister declared that Portugal could not "recoil from the prospect of reform." Of Portugal's African policy, he said: "It would not be permissible for us to abandon those of our brothers living in overseas territories, either natives of those territories or Europeans." He denied that Portugal was waging a colonial war in Africa. "We are defending order, social harmony and the labor of a population that shows each day its will to remain Portuguese," Caetano said.

(Caetano's speech coincided with a demonstration in Lisbon Feb. 21 against the war in the Portuguese African territories. Around 300 persons participated in the protest which called for "Peace in Guinea, Angola and Mozambique." Among those arrested was Mrs. Maria Eugenia Varela Gomes, wife of Joao Varela Gomes, a prominent opposition leader.)

Caetano scores Soares. In a nationwide broadcast April 9, 1970, Premier Caetano warned against left-wing groups which acted outside the law and against Mario Soares, the Socialist leader, who was accused of denigrating Portugal while abroad.

Claiming that he "did not wish to be a dictator," Caetano said he could not allow the substitution of "revolutionary groups for the authority of the state." Referring to Soares, who had been tour-

ing Latin American countries and the U.S., Caetano branded as "utterly false" the Socialist leader's assertions that "the government is forcing the defense of the overseas territories on the people." He said he would not tolerate "propaganda against the homeland." (Soares had told an audience at the Brookings Institution in Washington April 2 that Portugal was waging colonial wars in Africa, and they were an irritant to those who served in them and a drain on the economy.) A London Times report April 9 said Soares had declared he expected to be arrested on his return to Portugal.

The French newspaper Le Monde reported May 6 that Portuguese police authorities had announced that a suit would be brought against Soares on charges that he had made "false statements affecting the prestige of the nation" and "threats against the territorial integrity of the Portuguese state."

Soares exiled again—The Caetano regime ordered Soares Aug. 3, 1970 to leave Portugal within eight hours or be arrested. Soares, it was reported, crossed into Spain with his family that night.

Soares had returned to Portugal Aug. 1 to attend funeral services for his father. Security forces then told him that he faced arrest without bail on charges of "crimes against the security of the state."

Palma convicted in absentia. Revolutionary leader Herminio da Palma Inacio went on trial in absentia Jan. 7, 1970 for the biggest bank robbery in Portuguese history. Press reporting of the trial was banned.

Twenty-three persons were incriminated in the theft of an estimated $1 million from the Bank of Portugal in Figueira-da-Foz in 1967. Palma had claimed responsibility for the theft.

Sixteen of the defendants were found guilty Feb. 13 and sentenced to prison terms ranging from six months to 20 years. Six of the seven principal defendants were sentenced in absentia, including Palma, who received a 16-year sentence.

Action against others. Lisbon police Feb. 19, 1970 arrested oppositionist Salgado Zenha (who ran as a Socialist in the October 1969 elections). A police statement said Zenha had been the sole participant in a banned demonstration organized by Communist elements. The police were investigating Zenha's activities as an instigator of protests against Portugal's wars in Africa. It was the first arrest of a prominent oppositionist since Caetano came to power.

■Jose Pons Queiroz da Cruzeiro, a member of the patriotic front for national liberation, was turned over to the Portuguese political police by Spanish authorities Jan. 12, 1970. He had served a 15-month term in Spain for carrying a false passport. Spanish authorities approved the Portuguese request for extradition.

■ The Abbott Felidicade Alves, a leader of the liberal Roman Catholic movement Studies & Documentation Group (Gedoc), was arrested at his home March 20, 1970 but released on bail March 29. Another Gedoc member, the Rev. Abilio Tavares Cardoso, was arrested at his home June 16. Cardoso's lawyer said in a protest to the government that he was being impeded in preparing his case for the defense, according to a July 25 report. Joaquim Pires de Lima said he was refused permission to examine the documentation on the case, and censorship had suppressed his protest to the newspapers that the police accusation against Cardoso had not specified an offense.

■Three members of the Popular Action Front, a Marxist-Leninist faction of the Portuguese Communist Party, were sentenced May 12, 1970 to 15-20 years in prison on charges of "an attempt on the security of the state." The three men—Francisco Martins Rodrigues, Rui d'Espiney and Joao Pulido Valente—were charged with having "prepared an armed revolt against the government."

■A national committee for help to political prisoners May 14 released a circular accusing the government of continuing police repression and of ill treatment of those arrested. Another document, signed by 28 members of the Socialist and Social Democratic opposition, also charged the government with repression, particularly "against intellectuals, students, priests or politicians."

Political prisoners. The National Commission for Aid to Political Prisoners, a nonpartisan group formed in 1969, distributed a statement to foreign reporters in Lisbon Sept. 1, 1971 charging that the number of political prisoners in Portugal had increased from 79 in January to 160 by Aug. 15. It said 70 persons were serving court-imposed sentences and 90 were under preventive detention. The figures did not include detentions in Portual's African territories. The commission charged that a "brutal wave" of arrests was taking place, involving "indiscriminate jailing, torture and beating, and the systematic refusal of legal aid as well as other illegalities." The commission, consisting of lawyers and other professionals, gave legal aid to detainees and financial aid to their families.

The commission had published a letter May 5 to Premier Marcello Caetano asking, among other things, for the revocation of "security measures," of "anticonstitutional" laws authorizing police to open judicial inquiries and of Portugal's "exceptional" laws providing for special political trials.

Violence

Dissident group claims bombings. A series of bomb explosions affecting Africa-bound freighters and political and cultural installations marked the formation of a new revolutionary group pledged to violence against "the colonial war machine of the fascist government."

The group, which called itself the Armed Revolutionary Action (ARA), in a statement Oct. 27, 1970, claimed responsibility for two explosions aboard the cargo ship Cunene the day before. The Cunene, anchored at a Lisbon dock, regularly sailed the Portuguese-Africa run, carrying supplies for functionaries and military personnel of the Portuguese colonial presence in African territories. The ARA statement, distributed to foreign news agencies, said the

Cunene had been "immobilized" because it helped "supply the war of colonial oppression."

A second explosion aboard the freighter Vera Cruz at Lisbon Oct. 29 resulted in the death of one dockworker. The ARA claimed responsibility for the action, charging that the Vera Cruz was used to transport troops to the African territories.

Three bombs exploded Nov. 20, damaging the U.S. cultural center in Lisbon, the Portuguese political police training school and a dock. One man was reported killed and four others injured. Police said the dead man, who could not be identified, was responsible for the bombing of the police school and was killed while trying to set a second charge.

The dock explosion, which caused extensive damage, resulted from a bomb placed in a metal suitcase. The suitcase was to have been loaded onto the liner Niassa, scheduled to leave for Africa Nov. 21 with soldiers aboard.

A Nov. 22 report said the director of Portuguese security police attributed the bombings to the ARA. Later, in a letter to the press, the ARA claimed responsibility for the three incidents, according to a Nov. 25 report.

Observers speculated that the ARA grew out of a split within the Portuguese Communist party between the orthodox Communist hierarchy and activists dissatisfied with the party's failure to organize to overthrow the dictatorship of Premier Marcello Caetano.

The Moscow-based party leadership transmitted its philosophy over Radio Free Portugal, broadcasting from Bucharest, with claims to be the "only voice of Portuguese resistance" and denunciations of the dissidents as "romantic revolutionaries." The dissident Patriotic Front, broadcasting from Algiers over the Voice of Liberty, accused the Portuguese party of "showing more interest in imposing its control over resistance organizations than in carrying out acts of resistance."

Security police linked the new ARA to recent infiltrations reported Oct. 27. The police said 30 armed men entered Portugal illegally in August. Three of them, arrested in September, were found to be armed with Czechoslovak weaponry and were carrying "a significant quantity" of munitions.

Guerrillas raid air base. Bomb explosions in a hangar at the Tancos air base, 100 miles northeast of Lisbon, destroyed six helicopters and two training planes March 9, 1971.

The next day the ARA claimed responsibility for the sabotage, which it said had destroyed at least 14 helicopters and three training planes.

The ARA said the action was to protest "the shameful colonial war . . . waged by the Portuguese fascists and colonialists against the peoples of Angola, Portuguese Guinea, and Mozambique . . ." The statement attributed the success of the operation to "growing anticolonialist feelings among Portuguese soldiers."

Observers speculated that the ARA terrorist action had become increasingly well-organized.

Bomb explosions interrupted communications between Lisbon and the rest of the world for nearly 12 hours June 3. The blasts occurred at a telephone substation in Sacavem, a suburb of the capital, and at the main Lisbon post office. The ARA claimed responsibility for the blasts June 7.

Caetano denounces terrorism. Premier Caetano, in a nationwide TV address June 15, 1971, called on the entire nation to unite in combating sabotage and terrorism. He disclosed that incidents, earlier reported as accidents, were actually the result of sabotage. One of the most serious was an explosion April 26 on board a ship off the Mozambique coast, resulting in the death of 23 crew members.

Subversion law invoked. The government's announcement that it would invoke Article 109 of the revised constitution to halt subversive acts was reported by the New York Times Nov. 17. The constitution authorized the government to take any measures necessary to curb subversion and provided for National Assembly debate in the event of prolonged incidents. The Times report said the government had asked the assembly to debate Portugal's "state of subversion."

The government acted following bomb explosions in the new North Atlantic Treaty Organization (NATO) headquarters outside Lisbon Oct. 27 and at a NATO military base at Caparica Nov. 8.

Communists sentenced. A court in Oporto sentenced five persons belonging to a group called Communist Revolutionary Action to prison terms ranging from four to 22 months and to a deprivation of political rights for 3–5 years, the French newspaper Le Monde reported Dec. 10, 1971. They were charged with subversive activities.

Labor Unrest

Suspension of labor leaders protested. Some 20 workers' syndicates addressed a petition to the government, expressing their opposition to a court decision to suspend the leaders of a metallurgical workers' union, it was reported Nov. 20, 1970.

The union leaders had proposed a collective contract which was unacceptable to management. The Ministry of Corporations filed suit against the leaders, and the court ordered them suspended from their leadership posts. It was the first time since the promulgation of a new, looser labor law in 1969 that the government had suspended delegates elected by the workers.

The labor leaders, who represented several thousand Lisbon metallurgical workers, were replaced by an administrative commission.

The court decision to suspend the men cited a "class struggle" which it claimed was sparked by the syndicate's action. It charged that the proposed contract was contrary to the "spirit of Portuguese corporatism."

The protesting labor groups sought revocation of the court decision. In addition, the groups protested recent proposals to the labor law which would prolong the time of contract renewal, allowing the government to interfere in contract talks, especially in naming representatives to arbitration commissions.

Labor protests. Fresh labor protests were reported in 1971:

■ Nearly 3,000 saleswomen demonstrated peacefully March 15 before the National Assembly in Lisbon to demand a 44-hour work week to replace the 48-hour week. Armed policemen with dogs dispersed the demonstrators.

■ The French newspaper Le Monde reported April 10 that 21 trade union organizations sent a statement to Premier Marcello Caetano demanding the right to strike; the liberty for workers to join national or international labor organizations; and the right to elect representatives who would not be subject to suspension or dismissal. They also requested that trade unions not be subject to administrative dissolution or suspension.

■ Police clashed in Lisbon July 26 with about 1,500 bank clerks who were staging a silent protest march against the arrest of Daniel Cabrita, the secretary of their union. Police clubbed the demonstrators, who responded by throwing stones. Other clashes occurred July 27 in Lisbon and Aug. 6 in Porto.

Cabrita had been arrested June 30 and held without formal charges after sending a letter to the International Labor Organization in Geneva protesting the composition of the Portuguese union delegation, whose members, he said, had been designated by the government without adequate consultation with the workers.

Cabrita's arrest sparked a growing dispute between the government and Portuguese unions.

The Interior Ministry published a communique July 26 charging Communist infiltration of the bank clerks' union. It closed the union in Lisbon and Porto July 29 "for an indefinite duration" because of the union's alleged "seditious" activities. The union's officials in Lisbon and Porto were suspended from their posts Aug. 9.

(The International Confederation of

Free Trade Unions sent a telegram to the Portuguese premier protesting Cabrita's arrest, the French newspaper Le Monde reported July 28.)

Press liberalization planned. The Caetano government Nov. 26, 1970 released the text of a proposed law abolishing press censorship for all but military matters. The draft law set strict limits on the new liberties and sought to impose penalties of stiff fines and prison terms of a year for any infraction of the rules.

Informed sources had disclosed Aug. 28 that press censorship would be extended to labor union publications, newsletters and magazines.

Crackdown on unions. An apparent crackdown on the union movement took place in Portugal in August 1971.

The Caetano government Aug. 4 arrested Antonio dos Santos, secretary of the journalists' union. No reason for the arrest was disclosed. His wife, a member of the store clerks' union, was also arrested, according to a Le Monde report Aug. 14.

The Interior Ministry declared Aug. 12 that the arrests of the union leaders were linked to a government inquiry into the sabotage of the Tacos air base. It implied the union leaders were tied to the clandestine Communist party, and said the Communists were linked to the Armed Revolutionary Action, an anticolonialist group that had claimed responsibility for the Tancos attack.

Interns placed under military orders. The regime decreed Nov. 27, 1971 that interns would be placed under the military orders of the defense and health ministers. The action was taken because the doctors had launched a strike Nov. 15, reportedly to protest the lack of positions available for medical residency.

Student Discord

Shots fired at university. Thirteen students were injured in rioting at Coimbra University May 9, 1970.

The disturbance erupted when members of a left-wing theatrical group broke into a performance by a group of right-wing students who had broken a student strike and gone on tour to Angola.

In response to student demands, the government May 13 ordered an investigation into the clash. In another order May 14, the government ordered all universities closed until final examinations.

Institute closed. The Advanced Technical Institute in Lisbon was closed Jan. 18, 1971 for an indefinite period of time. Lisbon University authorities announced Jan. 17 that "as it has become difficult to ensure the proper conduct of classes and other scholastic activities, the directors of the Advanced Technical Institute have decided to close the buildings and suspend the establishment's activities as from Monday [Jan. 18]." Student disorders had disrupted various sectors of the University of Lisbon during December 1970 and January, and university students had scheduled a meeting at the institute Jan. 18.

Warning to students. Education Minister Jose Veiga Simao issued a communique Jan. 22, 1971. He ordered student groups to stop their growing political activities or be liable to legal sanctions. He noted that the associations were increasingly involved in the distribution of revolutionary propaganda.

The warning came amid continuing student unrest at the University of Lisbon, where clashes between students and police had erupted again Jan. 20. The presidents of student associations decided the same day to demand the normalization of relations between students and the administration, the release of arrested students, and an exclusive meeting with Education Minister Simao. The education minister said he would meet jointly with students and university administrators only when classes returned to normal.

Actions against students. Among government actions against students during 1971:

■ A Lisbon court sentenced two women students and two men to 22 months correctional imprisonment for being members of the outlawed Portuguese Communist party and for subversive activities in the Lisbon Higher Institute of Economic and Financial Science, it was reported Jan. 27. They were also deprived of their voting rights for five years.

■ About 9,000 students of the University of Coimbra struck Feb. 16–17 to protest the arrest of eight students who had attended an unauthorized meeting protesting a political trial in Lisbon.

■ Alberto Costa, a Lisbon law student, was arrested April 9. Costa, whose candidacy in the 1969 legislative elections had been rejected by the government, was a member of the liberal intellectual opposition.

■ The arrest of several university students, including the vice president of the Lisbon law students' association, was reported by the "commission against repression", according to an April 22 report in Le Monde.

Six students of the Lisbon University law school were sentenced Dec. 21 to prison terms of 16–24 months and the deprivation of their civic rights for 5–15 years on charges of belonging to the banned Communist party. Four of the sentences were suspended.

Educational reform. Education Minter Veiga Simao announced a major educational reform system, it was reported Jan. 8, 1971. The planned reforms included an extension of required schooling from six to eight years, two years of optional kindergarten education, and abolition of university entrance examinations. In addition, Simao reported that a chain of polytechnic schools would be established to operate alongside the three existing universities and that higher education would be made available to all classes of society. Although pledging full autonomy to universities, Simao warned students against using schools and universities as a forum for political dissidence.

Salazar Dies

Ex-dictator's end. Former Premier Antonio de Oliveira Salazar died in Lisbon July 27, 1970 of a pulmonary embolism. He died without knowing that he had been replaced as Portugal's chief of state. Since the illness in 1968 that had made his replacement necessary, government officials had met frequently with Salazar and had pretended to him that he was still in charge of the government.

Mounting Problems

Troubles at Home & Abroad Reflected in U.N. Action

By the time the Caetano regime had struggled half of the way through its 5 1/2-year existence, its troubles both abroad and at home were increasing at an accelerating rate.

Rebellion in the African territories remained Portugal's most serious problem as well as the principal cause of both the spread of anti-Portugal sentiments abroad and the growth of frequently violent dissent at home.

United Nations agencies were frequently a forum for attacks on Portugal's African policy:

'Genocide' seen in Africa. A six-man working group reported to the U.N. Human Rights Commission in Geneva Feb. 23, 1971 that "elements of genocide" in the treatment of black Africans existed in Portugal's African territories as well as elsewhere in southern Africa.

The team of experts, appointed in their personal capacity by the Human Rights Commission, had completed a four-year investigation.

The report cited actions in South Africa, Rhodesia and the Portuguese African territories as examples of the genocide" alleged. The team's report charged that in the Portuguese territories of Angola, Portuguese Guinea and Mozambique "Portugal had carried out mass executions of civilians and of persons suspected of opposing the regime and had carried out collective punishment against the civilian population." (The Portuguese delegation to the U.N. had denied these charges before the report was submitted.)

Members of the investigation team were: Luis Marchand-Stens, international law professor attached to the Peruvian embassy in Washington, D.C.; Ibrahim Boye, government prosecutor and Senegal representative at the U.N.; Felix Armacora, law professor in Vienna; Branimir Jankovic, law professor at the University of Belgrade in Yugoslavia; N.N. Jha of the Indian Foreign Trade Ministry; and Waldo E. Waldron-Ramsey, lawyer and high commissioner of Barbados in Great Britain.

Portugal quits Unesco. Portugal announced its departure from the U.N. Educational, Scientific & Cultural Organization (Unesco) in May 1971 in response to Unesco criticism of Portuguese actions in Africa.

Portuguese Foreign Minister Rui Patricio was reported May 30 to have said that

Portugal's delegate to Unesco had already informed the organization's interim director general May 28 that his country was withdrawing from the organization. Patricio said Portugal "would no longer participate in the work of the organization" and said he was closing his bureau immediately. He also extended an invitation to the members of the U.N. Committee on Colonization to visit the provinces of Angola and Mozambique to ascertain whether the charges of derelict administration were valid.

U.N. probes. The U.N. Security Council Sept. 29, 1971 received reports from missions sent to investigate charges by Guinea and Senegal of hostile Portuguese activities in West Africa.

A two-member mission to Guinea had been sent to investigate charges by Guinean President Sekou Toure that his country was about to be invaded by Portuguese forces in the neighboring territory of Portuguese Guinea. The mission's report recounted meetings in Guinea but contained no recommendations.

A six-member mission to Senegal investigated a report July 6 charging that the Portuguese had laid mines along her borders and flew aircraft over Senegal territory. The report called on the Council to force Portugal to cease hostile activity.

The council Oct. 23, 1972 voted 12–0 to condemn Portugal for a border violation against Senegal which occurred Oct. 12. The U.S., Britain and Belgium abstained.

In the incident, armored vehicles stationed in Portuguese Guinea opened fire on the Senegalese border post at Nianao, killing one soldier and wounding another soldier and a civilian. In a letter to the Security Council's president acknowledging the violation, Portugal explained that "mental agitation" on the part of the unit commander had been responsible.

The council had held a special session Jan. 28–Feb. 4, 1972 in Addis Ababa, Ethiopia. It was the council's first session outside New York in 20 years and the first in Africa. A resolution similar to earlier ones passed by the council

asking Portugal to withdraw from her African territories was adopted 9–0. Argentina abstained, as did Portugal's five NATO allies—the U.S., Britain, France, Italy and Belgium.

Portuguese Foreign Minister Rui Patricio declared Feb. 9 that his country would withhold its share of the cost of the Addis Ababa meeting, which he described as "a pure propaganda operation" and "another step in the process of degradation and abasement of the U.N." Patricio said the Security Council had overlooked several "hot spots not far from Addis Ababa," including the "ferocious repression" of Ethiopian nationalists and the "massacre" of Catholic blacks in southern Sudan.

The Security Council Aug. 2 received the report of a special U.N. decolonization committee mission to Portuguese Guinea, which urged the U.N. to apply pressure to Portugal to end its policy of reprisals against the population of the colony's "liberated regions."

Portugal scores U.N. Responding to a committee decision to allow representatives of insurgent movements in Portuguese African territories to attend U.N. General Assembly sessions as observers, Portuguese Foreign Minister Rui Patricio Oct. 2, 1972 said the U.N. was an "organization without law and without regulations."

Patricio told the assembly that the African territories of Angola, Mozambique and Portuguese Guinea were not colonial dependencies but integral parts of Portugal, with the same "system of juridical, political, social and ethnic values [as] all parts of Portuguese national territory." That some countries did not recognize this situation did not give them the right "to seek to overturn by violent means" the Portuguese government in Africa, Patricio asserted.

Nigerian delegate Okoe Arikpo told the assembly later that "assistance should be given on such a massive scale as to remove, without further delay, the forces of oppression and racism" from the Portuguese territories, Rhodesia and Namibia. Jamaican Prime Minister

Michael Manley added a sharp attack on Portugal as a "colonialist oppressor," saying his government would take steps "to bring all trade with Portugal to a halt until her African colonies have won their freedom."

Rebel forces backed. The U.N. General Assembly voted Nov. 2, 1972 to recognize the "legitimacy" of anticolonial armed struggles. The resolution, passed 99–5, also called on the U.N., its world agencies and all countries to withhold all assistance from Rhodesia, Portugal and South Africa, and urged colonial powers to withdraw military installations from colonial territories.

The resolution was opposed by the U.S., Portugal, South Africa, Great Britain and France. George Bush, the chief U.S. delegate, said after the vote that while the U.S. supported independence for colonial peoples, it felt support for "liberation armies" was contrary to the U.N. Charter.

The General Assembly also approved Nov. 2 three resolutions seeking support against colonialism outside the U.N., opposed only by Portugal and South Africa. One called for expanded dissemination by the U.N. of information on colonialism; another, for U.N. co-sponsorship, with the Organization of African Unity, of a 1973 conference to speed the end of colonialism and of official policies of racial separation; and a third, for an annual "week of solidarity" with African colonies in their fight "for freedom, independence and equal rights." The week would begin May 25, designated African Liberation Day.

The General Assembly Nov. 14, by 98–6 vote with 8 abstentions, resolved to condemn Portugal for waging "colonial wars" in Africa and called on U.N. members to give "all moral and material" assistance to armed rebel movements in Portugal's African territories.

Portuguese colonial talks urged. The Security Council, unanimously adopting a compromise resolution, urged Portugal Nov. 22, 1972 to stop immediately "military operations and all acts of repression" in Africa and begin negotiations leading toward self-determination and independence for its African territories of Angola, Mozambique and Portuguese Guinea.

Portugal rejected the resolution Nov. 23, saying it could not "abdicate" from Africa without causing "grave injustice and irreparable damage to the populations" of Portuguese "provinces" there. It chided the Security Council for "anti-Portuguese propaganda," and charged the body was "not competent to deal with the internal affairs of any state." However, Portugal renewed its offer to the U.N. to send observers to verify that claims by rebel movements of control over "liberated zones" in its colonies were without foundation.

Portuguese Premier Marcello Caetano had declared Nov. 14 that negotiations with rebel movements in the nation's African territories would amount to

ICAO suspension. The International Civil Aviation Organization, meeting in New York March 1, 1973, voted to suspend participation by Portugal in ICAO activities, including navigation committees, until Portugal abided by United Nations resolutions on decolonialization. All the Western nations voted against the resolution, while Japan and the Latin American countries abstained in the 68–26 vote.

Nonaligned states charge torture. A report compiled for the U.N. Human Rights Commission by diplomats from six nonaligned countries charged Portugal with torture and the use of napalm, defoliants and herbicides against black guerrillas in Angola and Mozambique, it was reported March 26, 1973. The report said that captured guerrillas were "maimed and forced to eat parts of their own bodies" and that their wives were "raped in their presence and killed."

During a discussion of the report April 2, Clarence Clyde Ferguson Jr., a U.S. deputy assistant secretary of state for African affairs, told the commission that the allegations were "largely unsubstantiated." The working group, appointed by the commission, had visited Portuguese territories and interviewed witnesses. Its members were from Senegal, Yugoslavia, Austria, India, Peru and Tanzania.

Portugal, South Africa curbs vetoed. The U.S. and Britain May 22, 1973 vetoed a Security Council resolution that would have extended trade sanctions against Rhodesia to include South Africa and Portuguese territories in Africa.

The resolution, put forward by African delegates, was backed by 11 of the 15 council members, with Austria and France abstaining. It called for limiting imports from South Africa, Mozambique and Angola to 1965 levels; denying landing rights to airlines of countries which granted such rights to the Rhodesians; and extending Great Britain's blockade of the port of Beira, in Mozambique, to the territory's other port, Lourenco Marques.

The U.S. ambassador to the U.N., John Scali, charged it was unrealistic to call for broader sanctions in Africa until all governments took more seriously the existing sanctions against Rhodesia. "To pass resolutions which are clearly unenforceable would seriously damage the reputation and credibility of the United Nations and further erode public confidence in the United Nations to act in any meaningful way," he asserted.

The British delegate, Sir Colin Crowe, had argued that the measure amounted to a "declaration of economic warfare against the whole of southern Africa." British officials also admitted they simply could not afford the extension of the sanctions, the Times of London reported May 23.

Proponents of the resolution argued it would help enforce the Rhodesia sanctions, since South Africa and Portugal had allowed Rhodesian goods to move through their ports in violation of the trade embargo.

Foreign Relations

Arms from abroad. Portugal continued to experience difficulty in buying foreign

planes and weapons. In most cases, arms were sold to Portugal on condition that they were not to be used in Africa.

The U.S. approved the sale of two Boeing 707 jets to the Portuguese government in what was believed to be the first such sale since the imposition of a partial arms embargo in 1961, the Washington Post reported Jan. 5, 1971. State Department officials said the arms embargo, which applied to arms for use in the Portuguese overseas territories, did not apply to 707s. However, informed sources indicated that the planes would probably be used for transport to and from Africa. The transaction, approved in July 1970, was concluded directly with the Portuguese government. Former aircraft sales had been to the Portuguese commercial airline, Transportes Aereos Portugueses.

In another development affecting Portuguese territories, the Washington Post reported April 4 that government troops in Angola had received three French-manufactured SA-330 helicopters in March. The Post quoted a Portuguese officer as saying that the aircraft, each capable of carrying 24 soldiers, would be "enough to enable our patrols to disrupt the guerrillas' supply lines."

A Bonn protest to Portugal against the use in Mozambique of Fiat G 91 jet fighters sold by West Germany to Portugal in 1966 under a NATO agreement was reported in the London Times Aug. 4, 1971. The report was based on material in the West German Press. The West German Ministry of Defense had denied knowledge of the location of the aircraft, but the semi-official Lisbon newspaper Diario de Noticias had reported the planes were in Mozambique. The original sale agreement had contained a clause stipulating that the jets were to be used only in Portugal and for defense missions under NATO. Portugal reportedly replied that Angola, Mozambique and Portuguese Guinea were all Portuguese provinces.

In a related development, the Washington Post reported Aug. 17 that the Malawi government had turned over two gunboats to Portuguese authorities who were using them to patrol Lake Malawi against guerrilla attacks by Frelimo.

A U.S. grand jury indicted the Chrysler Corp. Jan. 16, 1973 on charges of violating the U.S. Munitions Control Act by shipping 100 engines designed for amphibious armored cars to Portugal without a license or permission from the State Department.

Portugal had been denied permission to buy the completed vehicles in 1965, but subsequently secured spare parts, blueprints and a prototype, which led to U.S. indictments of a Detroit freight forwarder and two former Chrysler employes in 1971–72.

The new indictment charged Chrysler with two illegal shipments, in June 1968 and September 1970, with total export values of $177,474.

Diggs vs. Azores deal. Rep. Charles C. Diggs Jr. (D, Mich.) resigned from the U.S. delegation to the United Nations Dec. 17, 1971 in protest against Nixon Administration policies in Africa. At a press conference held Dec. 17, Diggs, who was also chairman of the Congressional black caucus, cited a series of Administration actions that brought him to a public break. The "watershed," he said, came when the U.S. announced Dec. 10 that it had made a decision to provide Portugal with up to $436 million in economic credits in return for the continued use of military bases in the Azores.

Diggs called this "an open alliance with Portugal," which would use the money to "wage war against the black peoples" in its African territories.

Portuguese Foreign Minister Rui Patricio said Oct. 5, 1973 that the lease on the U.S.' Azores base might not be renewed beyond the end of 1973.

Patricio said the base was unpopular in Portugal. He also said it was not important to the U.S. or NATO and added that the U.S. had not requested renewal negotiations. He charged that of the $436 million U.S. commitment made in exchange for the lease's renewal in 1970, $400 million was in credits for imports

from the U.S., none of which was used, and the rest was in scholarships and surplus equipment, some of which had not beer delivered.

Portuguese opponents of the regime's African policies had charged that the base had been used by the government to extract tolerance from the U.S. government for the African policies.

The Azores base suddenly assumed immediate value to the U.S. later in October 1973 when it was used to refuel U.S. aircraft used in a massive airlift to rearm Israel after the outbreak of war in the Middle East. Spain had barred the use of its bases for this purpose. (Arab oil nations Nov. 28 announced a retaliatory embargo on oil exports to Portugal.)

Youth conference backs rebels. Representatives of 32 leftwing youth and student organizations from Africa, Asia, Latin America and Europe met in Brazzaville, the Congo April 22–24, 1971 for an international conference of solidarity with the liberation movements in Portugal's African territories.

Bernard Combo-Matsiona, chairman of the Congolese Socialist Youth Union, opened the conference with a speech in which he declared: "We describe as imperialist agents all those who are calling for a dialogue as a means of liberating the so-called Portuguese colonies. The experience of liberated peoples has shown clearly that imperialism has no human feelings and its domination can be destroyed only by popular armed struggle...."

Conference resolutions condemned exploitation and oppression by Portuguese colonialists, the alleged Lisbon-Salisbury-Pretoria alliance and the reported Portuguese raids on African countries bordering on Portugal's African territories.

Rift with Denmark. A Portuguese rift with Denmark took place in 1972.

The government's recall of its ambassador to Denmark for consultations because of Denmark's alleged promise of aid to African nationalists was reported by the French newspaper Le Monde March 22. Le Monde said the ambassador had submitted before his departure a protest against the "unfriendly" attitude toward Portugal taken by Danish Foreign Minister Knud Andersen during a tour of East Africa. He had reportedly pledged nearly $900,000 to Frelimo while visiting Tanzania.

China claims Macao & Hong Kong.

China officially claimed the British Crown Colony of Hong Kong and the Portuguese colony of Macao in a letter filed with the U.N. Committee on Decolonization, which was made public March 10, 1972.

The letter, from Huang Hua, China's chief delegate to the U.N., stated that the two islands just off the China mainland "belong to the category of questions resulting from . . . unequal treaties . . . which the imperialists imposed on China." The letter added: Hong Kong and Macao were "part of the Chinese territory, occupied by the British and Portuguese authorities. They should not be included in the list of colonial territories covered by the Declaration on the Granting of Independence to Colonial Countries and People."

Huang said the U.N. had no right to discuss the question of Hong Kong and Macao.

Portugal-Brazil ties.

A convention conferring mutual rights of citizenship on Portuguese and Brazilian citizens, approved in 1971, went into effect April 22, 1972.

The two countries also agreed on a number of measures to strengthen economic ties, including customs-free zones for each other's exports, the newsletter Latin America reported July 7, 1972.

The agreement would establish customs-free zones in the Brazilian ports of Sao Paulo and Rio de Janeiro, as well as in Lisbon and the Portuguese colonies of Angola and Mozambique. Other measures included easier flow of capital between the two countries, particularly to Portugal's colonies; direct participation of Portuguese capital in Brazilian development, notably in cement, beer and heavy machinery; investment by Brazil's

state oil company in exploration in Africa; and increased shipping services.

Brazilian and Portuguese officials admitted one of the goals of the agreement was to enable each country to infiltrate other "regional economic blocs." Brazil had reportedly had difficulty penetrating European markets, and was also interested in trade with Africa. The agreement provided for a multinational investment bank which would operate not only in the Portuguese colonies, but in Rhodesia and South Africa.

Church grants to rebels.

The World Council of Churches Jan. 22, 1973 announced grants of about $210,000 to organizations around the world opposed to racism.

A grant of about $25,000, one of the largest for a single group, was to go to the African party for the Independence of Guinea and Cape Verde (PAIGC).

Churches to aid deserters—The central committee of the World Council of Churches approved Aug. 27 a $500,000 five-year program to aid Portuguese army deserters and draft evaders, who had been leaving Portugal at the rate of 16,000–20,-000 a year to avoid service in Africa.

Oslo conferees back rebels.

Delegates from more than 50 countries met in Oslo, Norway in April 1973 to discuss racism and colonialism in Africa.

Leaders of nine nationalist groups from South Africa, South-West Africa (Namibia), Rhodesia and the Portuguese African territories met for the first time at the Oslo conference, the London Times reported April 16. Their call for support for armed struggle in Africa reportedly won the backing of the U.N. members in attendance.

In the Portuguese territories, the conference declared, support should be given to the "liberation movements" recognized by the Organization of African Unity, enabling them to carry on their armed struggle. Delegates recommended an embargo on sales of weapons to Portugal, backed by the U.N., and action by the Vatican to renounce the concordat and missionary agreements with Portugal relating to its African territories.

Protests during visit to Britain. Portuguese Premier Marcello Caetano, visiting Britain July 16–19, 1973, encountered strong protests over a recent London Times report that Portuguese troops had massacred civilians in the Portuguese territory of Mozambique.

Caetano's visit was planned to celebrate the 600th anniversary of the alliance between Portugal and Britain. The premier met with Prime Minister Edward Heath July 16, reportedly discussing trade problems among other topics, and attended a banquet given July 17 in Caetano's honor by Queen Elizabeth and Prince Philip.

Reports of the massacre led the opposition Labor party to force a debate in the House of Commons July 17 on whether the government should have canceled Caetano's visit. Party leader Harold Wilson denounced the alleged massacre as a "most outrageous and bestial atrocity," which would justify Portugal's expulsion from the North Atlantic Treaty Organization. He said Heath's government should have insisted on a Portugese inquiry into the charges before entertaining Caetano. Foreign Secretary Sir Alec Douglas-Home countered by questioning the validity of the news account, which he said was based on "second- and third-hand reports." "To have canceled the visit," he maintained, "would have been to . . . prejudge the case against an old and loyal ally."

The largest demonstration, on July 15, involved a march to the Portuguese embassy in London by 5,000 protestors.

Australians protest trade mission— Police clashed with a large crowd of demonstrators protesting the arrival in Melbourne of a Portuguese trade mission Sept. 20. The crowd shouted slogans condemning the alleged massacre of civilians in Mozambique. This was the second Melbourne demonstration in a week against the visit of the mission. Portuguese offices in the city had been damaged.

A spokesman for the World Council of Churches criticized the Australian government Sept. 20 for permitting the visit.

African Areas Get Autonomy

Constitutional reforms approved. A special session of the National Assembly, convened June 15, 1971 by decree of Premier Marcello Caetano to vote on constitutional reform proposals, approved a government bill authorizing greater autonomy for Portuguese overseas territories, the Washington Post reported July 9.

The reform, which applied particularly to Angola and Mozambique, authorized the territories to legislate locally, to organize their own administration and to raise revenue from a budget drafted and approved by locally elected assemblies. The central government would retain control over defense, guarantee rights for the territories' ethnic groups and preserve the national unity. The bill evoked harsh criticism from both the extreme right and the liberals.

Domestic liberties— Legislation giving Portuguese citizens additional liberties was also adopted during 1971.

A bill guaranteeing freedom of worship to minority religions was approved by the assembly July 22. Under the new measure, the Portuguese government recognized the juridical identity of religious groups other than the Roman Catholic Church and granted them the right to meet without previous authorization. Compulsory religious education in public schools was abolished.

The assembly approved a bill Aug. 5 abolishing formal press censorship—in existence 40 years—and instituting in its place new rules safeguarding "the national interest." Journalists who published articles undermining the constitution, institutions, unity and independence were made subject to fines and prison terms. Censorship would be resumed in states of emergency, when martial law was declared or when "grave acts of subversion occur in any part of the national territory." The law required all publications, professional journalists and foreign news agencies to register with the central information services.

(The French newspaper Le Monde had reported May 22 that 120 Portuguese intellectuals had formed a commission to act as a pressure group in defense of the freedom of expression during parliamentary discussion of the press law.)

Alternative bills and amendments advocated by parliamentary liberals for the three reform proposals were defeated. About 60 parliamentary members of the Social Democratic opposition had written a letter to the president of the National Assembly urging amendments to the constitutional proposals that would permit "the permanent and free expression of different currents of opinion," Le Monde reported July 4. They criticized the law granting autonomy to overseas territories as "a timid step" and urged the reduction of preventive detention from six months to 24 hours and the direct election of the president by universal suffrage.

Overseas territories bill approved. The National Assembly approved legislation designating Portugal's overseas territories as states and giving them more autonomy, the London Times reported May 2, 1972.

The regime officially proclaimed legal autonomy for the African overseas provinces of Mozambique, Angola and Portuguese Guinea, the Washington Post reported Dec. 24. It called for local elections in the provinces by April 1973.

Guerrillas given amnesty. An official communique said July 10, 1972 that 1,500 guerrillas and sympathizers of anti-colonial movements in Angola, Mozambique and Portuguese Guinea were freed in an amnesty campaign. The government July 5 had called for the surrender of guerrillas in its African territories and promised amnesty for all those not already facing criminal charges.

Portuguese African elections. Two days of voting for legislative assembly representatives in Portuguese territories took place March 26–27, 1973.

The balloting took place for 53 seats in Angola, 50 in Mozambique, 17 in Portuguese Guinea, 21 in Cape Verde and 16 in Sao Tome and Principe, islands

located off the coast of Gabon. In Angola and Mozambique, more than half the seats in the assembly were filled by the governor and the remaining candidates were nominated by him. There were no opposition parties.

The Portuguese government reported later that the legislative elections in its overseas territories had produced native-born majorities in all except Angola.

Mozambique elected a non-white majority of 26, including five Asians, out of 50 seats, according to an April 29 report. Candidates were elected in separate racial categories and by tribal and economic groups. Whites constituted about 3% of the population.

Struggle in Mozambique

7-month toll. A Jan. 19, 1971 bulletin from Portuguese army headquarters in Laurenco Marques said that in June–December 1970, a total of 1,804 rebels had been killed and 651 wounded. The dispatch listed government losses as 132 killed.

Le Monde of Paris reported Jan. 30 that 18 black nationalists, including Joel Monteiro, a leader of Frelimo, the insurgent Mozambique Liberation Front, had been killed in prison in Lourenco Marques after torture by police.)

New rebel offensives. Increasing insurgent activity took place in Mozambique in early 1971.

Guerrilla forces were reported Feb. 1 to have opened offensives on two fronts— one south of the Messalu River and the other in the Tete district. A Portuguese military communique said pursuit of rebel infiltrators was continuing "with the greatest intensity." General Kaulza de Arriaga, Portuguese military commander in Mozambique, said during a visit to Lisbon March 15 that his army had sealed off the main guerrilla infiltration points along the Tanzanian border and had captured the principal guerrilla bases in northern Mozambique.

(A Portuguese army deserter, Capt. Jaime Morais, said Feb. 1 in Stockholm that he had participated in 1970 in the "so-called victorious campaign in northern Mozambique. The truth is that we scored no success, but suffered losses, and when we withdrew the region was no longer under control. This campaign was an invention of the commander-in-chief who wanted to gain prestige in Portugal.")

Frelimo defectors. Several Frelimo leaders were reported to have defected to Portugal by the end of 1970. They included two former members of Frelimo's Central Committee, Dr. Miguel Artur Murupa and Manuel Mussa Katur, as well as Lazaro Kavandame, a Caconde tribal chieftain and the first Frelimo member to defect (in 1969) to Portugal.

Murupa was the former head of Frelimo's foreign relations department and a holder of economics and sociology degrees from Howard University (Washington, D.C.). In an interview published in the Washington Sunday Star May 2, 1971, Murupa was quoted by James J. Kilpatrick as saying that Frelimo had split into Russian and Chinese Communist factions after the assassination of Frelimo leader Eduardo Mondlane in 1969.

Zambia accused re rebel abductions. Portugal and Zambia traded charges March 5–8, 1971 over 11 farm workers of Portuguese nationality said to have been kidnaped from Mozambique in January by members of COREMO, the Mozambique Revolutionary Council.

The Portuguese Foreign Ministry March 5 accused Zambia of responsibility for the incident. It said that five of the kidnaped men, all black Mozambicans, had escaped and a Portuguese had died. The Portuguese note said Portugal had tried to contact Zambian officials in London and Malawi on the matter, but "now we have lost hope in silent diplomacy."

Zambian Home Affairs Minister Lewis Changufu said March 5 that the captured Portuguese had never been in the country, and his government had refused

a COREMO request to bring the men into Zambia. Changufu March 8 accused Portuguese authorities of taking five Zambian hostages from villages along the Mozambique frontier.

Zambian President Kenneth Kaunda March 22 asked diplomats of more than 30 nations for help in fighting what he said was a Portuguese blockade of Zambian imports levied in reprisal for the COREMO abductions.

At a press conference in Lusaka, Kaunda expressed his "grave concern" over the blockade, which he said was resulting in the pileup of Zambian goods, including maize, at Nacala and Beira in Mozambique and at Lobito Bay in Angola. He said Zambia was in no way involved with the capture of the Portuguese, whom he described as soldiers, but that his government would have tried to secure the release of the men had Portugal made a request through normal diplomatic channels. Kaunda spoke of the danger of a Portuguese invasion of Zambia and accused authorities in Mozambique of holding three Zambians.

A spokesman for the Portuguese Foreign Ministry declared March 22: "We reiterate what we have said in previous communications. There is no blockade of Zambian goods in Beira. Perhaps traffic congestion has caused delays but there is no blockade by Portugal."

An official Portuguese government note, printed in Lisbon newspapers March 25, said Kaunda had "presented a version of the facts completely contrary to the reality." The note asserted that diplomatic channels had been used to approach Zambia and that, in denying this, Kaunda showed "a complete lack of knowledge of what goes on in the highest sphere of his country's administration." Portuguese ports in Africa were described as remaining open to Zambian goods "so long as that country does not antagonize us directly."

Portugal expels priests. The Portuguese government May 25, 1971 told the White Fathers, an order of Roman Catholic priests, they had 48 hours to leave Mozambique after the order had earlier announced its intention of withdrawing from the territory.

Rev. Theo Van Asten, the White Fathers' superior general, said in a May 15 letter to the order's priests in Africa that the nine parishes in Mozambique were being closed and the 40 missionaries withdrawn because of the "basic ambiguity" in being identified with Portuguese colonial rule.

In explaining his government's decision May 28, Portuguese Foreign Minister Rui Patricio accused two White Fathers of recruiting terrorists for Frelimo and of "insulting the Portuguese flag and the name of Portugal." Patricio said that after the two had been expelled and other priests supported them, the Portuguese government received notice that the White Fathers were leaving Mozambique.

Three members of the order said in Rome June 5 that Portugal had expelled 11 White Fathers from Mozambique in recent years.

Portugal accused of massacres. The London Times reported July 10, 1973 that Portuguese troops had been "carrying out the systematic genocidal massacre of people in villages thought to have helped Frelimo." The charges, denied by the Portuguese, recalled accounts of other atrocities, some allegedly by Frelimo forces, compiled by European missionaries in Mozambique.

The July 10 article, by a British Roman Catholic priest, Adrian Hastings, cited Spanish missionaries as the source of the charge that "a whole series of massacres," each "rivalling that of My Lai," had been perpetrated by Portuguese forces in west central Mozambique between May and November 1971. More recently, Hastings said, security forces killed at least 400 men, women and children in the village of Wiriyamu Dec. 16, 1972. A July 14 report from Lourenco Marques said villagers who had escaped the massacre charged

the killing was done by black troops under the command of European officers.

Hastings charged that two Spanish missionaries had been jailed without trial for the past 18 months in Lourenco Marques for having protested the earlier killings, and all missions in the region had been closed. Three Spanish missionaries expelled from Mozambique said in Madrid July 11 that they were the source for Hastings' article. They said the Wiriyamu incident was the worst of four such events in the area in the past two years.

A 400-page report on atrocities was released July 13 by the Rome headquarters of the Missionaries of Africa, known as the White Fathers. The order had left Mozambique in May 1971, but one missionary who remained in the area reported on subsequent events.

Among other charges, the White Fathers claimed that Rhodesian troops had crossed the border on at least one occasion to assist Portuguese forces, killing 18 persons Sept. 3-9, 1971. Some of the Portuguese killings were said to be in retaliation for the killing by Frelimo of two African chiefs and civilians. The documents charged that Portuguese bishops in Mozambique had ignored missionary protests.

Frelimo charged July 13 in Dar es Salaam, Tanzania that Portuguese massacres began in 1960, when 500 villagers in northern Mozambique were killed after a pro-independence demonstration.

Another massacre, the same day as the Wiriyamu incident, was reported to have taken place at the nearby village of Chawola, where at least 53 corpses were later counted, according to the July 15 Sunday Observer of London. The report was said to have originated with survivors interviewed at a hospital.

The July 10 report was denied the same day in a statement by the Portuguese embassy in London, which called the charges "hearsay allegations." The Portuguese government said the next day it would hold an inquiry "in the established way." Gen. Kaulza de Arriaga, commander of Portuguese forces in Mozambique, denied that his troops had committed a massacre. But he said his troops had toured the area for 10 days before military operations took place in December, inviting residents to come to "security areas."

(Frelimo Vice President Marcelino dos Santos had charged in London June 19 that three battalions of South African troops had been serving in Tete Province, Mozambique in the vicinity of the recent massacres, protecting the Cabora Bassa dam construction project.

(South African Defense Minister Piet W. Botha denied June 20 that any South African troops were aiding the Portuguese in Mozambique.)

Massacre charges repeated at U.N.—Speaking before the United Nations decolonization committee July 20, the Rev. Hastings testified that the massacre was the worst atrocity in modern colonial history and said the Portuguese government's reaction showed how blind it was to the seriousness of the charges.

Prior to the committee hearing, Hastings met with U.N. Secretary General Kurt Waldheim who said the priest's report, "based on the testimony of missionaries in Mozambique, has aroused the conscience of mankind." He urged "all member states to lend their support to the committee in its inquiry into the tragic report."

(The Portuguese mission to the U.N. had asserted July 17 that Hastings had an "anti-Portuguese bias" and that his report of massacres in Mozambique was "less than plausible.")

After hearing Hastings' testimony, the U.N. Committee on Colonialism July 20 demanded that Portugal permit an on-the-spot investigation of the massacre reports.

At a press conference during an official visit he was making to London July 18, Portuguese Premier Marcello Caetano said he would not permit a U.N. team to investigate allegations of the massacre since he was certain any U.N. team would be opposed to a real inquiry into the facts.

Trial witnesses confirm massacre—Witnesses at the trial of two Spanish Burgos priests in Lourenco Marques, capital of Mozambique, confirmed allegations of the massacre. Ten witnesses, including three

nuns, two bishops and a priest, had testified under oath that four massacres took place in the Mukumbura area of the Tete district in 1971. The witnesses also testified to other atrocities in the area, the Washington Post reported July 24.

The testimony came in preliminary proceedings against the two priests, who had gone on trial on treason charges in connection with their protest against earlier massacres in the region.

The two Burgos priests, who had initially told Hastings about the Portuguese massacre, said, according to a July 24 report, that they were backing their allegations of widespread killings and torture because "We side with blacks and as Christian missionaries our duty is to denounce the white colonialist murders." The two priests said they were angry and distressed because "our documented denunciation" had been challenged by the Portuguese as a fabrication.

Missionary names 5 survivors—The London Times reported Aug. 6 that a Spanish missionary who helped prepare a report on the alleged massacres disclosed the names of five survivors who he said could give testimony to any international inquiry "if the Portuguese government has let them live."

The Rev. Vincente Berenguer Llopis said the survivors of the Wiriyamu massacre were admitted to a missionary hospital after the massacre where they disclosed the killings.

The Times Aug. 5 had published an interview with a teenage boy who claimed to have survived the massacre. British journalist Peter Pringle said the recording of the interview had been confiscated by Portuguese military police.

Portuguese probers deny massacre—The Portuguese Ministry of Defense issued a communique Aug. 19 asserting that a "rigorous inquiry" by Portuguese authorities into accusations against the Portuguese army showed a "total absence of the alleged facts in the places alleged by the accusers."

The communique said the inquiry determined that isolated forces had disobeyed orders and had committed at least one "retaliatory act," but not at the place alleged by the Spanish missionaries. The report said those responsible for the "reprehensible acts" would be punished.

Portuguese defense headquarters had confirmed July 24 that Gen. Thomas Jose Basto Machado would replace Gen. Kaulza de Arriaga as chief of the armed forces in Mozambique. De Arriaga had denied that his troops committed a massacre.

In a July 29 interview in the London Times, de Arriaga said rumors of the massacre were investigated "immediately—maybe in January" and that the investigation "obviously" would not be made public. He maintained that the war in Mozambique was a constructive war in which the army did not even kill terrorists if it could be avoided. He said the intention of the Portuguese was to bring peaceful unity to the territory and this could not be done by massacring guerrillas or civilians.

Portuguese confirm massacre. A Portuguese government inquiry confirmed that Portuguese troops had been responsible for the Tete village massacre, the Johannesburg (South Africa) Star reported Sept. 25, 1973.

The Star cited undisclosed Portuguese sources for a report that bodies of about 70–80 murdered persons were found in the village, and that details of the massacre were confirmed by about 30 survivors. The report said black and white troops had shot the victims during a search for guerrillas, after a successful rebel ambush in the region.

Col. Armindo Martins Videira, governor and military commander of the Tete district, had left Mozambique Sept. 9. According to the Star report, he had been ordered fired by Premier Caetano, who had not heard of the massacre until after it was revealed by the London Times. Videira had been rebuked by Gen. Kaulza de Arriaga, head of Portugal's troops in Mozambique, shortly after the incident, according to the Star version.

Patriarch condemns violence—The London Times reported Sept. 20 that Antonio Cardinal Ribeiro, patriarch of Lisbon, had condemned the use of violence

in a statement about the massacre suppressed by the Portuguese government.

According to the Times, Ribeiro quoted a letter by the bishop of Tete, endorsed by all the bishops of Mozambique, expressing "vehement indignation" over the incident, and citing the "more and more widespread" situation of civilians caught "in the cross fire."

Reaction abroad—Among developments abroad:

■ Alluding to reports by Roman Catholic priests of the Portuguese massacres, Pope Paul VI July 22 expressed support for the cause of missionaries who condemned "misdeeds perpetrated against defenseless populations."

■ Swedish Foreign Minister Krister Wickman, calling for an immediate U.N. investigation into the alleged massacre, said July 15 that Sweden would double its aid to Frelimo.

Wickman said no company operating in South Africa or Portugal would receive state financial support, and warned those companies of possible reprisals from labor.

■ The West German Social Democratic party announced its support of Frelimo, according to an Aug. 8 report. The party would also support a ban on any West German arms deliveries to Portugal.

■ The Soviet Communist party newspaper Pravda Aug. 14 denounced the "total support" given by the North Atlantic Treaty Organization (NATO) to Portugal for its colonial wars in Africa. The paper said NATO's support for Portuguese colonialism stemmed from strategic and economic considerations.

Other massacres—Frelimo issued a statement listing these other alleged atrocities of the Portuguese in Mozambique:

In June, 1970, the Portuguese troops arrived in the village of Joao, in Tete Province, gathered everybody they could find (about 60 people, among them children), and told them dig a big hole "for us to hide from the bandits". The people, unaware, obeyed. At a certain point the Portuguese told the people to enter into the hole "to see if all of us will fit into it". The hole was still not big enough. The people enlarged it. Then the soldiers said: "Let us try again". The people entered again, and now there was room for all. When our people were inside, the Portuguese started shooting at them. They killed all 60 Mozambicans and buried them in the hole.

In another village, in Xidecunde, in February 1972, the Portuguese soldiers locked 16 people—men, women (some with babies) and children—in a house and threw grenades inside. 15 people were killed—among them 4 pregnant women and 6 babies. Only one woman survived, with the loss of an arm, blown off by the grenade.

On September 28, 1972, in Angonia, Tete, the Portuguese locked up about 30 people inside a house, set fire to the house and burnt all of them to death. The people were accused of knowing the hide-outs of the FRELIMO guerrillas.

In early December, 1972, as a reprisal against FRELIMO's successful attack against the town of Tete, the Portuguese troops rounded up the neighbouring villagers and arrested 60 people. They were locked inside a house and burnt to death.

In May, 1973, Rhodesian troops in Mucumbura massacred 15 people from a village. They took others away in their helicopters, and they were never seen again.

By the end of 1971, Portuguese soldiers in Tete ordered civilians to leave their villages and the day when they were on their way to other places, they were attacked by helicopters and savagely slaughtered. On that occasion, several mothers were caught with their children and forced by the Portuguese troops to crush their babies in mortars. (Reported also in the South African newspaper The Star, November 6, 1971).

In our reports we have also denounced an infamous practice which has become common among Portuguese soldiers: killing all pregnant women by ripping open their abdomens with bayonets to take out the fetus in order, in their own words, "to prevent the birth of new terrorists". Sometimes they place explosives inside the woman's dead body as a booby-trap, to kill other villagers when they bury her.

More recently other voices have also been raised in Mozambique, especially those of priests, condemning these crimes. We recall the overwhelming evidence given by the White Fathers Missionary Congregation, who decided to leave Mozambique in May, 1971, appalled by the crimes and torture inflicted on Mozambicans. In October, 1972, a Portuguese priest, Father Afonso da Costa, revealed in a Press Conference in Europe, after being expelled from Mozambique, that he had irrefutable information that over one thousand Mozambican civilians had been massacred in Tete Province alone, between March 1971 and May 1972.

Neighboring countries involved. Additional reports during 1973 indicated that neighboring countries were becoming increasingly involved in the events in Mozambique.

The New York Times Feb. 28 published what it described as unconfirmed reports that Rhodesian Air Force jets had strafed suspected guerrilla bases the previous weekend in the Centenary area bordering Mozambique.

Portuguese troops clashed with Malawi forces May 4. Portugal had recalled its ambassador to Malawi in December 1972 after charging that Malawi was harboring guerrilla bases.

The London Observer charged Sept. 2 that Rhodesian troops, helicopters and bombers had systematically killed Mozambique civilians in an attempt to cut off supplies for the guerrillas. Lisbon had denied that any Rhodesian or South African troops were involved in the war, it was reported Aug. 24.

Mozambique expels bishop, priests. Manuel Vieira Pinto, Bishop of Nampula, was expelled from Mozambique April 15, 1974 during a deportation campaign mounted by the government. Since March, more than 20 priests and Roman Catholic missionaries had been expelled for allegedly supporting Frelimo.

(The Vatican announced April 16 that it was following "with particular, extraordinary attention the situation of the church and of the missions" in the area. No member of the Portuguese clergy received the bishop of Nampula on his arrival in Lisbon.)

The bishop had been responsible for a highly critical document presented at an episcopal conference in Quelimane March 28. In the statement, Pinto and 34 other priests denounced the church hierarchy in Mozambique for failing to condemn government massacres and accused the church of complicity in "a system leading to cultural genocide of the Mozambique people."

A nun who was deported to Rome March 21 said the government-established resettlement villages, or "aldeamentos," were "concentration camps." Among those deported, several missionaries charged the authorities with denying fundamental human rights and torturing prisoners.

Angola Developments

Rebel reconciliation. The annual Organization of African Unity (OAU) summit conference, held in Rabat, Morocco June 12-15, 1972, served as a vehicle for a reconciliation of two rival guerrilla movements in Angola.

The leaders of the two Angolan movements—Holden Roberto of GRAE (Revolutionary Government of Angola in Exile) and Agostinho Neto of MPLA (Popular Movement for the Liberation of Angola) addressed the conference June 14 in a demonstration of unity between their respective groups. The reconciliation had been announced June 8 in a communique signed by Zaire President Mobutu Sese Seko and Congo (Brazzaville) President Marien Ngouabi, who mediated the settlement of differences.

The pro-Communist MPLA and the Western-oriented Angolan Nationalist Liberation Front (FLNA) signed an agreement in Kinshasa, Zaire Dec. 13 to form a united Supreme Council.

It was agreed that each would appoint 14 members to the ruling council and seven members each to the United Military Command and the Angolan Political Command. MPLA was to name the military leader and FLNA would choose the political chief. A committee composed of representatives from Zaire, Congo (Brazzaville), Tanzania and Zambia was to supervise application of the agreement.

South Africans in patrols. An MPLA communique said Feb. 10, 1972 that the Cunene District of Angola, near the Ovamboland area of Namibia (South-West Africa), had been in "armed revolt" since Jan. 12.

The dispatch said Camilo A. Rebocho Vaz, Angola's governor general, had visited the area Jan. 31 to study the situation. According to the New York Times Feb. 12, which confirmed Rebocho Vaz' visit, Portuguese and South African forces were conducting joint patrols in the region with the aim of preventing unidentified "outsiders" from spreading unrest.

Massacre charged. GRAE charged in Zaire July 23, 1973 that over 200 persons had been killed by Portuguese troops in attacks on two villages.

The massacres had been reported earlier by two Dutch Roman Catholic missionaries. The government in exile also charged that Portuguese troops had used chemical warfare, with over 200 deaths reported in the first eight months of 1973 resulting from ingestion of food containing chemical residues.

Agence France-Presse reported July 20 that over 128,000 refugees had left Angola for Zaire during the first six months of 1973.

Chinese to help. GRAE leader Holden Roberto, who had returned to Kinshasa, Zaire, said Dec. 24, 1973, after an 18-day visit to China, that Chinese leaders had pledged aid and cooperation with the independence movement.

Portuguese Guinea: Guinea-Bissau

Cabral killed in Guinea. Amilcar Cabral, who had headed the nationalist movement opposed to the government of Portuguese Guinea, was assassinated Jan. 20, 1973 in front of his home in Conakry, capital of the neighboring Republic of Guinea.

The news was revealed in a radio speech Jan. 21 by Guinean President Sekou Toure, who said Cabral had been killed "in a cowardly and horrible manner" by "the poisoned hands of imperialism and Portuguese colonialism." The "principal killers" had been arrested soon after the assassination.

In a broadcast Jan. 22, Toure identified those responsible as Portuguese soldiers who had infiltrated Cabral's group, the African Party for the Independence of Guinea and Cape Verde (PAIGC), while posing as deserters. Toure said they confessed that they captured Aristide Pereira and several other top Cabral lieutenants and headed north in boats to Portuguese Guinea before being turned back to Conakry by naval vessels of the Toure government.

Cabral had told newsmen in Conakry May 19, 1972 that PAIGC was seeking, for the first time, to hold elections in the "liberated zones" of Portuguese Guinea. He reported that PAIGC had "already chased the Portuguese out of Guinea-Bissau morally" and that it "must now answer the needs of a state." He said his group was "ready to enter negotiations with the Portuguese at any time" to settle the independence issue.

Independence declared. PAIGC said in Dakar Sept. 27, 1973 that a 120-member popular assembly had met and proclaimed an independent "Republic of Guinea-Bissau" Sept. 24 in territory that was liberated by guerrillas from Portuguese control.

The guerrillas had claimed they controlled three-quarters of Portuguese Guinea, a claim denied in Lisbon by the Foreign Ministry Sept. 26.

PAIGC Secretary General Aristides Pereira informed U.N. Secretary General Kurt Waldheim of the independence proclamation, which he said had been encouraged by General Assembly and Security Council resolutions. But Guinea-Bissau did not apply for immediate U.N. admission.

Among the countries recognizing Guinea-Bissau that week were the Soviet Union, China, most of the Communist nations and many of the African and Arab nations. PAIGC leaders claimed recognition for Guinea-Bissau from 54 nations by Oct. 10, and the Organization of African Unity admitted Guinea-Bissau as a full member Nov. 19.

U.N. status. U.N. Secretary General Kurt Waldheim March 15, 1974 granted U.N. observer status to Guinea-Bissau.

The Government
& the Opposition

Dissenters on trial. A court in Oporto Feb. 17, 1971 acquitted the Rev. Mario Pais de Oliveira, a former army chaplain in Portuguese Guinea, of charges of subversive activities against Portugal's policies in its African territories. He was the first priest to be tried for opposition to the war in Africa.

During the two-month trial, Pais de Oliveira declared his opposition to war and his support for self-determination of peoples, but said, "I didn't preach against the [Portuguese] wars and I respected the opinions of others."

The acquittal was seen as a victory for the liberal minority in Portugal's Roman Catholic Church. The bishop of Oporto, Antonio Ferreira Gomes, one of the leaders of the liberal faction, testified four times on behalf of Pais de Oliveira during the trial. (The bishop had been exiled for his liberal social views by the late Premier Antonio Salazar. Gomes was attacked again March 8 when he was accused of maligning the armed forces. The charge was made by Adm. Armando Reboredo e Silva, former navy chief and currently a member of the National Assembly, in a speech in the assembly. Reboredo e Silva said the bishop, whom he did not name, had "unjustly and wrongly treated the armed forces of Portugal, slandered military virtues and offended the military chaplains" in a "homily on peace" delivered in Oporto Cathedral Jan. 1. The bishop's address had denounced "war as sin" and criticized the "military virtues" shown by some of the chaplains in the armed forces. The bishop's statements were interpreted as criticism of Portugal's military role in Portuguese African territories, despite the fact the bishop had made no specific reference to the territories.)

A month and a half later the Lisbon court of political crimes March 30 convicted the Rev. Joaquim da Rocha Pinto de Andrade, an Angolan priest, and eight others from Portuguese Africa on charges of membership in a Lisbon clandestine organization that supported the African nationalist group, the Popular

Movement for the Liberation of Angola (MPLA). One other person was acquitted. The trial had opened Feb. 11.

Pinto de Andrade, former chief administrative officer of the Archdiocese of Launda, was sentenced to three years in prison and loss of political rights for 15 years. The prosecution alleged that he was named an "honorary president" of the MPLA in 1962, and had retained membership in the organization since then. The defense pointed out that Pinto de Andrade was in prison in 1962 and denied charges of his membership. His brother, Dr. Mario Pinto de Andrade, was one of the founders of the MPLA.

The seven others found guilty of such "subversive activities" as sending letters abroad for the Angolan nationalist movement and collecting funds and medicine for the nationalists received prison sentences ranging from 16 months to four and one-half years.

The sentences were considered more severe than expected. Observers felt that the verdicts reflected government concern over the increasing domestic opposition to Portugal's African policies.

One defense lawyer, Joaquim Pires de Lima, withdrew from the case March 3 on the ground that the court had violated "the principles of liberty and the rules of evidence." The prosecution based its case largely on the confessions of three of the defendants while under preventive detention. Pires de Lima charged that the prisoners had been subjected to torture.

A Lisbon court sentenced 11 persons charged with "subversive activities" to prison terms of 14 months to six years April 27, 1972. They were accused of membership in the Armed Revolutionary Action, an anti-colonialist urban guerrilla group.

Twelve persons were sentenced May 23 in Lisbon to prison terms ranging from 18 months to two years and to deprivation of civic rights of from five to 15 years for "subversive activities and membership in the Communist party."

Increase of political prisoners. The National Commission of Aid to Political Prisoners said May 29, 1972 that the number of political prisoners rose in Portugal from 70 at the end of 1970 to 135 in 1971. Fifteen detained persons had not yet been tried.

(Orbilio Barbas, deputy director general of prisoners, disclosed that 130 political prisoners were in Portuguese jails, of whom 48 had been sentenced, the New York Times reported Nov. 26. Opposition sources derided the figure as lower than the true one.)

Security curbs eased. The government Nov. 16, 1972 published a decree abolishing the so-called "security measures" that permitted authorities to extend the original sentence of certain political prisoners indefinitely. Along with the abolition, the decree codified relatively minor offenses and spelled out specific penalties.

The decree established prison terms of six months to three years for forming, subsidizing or belonging to a subversive group, and imposed small fines on persons meeting in illegal places or causing a disturbance and slightly higher fines on persons writing, printing or distributing subversive literature.

Education minister resigns. Education Minister Jose Veiga Simao resigned May 23, 1972.

His resignation followed a clash May 16 at Lisbon's Institute of Economic and Financial Science when police forcefully dispersed a student meeting. Students staged a protest May 17 in Lisbon against the alleged police brutality in the incident.

The previous week the students had demonstrated against Portugal's wars in its overseas African territories and against U.S. involvement in Vietnam, Le Monde reported May 19.

New censorship law decreed. The government announced new censorship regulations May 5, 1972 enacting provisions of a press law that had been approved by the National Assembly in August 1971. The new legislation, effective June 1, abolished the old board of censors and replaced it with a "commission of previous review," which would retain the right of censorship prior to publication during a state of emergency. (A state of emergency had been in effect in Portugal since November 1971.)

The law would impose heavy fines and prison sentences of up to two years on journalists and newspaper owners and publishers for breaking the regulations. The accused persons would have recourse to the courts.

Information State Secretary Cesar Henrique Moreira Baptista, according to the French newspaper Le Monde June 1, cited as prohibited articles those deemed injurious to national integrity and independence, disclosures of state secrets, statements potentially injurious to Portugal's relations with foreign nations, false or tendentious information, and offenses against foreign or Portuguese government officials.

Caetano regime criticized—About 50 government opponents published a document July 21 sharply criticizing Premier Caetano's government for failing to effect social, economic and political reforms. The document called for "a structural reform of the state and society, requiring the installation of a democratic political order and the socialization of key sectors of the national economy."

Price controls imposed. In an effort to halt growing inflation, the government decreed authority to the commerce minister to fix prices on certain products and services and to require the submission by businesses of their price list on other products for approval, the Journal of Commerce reported June 14, 1972.

The new law also imposed taxes on high profits and an additional surtax on high incomes.

Those persons accused of breaking the law would be charged with speculation and subject to fines ranging from the equivalent of $37–$370. Repeat offenses would carry the risk of the closure of the business or stores for up to six months.

Thomaz installed for third term. President Americo Thomaz, 77, was sworn in for a third term Aug. 9, 1972.

Several hours before the investiture ceremony, bombs had damaged power pylons in various parts of the country, reducing Lisbon's hydroelectric power supply by 30% and briefly cutting Oporto's electrical supply. No group claimed responsibility for the attacks.

Bombs had previously exploded July 25 in the center of Lisbon to protest Thomaz' uncontested election that day by a 616–29 vote in the electoral college.

In an earlier terrorist incident, time bomb explosions had destroyed 13 army trucks at a depot in the Lisbon surburb of Olivais July 11. A group calling itself the International Revolutionary Brigade telephoned news agencies and newspapers to claim responsibility for the blasts as a blow against "the Portuguese colonial army."

Cabinet shuffled—A slight Cabinet shuffle was announced Aug. 10 after Thomaz asked Premier Marcello Caetano to remain in office. Caetano had offered the traditional resignation of the government to coincide with the new presidential term.

Finance Minister Joao Augusto Dias Rosas resigned, reportedly for personal reasons, and was replaced by Manuel Cotta Dias, a member of the National Assembly and president of the executive commission of the National Popular Action (ANP), Portugal's only authorized political movement. Other changes involved appointment of Alexandre de Azevado Vaz Pinto, an economic planner, and Hermes Dos Santos, a member of the ANP executive commission, as secretaries of state for commerce and national industry, respectively, replacing Xavier Pintado and Rogerio Martins. Pintado and Martins had been considered leading liberal technocrats in the previous government.

Skeletal opposition group formed. A group known as the Democratic Opposition met in the coastal town of Aveiro to plan a congress that would nominate candidates to run in the 1973 elections for the National Assembly, the New York Times reported Dec. 13, 1972.

The opposition leaders were identified by the Times as Alvaro Seica Neves, chairman of the group's executive committee; Santos Simoes, chairman of the national commission; and Antonio Neto Brandao, commission secretary.

14 held in peace vigil. About 14 persons were arrested Dec. 31, 1972 in a Lisbon church for participating in a peace vigil. The detained included opposition figures Prof. Francisco Pereira de Moura, who was freed Jan. 11 on $800 bail, and Teotonio Pereira, and two priests.

A council of ministers communique announced Jan. 10 that those arrested would be fired from their jobs.

The vigil was called to discuss a document prepared by Catholics in Oporto and approved by the bishop of Oporto, calling for a peaceful solution to Portugal's African wars, and welcoming the possibility of independence for the colonies.

Bombs explode. Ten plastic bombs exploded at various public points in Lisbon Dec. 31, 1972 and 16 more were detonated Jan. 6. Pamphlets were found near each bomb opposing Portugal's Africa policies. Some of the leaflets were signed "revolutionary workers." Four children were injured in the explosions.

Two men were killed and eight injured when three bombs exploded at military offices in Lisbon March 9-10, 1973.

Liberals resign. Dr. Francisco Sa Carneiro, a liberal critic of the government's political prisoner policies, resigned from the National Assembly because of persistent failure to obtain changes in the press law, or passage of an amnesty law for political prisoners, it was reported Jan. 28, 1973.

Sa Carneiro said he could no longer serve with "dignity" because of limitations of public and political liberties. He had been personally recruited by Premier Marcello Caetano to run on the governing party ticket in 1969, but subsequently helped lead a group of nine liberal deputies in the 130-member Assembly in opposition to government policies.

Dr. Miller Guerra became Feb. 6 the second liberal to quit the National Assembly within ten days, on the grounds that he could do nothing within the Assembly to liberalize political or press policies.

Rightists curbed. Nine organizers of an independent association of 11,000 rightist veterans of the African wars resigned in protest when the government imposed its own chairman for the organizing committee of the new group, which had begun a meeting in Oporto June 1, 1973. The regime reportedly feared the group might evolve into a rightist opposition movement that would oppose some aspects of the government's overseas policy. A leader of the group had protested in an April 24 interview against unemployment among 1½ million veterans who had served in Africa since 1961.

Elections shunned by opposition. The government claimed that about 70% of the electorate voted in National Assembly elections Oct. 28, 1973 in Portugal proper and the overseas provinces. All 150 seats were won unopposed by candidates of the government Popular National Action party.

A bomb had exploded in the military headquarters of the Oporto district and another was found unexploded in Lisbon Oct. 26, in apparent protest gestures.

All 66 opposition candidates had withdrawn from the elections Oct. 24, charging government harassment and suppression of all discussion about independence for Portugal's colonies during the official month-long campaign. The opposition Democratic party said Oct. 22 that over 10,000 Portuguese citizens had been killed in the colonial wars and more than 50,000 injured.

Premier Marcello Caetano had issued a decree Sept. 11 providing for five years suspension of political rights for any parliamentary candidate who pulled out of the race or encouraged voters to abstain. Most of the opposition candidates were considered farther to the left than opposition candidates in the 1969 general elections, none of whom were elected.

Several thousand delegates attending the first opposition gathering permitted by the regime in four years, in Aveiro April 4-9, had called for an end to the colonial wars and for the eventual independence of the colonies. The delegates, ranging from monarchists to Communists but predominantly leftists, also called for the restoration of political and civil rights in Portugal and for a "struggle against the absolute power of monopolistic capitalism." About 20 people were injured when police broke up a march of about 2,-000 delegates April 8. Government censorship limited reports of the meeting's actions.

Almost none of the new deputies were known liberals. About 200 liberals, including three assembly deputies, met July 28-29 to discuss domestic and overseas reforms, but no common program was adopted. The government refused to allow the meeting to be held in a hall that would accommodate more delegates.

Registered voters totaled 2,091,064 in Portugal itself, and 962,854 in the colonies, the latter an increase of 658,832 over 1969.

Interior minister replaced. The government announced Nov. 7, 1973 that Minister of the Interior Antonio Rapazone had been replaced by Cesar Moreira Baptista, head of the Information Department.

Rightist plot reported. The British newspaper the Guardian reported December 31, 1973 that "contradictory" rumors had indicated that a right-wing group had planned to overturn the government of Premier Marcello Caetano and impose harsher domestic and colonial policies.

Several generals had reportedly been put under surveillance after the plan was uncovered, including former Mozambique commander Gen. Kaulza de Arriaga. Most of the generals named were not on active military duty.

Arrests. The police said Jan. 19, 1974 that 29 members or associates of the revo-

lutionary group LUAR (Line of Revolutionary Unity and Action) had been arrested since apprehension of the group's leader, Herminio da Palma Inacio, Nov. 22, 1973.

According to police, the group had been responsible for bombings, and was planning an airplane hijacking and a bank robbery. LUAR charged that Inacio had been beaten into a coma and transferred to a hospital in December 1973.

Inacio was charged with directing a 1968 bank robbery and various terrorist activities.

Spinola Dismissed, Coup Suppressed

Spinola ousted in book dispute. Gen. Antonio de Spinola was dismissed as deputy chief of the general staff March 14, 1974 for writing a book that severely criticized Portugal's economic, social, political, military and diplomatic policies. Spinola was particularly critical of the government's colonial wars, arguing it could not win a military victory over rebel movements in Portugal's African territories.

The book, titled "Portugal and the Future," became an instant best-seller when it was published Feb. 22. It infuriated right-wing military officers and government officials, including President Americo Thomaz, who forced Premier Marcello Caetano to fire not only Spinola but his immediate superior, Gen. Francisco de Costa Gomes, who also called for modifications in the government's colonial policies.

Military rebellion fails. An estimated 200-300 members of the army's 5th Infantry Regiment rebelled briefly March 16, 1974. They yielded without bloodshed after other military units refused to join them.

The rebels, led mainly by junior officers, were supporters of Gen. Antonio de Spinola.

The revolt began at the 5th Regiment's headquarters at Caldas da Rainha, some

50 miles north of Lisbon. The rebels
locked up the regimental commander, his
deputy and three majors, and departed
for the capital in 10 trucks.

The rebels failed to gain expected military support, particularly from an
armored detachment based at Santarem,
30 miles northeast of Lisbon. They surrendered without a fight after being con-
fronted on the outskirts of the capital by
the mobilized 7th Armored Regiment.

Thirty-three officers including Lt. Col.
Joao Almeida Bruno, a much-decorated
supporter of Spinola, were arrested, according to official announcements. Some
180 enlisted men also were held, according
to the Washington Post March 20.

A state of alert was imposed March 16
to keep the armed forces in their barracks; it was lifted March 18. The government claimed after the rebels surrendered
that the situation throughout the country
was normal.

A similar alert had been imposed
March 9–12 after a series of meetings of
angry young officers—mostly captains
and majors—who had complained for
months of the army's war, pay and promotion policies, and who opposed reported government plans to discipline
Spinola. Their leaders were transferred to
remote areas, according to the London
Times March 15.

(Lt. Col. Carlos Fabiao, another supporter of Spinola, had been arrested 10
days before the aborted rebellion for
alleged "anti-government activities" in
northern Portugal, it was reported March
20. In December 1973 Fabiao had denounced what he called a right-wing plot
to kill Spinola, Costa Gomes and
Caetano.)

Besides Spinola and Costa Gomes, the
naval secretary of the Armed Forces Defense Staff, Adm. Tierno Bagulho, was
dismissed March 14 for opposing the
government's colonial policies. Costa
Gomes was replaced by Gen. Joaquim da
Luz Cunha, Portuguese commander in
Angola, who arrived in Lisbon March 19.
Spinola's position, created for him by the
government, was not filled.

The dismissal of the military academy
commandant, Reserve Gen. Amaro
Romau, was announced by the government March 18. He reportedly was fired

for allowing a group of dissident officers
to meet at the academy late March 15.

Caetano asserted March 15 that the
government's policy in the African territories would not change. He said: "We
have full confidence in our capacity to win
[a military victory]. I have the faith that
unity, serenity, and the national awareness
of the people will finally triumph over this
crisis."

Nevertheless, an estimated 300 officers
circulated a clandestine paper backing
Spinola's contention that the solution to
Portugal's overseas problem would be
political, not military, the New York
Times reported March 19.

Spinola talks with Cabral cited. A
Portuguese general in Bissau, Portuguese
Guinea reported that Gen. Spinola had
met secretly at least three times with the
late Amilcar Cabral, leader of the rebel
African Party for the Independence of
Guinea and the Cape Verde Islands
(PAIGO), the Washington Post reported
March 20.

Spinola was military governor of
Portuguese Guinea until mid-1973. Cabral
was assassinated in January 1973.

The unidentified officer said the meet-
ings were arranged by Senegal's President
Leopold Senghor, and apparently took
place inside Senegal. The officer said
Cabral was offered the leadership of
Portuguese Guinea if his insurrection
ended and the territory remained inside a
Portuguese "commonwealth."

80 new arrests. A dozen journalists and
members of the political opposition were
arrested in Lisbon April 18, 1974 for
alleged Communist activities. This increased to 55 the number seized within
several days and sent off to the Caxias
prison. Another 30 were reported arrested
in the capital and in Oporto April 21.

Among those seized April 18 were the
leading opposition politician, Jose Tengarrinha, and two political associates, Maria
Elena Neves and Ana Maria Alves. Ms.
Alves reportedly was released later because she was about to have a baby, and

was replaced in prison by her husband, Antonio Manso Pinheiro, a publisher.

Also arrested were Albano Lima, a journalist working for the Portuguese magazine Seara Nova and the French press agency Agence France-Presse, and at least three other journalists.

The arrests were said to be part of a government crackdown on opponents of its African policies. The outlawed Socialist Party had issued a statement April 17 calling for immediate negotiations with the liberation movements of the Portuguese territories of Mozambique, Angola and Portuguese Guinea.

Revolution of April 1974

Military Seize Power

The Portuguese dictatorship that Marcello Caetano had inherited from Antonio
de Oliveira Salazar was overthrown in
April 1974 by a group of young, disgruntled
military officers. Portugal's new rulers
promised to restore democracy and to end
Portugal's colonial wars in Africa.

Coup virtually bloodless. Rebel military
officers calling themselves the Armed
Forces Movement seized control of the
government April 25, ending more than 40
years of civilian dictatorship begun by the
late Premier Antonio Salazar.

The coup reportedly was virtually
bloodless and enjoyed widespread public
support.

Premier Marcello Caetano and President Americo Thomaz were arrested,
and leadership was assumed by a seven-
man "junta of national salvation" pledged
to bring democracy to Portugal and peace
to its African colonies. The junta apparently was dominated by Gen. Antonio
de Spinola, the former deputy general
staff chief, whose dismissal for opposing
Caetano's colonial policies had sparked an
unsuccessful coup attempt in March.

After seizing power, the rebels issued
the following proclamation:

Considering that after 13 years of fighting overseas
the present political system has been unable to define
an overseas policy leading to peace among Portuguese
of all races and creeds;

Considering the growing climate of total detachment of the Portuguese in relation to political
responsibilities they owe as citizens, the growing development of a situation of constant appeals to duty
with a parallel denial of rights;

Considering the necessity to clean up institutions,
eliminating from our system of life the illegal acts that
the abuse of power has legalized;

Considering, finally, the duty of the armed forces
and the defense of the nation, signifying also the civic
liberty of its citizens:

The Movement of the Armed Forces, which has
just achieved the most important civic mission in recent years, proclaims to the nation its intention of
completing a program of salvation for the country
and the restitution to the Portuguese people of the
civil liberties of which they have been deprived.

To effect this, the government will be handed over
to a junta of national salvation, which will carry out
the lines of the Armed Forces Movement plan, whose
details will be given to the nation later.

As soon as possible there will be general elections
for a constituent national assembly, whose powers, by
its representation and free election, will permit the
nation to choose freely its own form of social and
political life.

In the certainty that the nation is with us, supporting our aims, and will accept with good grace the
military government that will have to be in power in
this phase of transition, the Movement of the Armed
Forces calls for calm and patriotism from all
Portuguese and expects the country to support the
powers instituted for its benefit.

In this way we know we will have honored the past
in respect of policies assumed before the nation and
others, and we are fully conscious of having complied
with the sacred duty of restoring to the nation its legitimate and legal powers.

The coup began early in the morning when a raiding party seized a Lisbon radio station and broadcast an appeal to the Republican National Guard, the Lisbon police and other military units in the capital not to oppose the uprising and cause "unnecessary bloodshed."

Rebel forces simultaneously ringed Lisbon, seized the airport and took control of key government ministries. Other uprisings took place in Santarem, 50 miles north of Lisbon, where an armored unit departed for the capital; in Lamego, a base in north central Portugal, and in Tomar and Oporto.

Some shooting was heard in Lisbon, but no military casualties were reported. However, at least one civilian was reported killed and 20 were wounded in unclear circumstances, the New York Times reported April 26.

Military resistance collapsed quickly, although some National Guard units reportedly continued to hold out early April 26 in their barracks in downtown Lisbon, and some resistance was reported from policemen in charge of the Caxias prison, near the capital, where a large number of the government's political opponents were being held.

President Thomaz surrendered to the rebels in a lancers regiment barracks in Lisbon. Premier Caetano and several Cabinet ministers were arrested and taken to a barracks in nearby Pontinha.

Citizens of Lisbon reportedly welcomed the military take-over, and offered food and drink to the rebels. However, rebel officers ordered all shops closed and asked the population to remain at home until further notice.

A crowd of several thousand gathered outside the barracks of the National Guard, where Caetano and other officials had taken refuge. They shouted "assassin!" as an armored car thought to be carrying Caetano emerged, and gave Gen. Spinola a hero's welcome when he arrived to negotiate the premier's surrender. Caetano reportedly handed over power to the rebels "so that the government would not fall in the streets."

(Thomaz, Caetano and two ousted Cabinet officials—former Interior Minister Cesar Moreira Baptista and ex-Defense Minister Joaquim Silva Cunha—were then exiled April 26 to the Portuguese island of Madeira, where they were confined comfortably in a palace.)

Junta's plans. Spinola appeared on a radio-TV broadcast April 26 with five of the six other members of the junta. He pledged freedom of thought and speech and free elections.

(The newspaper Republica had announced in its April 25 issue, reporting the coup, that it was publishing without censorship for the first time.)

Spinola April 26 also held a press conference at which he announced that a provisional government of civilians, headed by a military man, would be formed within three weeks, and that free elections for a constituent assembly and a new president would be held within a year.

Spinola said the provisional government would include persons of varied political views, and he authorized the free formation of political associations to prepare for later political parties. Freedom of assembly and formation of trade unions were also allowed, and censorship was abolished except over disclosure of military secrets, Spinola said.

Political and labor organizing began immediately, and accelerated after April 28, when airports were reopened and land travel to and from Spain resumed, allowing the return of hundreds of political exiles. Among the first to return were Socialist Party leader Mario Soares April 28 and Communist Party leader Alvaro Cunhal April 30. Both received tumultuous welcomes from thousands of followers. They met after their arrival with Gen. Spinola.

Soares said the Socialist Party could agree to the program outlined by Spinola April 26, but he called for independence for Portuguese African territories as soon as possible. Spinola opposed independence, preferring to see the territories in a federation with Portugal.

Spinola said April 27 that "self-determination" for the colonies, which the junta had promised, "should not be confused with independence." He told representatives of the Portuguese Democratic Movement April 29 that the colonies were not yet ready for self-determination. Once self-determination was possible, he added, his government would press the colonies to vote to remain within the Portuguese orbit.

The Portuguese Democratic Movement, a coalition of Socialists, Communists and Christian Democrats, was an outgrowth of the opposition coalition which had sought unsuccessfully to contest elections for the National Assembly in 1973. Its representatives met with Spinola and then said the African territories were ready for self-determination immediately. This statement marked the first open disagreement between the junta and the opposition political forces, which had welcomed the military coup.

U.S. relations unchanged—The U.S. State Department said April 29 that the U.S. and Portugal had exchanged notes marking "the continuation of relations without interruption" between the two countries. State Department spokesman Paul Hare said, regarding Portugal's African territories, that the U.S. had "consistently stated that we believe the right of self-determination should be the governing principle of all people."

South Africa recognized the military junta April 28 and Spain followed suit the next day.

Old regime dismantled. The Portuguese junta issued a series of decrees April 29 which effectively dismantled the ousted civilian dictatorship.

The measures officially deposed President Americo Thomaz and all Cabinet members, including Premier Marcello Caetano; dismissed the governors of Angola and Mozambique; named replacements for the three military chiefs of staff; and dissolved the National Assembly, the Council of State and the only legal party under the old government.

Other decrees proclaimed an amnesty for all political prisoners and dismissed the heads of Portugal's six universities. An estimated 100 political prisoners, including major opposition leaders such as Jose Tengarrinha, had been released April

27, and their places in jail had been taken by members of the old regime's hated political police, which the junta abolished.

A nationwide manhunt for members of the political police was under way, it was reported April 29. Col. Fernando da Silva Pais, head of the state security service, and the leader of the paramilitary Portuguese Legion were said to have been captured and jailed.

Meanwhile, the country returned to relative normality with little bloodshed. A total of 10 deaths were reported by the London Times April 28, following reports of 35 wounded the day before. The casualties included policemen who resisted the coup and bystanders who were inadvertently shot by citizens celebrating the military take-over.

The junta issued warnings against violence by leftist demonstrators and attacks by citizens on members of the political police, and sent tanks into Lisbon streets to discourage unrest. A crowd had attacked the building of the reactionary newspaper Epoca April 26, and an arsonist later set fire to the building.

Massive demonstrations were planned for May 1, which the junta declared a national holiday. Leftist leaders warned their followers that violence would hurt their cause.

Shops, cafes and restaurants reopened April 26, but banks remained closed through April 30 to prevent a massive flight of capital. Border guards and airport security officers searched persons leaving the country and stopped those carrying large quantities of money.

Young officers reported in charge—A dozen liberal young military officers calling themselves the Coordinating Committee of the Revolutionary Plan had been the virtual rulers of Portugal since directing the military coup in April, the Washington Post reported May 5.

The officers, most of them 30–35 years old, appeared to be the governing body of the Armed Forces Movement, which organized and carried out the coup, the Post reported. They appointed Gen. Spinola acting head of the military junta and organized the provisional government he headed, according to the Post.

The officers, who refused to disclose their names for publication, said they were determined to allow Communists to assume public office "if that's what the people want." Whether the African territories became independent was "the decision of all the Portuguese people," they added.

Committee members said Spinola's advocacy of a federation of the African colonies with Portugal was "the general's own personal dream," the Post reported.

New rule in Mozambique, Angola. The new military governments of Mozambique and Angola affirmed their allegiance to the Portuguese junta of Gen. Spinola April 29 and began implementing a series of reforms in the African colonies.

(Gen. Basto Machado, commander in chief of Portuguese forces in Mozambique, announced the army's allegiance to the new Portuguese regime after, he said, carefully examining its program. Gov. Gen. Manuel Pimentel dos Santos had resigned April 27 after Portuguese paratroops barricaded the airport in Lourenco Marques to foil the governor's reported plan to declare the territory independent.)

Thousands participated in public rallies in Mozambique's capital April 29 and May 1, hailing the junta.

Newly appointed Acting Governor Col. David Ferreira issued a number of decrees April 29–30, including release of political prisoners. Upon their release May 1 from Machava prison, the more than 550 prisoners, most of them black, were told by Col. Antonio Maria Rebelo who April 29 was named head of the Directorate of General Security (DGS): "Never forget you belong to a great fatherland.... I know you are going to be good citizens. We trust you. You are free." Imprisoned members of guerrilla liberation movements were not released.

Ferreira also announced the lifting of press censorship; the dismantling of the DGS, which would be stripped of political power and reduced to a military intelligence unit; and dissolution of the Popular National Action Party, Mozambique's only legal political party. Ferreira suspended the territory's Legislative Assembly April 30 as it began to convene for a session.

In Angola, Gov. Gen. Augusto Santos e Castro announced April 27 that he had been suspended from office and ordered to turn control over to the army. Amid public demonstrations in support of the Portuguese coup, the new governor, Col. Soares Carneiro announced the release of 85 political prisoners May 1. The former governor sailed for Lisbon April 29.

African nationalists wary. In radio broadcasts April 26–28 from their headquarters in various African capitals, leaders of the rebel movements in Portugal's three African colonies expressed skepticism that the change of regime in Lisbon would substantially affect their activities.

While the groups hailed the coup because it removed the Caetano government, the spokesmen for the Front for the Liberation of Mozambique (FRELIMO), the Popular Movement for the Liberation of Angola (MPLA), the National Front for the Liberation of Angola (FNLA) and the African Party for the Independence of (Portuguese) Guinea and Cape Verde (PAIGC) all declared their opposition to the federative system of alliance with Portugal proposed by Gen. Spinola.

FRELIMO leaders said they expected no change in the government's policy and asserted, "We are not fighting to become Portuguese of black skin."

The MPLA announced that it would continue to strike at the Portuguese army and accused the coup of aiming to "perpetuate exploitation." The FNLA said it would be willing to negotiate with the new government, but only within "the historic context of total independence for Angola."

PAIGC forces vowed to step up their actions to "liquidate the largest possible number of Portuguese troops" and reiterated their opposition to any ties with Portugal.

Africa cease-fire offered. The military junta May 6 offered a cease-fire to guerrillas fighting for independence in Portugal's African colonies, on the condition that colonial liberation movements accept the "framework of the democratic program of the armed forces."

The proposal, made by Gen. Francisco da Costa Gomes, chief of the general staff and a junta member, was not immediately accepted by the liberation movements, leading to further appeals by the junta as the fighting continued.

Issuing a new appeal May 11, Maj. Jose Sanches Osorio, a junta spokesman, said the liberation movements had been asked to become legitimate political parties, and to seek satisfaction of their demands by peaceful and democratic means. Until the rebels laid down their arms, he said, Portuguese troops would continue to be sent to the territories to fight.

Sanches Osorio confirmed that junta representatives would investigate new reports of massacres by Portuguese troops in Mozambique between August 1973 and March 1974. The reports, by Dutch missionaries, followed charges by Spanish and British missionaries in 1973 of an earlier massacre in Mozambique.

The Socialist Party had issued a manifesto April 30 demanding an end to Portugal's colonial wars, and opening of negotiations with the "state" of Guinea-Bissau (Portuguese Guinea) and liberation movements of Angola and Mozambique to achieve self-determination for the colonies.

In a May 11 address in Mozambique, Gen. Costa Gomes reiterated the cease-fire offer. But he backed up his previous threat of intensified war by warning that "a majority of parties [in the forthcoming Cabinet] will surely be of the opinion that the fight must go on."

Soares on European tour. Mario Soares visited six European nations and conferred with leaders of three other countries during a whirlwind tour May 2–6. He traveled not as a representative of the junta but as leader of his Socialist Party.

Soares' first stop was London, where he met with British Prime Minister Harold Wilson and Foreign Secretary James Callaghan, and secured prompt recognition for the junta from Great Britain.

Soares later visited France, West Germany, the Netherlands, Belgium and Finland, conferring with leaders of those nations and, in Finland, with representatives of Norway, Denmark and Sweden, it was reported May 5.

Soviet & Chinese reaction. Soviet and Chinese observers hailed the overthrow of the Portuguese dictatorship as a defeat for colonialism and a major step toward independence for Portugal's African territories.

The Soviet government newspaper Izvestia charged May 6 that important civilian and military elements in Portugal sought to "castrate" demands for radical reform. It said the new Portuguese regime would have to accept complete independence for Portugal's overseas territories.

Chinese Premier Chou En-lai declared May 6 that the Portuguese coup "signals the ignominious failure of Portugal's notorious policy of colonialism and represents a major victory for the persistent and protracted armed struggle of the African people."

Liberal Trend?

Early actions of the ruling Portuguese military junta seemed to indicate that the country's new leaders intended to fulfill at least some of their promises to restore democratic processes. Some observers, however, expressed fear that an extreme leftist rather than liberal trend was developing.

Labor demands approved. The military junta May 10 approved labor contracts cutting the workweek to 40 hours and granting pay increases of up to 50% to thousands of industrial and construction workers.

The contracts embodied most of the workers' demands, and defused the threats of crippling strikes. The pacts had been negotiated with the ousted civilian dictatorship, but had been regarded as inflationary.

The junta had agreed May 9, after two days of meetings with representatives of 44 labor unions, to allow Portuguese unions to form a confederation. Junta spokesmen told the unions they would be recognized by the government and allowed to negotiate with management without official interference. Union leaders said they would call strikes only as a last resort, and warned against allowing "the enemies of the people, of democracy and of the workers to profit from the indiscriminate or undue use of strikes to spread confusion."

Steelworkers had called a strike for May 6, but had postponed it May 5 in exchange for a promise from management to consider their demands. Executives of the National Steel Co., owned jointly by the government and by banker Antonio de Champalimaud, a close friend of Gen. Spinola, announced a partial agreement with their employes May 10; workers would get a pay increase and be allowed to form a committee to review pay scales and working conditions and to participate in settlement of disputes.

Workers oppose 'collaborators'—The government faced other labor problems, stemming principally from attempts by workers to oust members of management who had collaborated with the ousted dictatorship.

The Timex watch manufacturing plant outside Lisbon was occupied May 9 by more than 2,000 women employes demanding the immediate dismissal of six supervisors whom they called "fascist tools" of the old regime. However, the women continued to work, asserting a production halt would only "damage the economy."

The Lisbon newspaper O Seculo did not publish May 10 because its management refused to give up control of news columns to the editorial staff. A similar problem had arisen earlier at the reactionary paper Epoca, and the junta had ordered the publication closed and its plants sold.

Workers in five key public services—postal, railways, electricity, telephones and the national airline TAP—had succeeded in ousting their top managements

because of connections with the former regime, it was reported May 4.

The junta had pledged May 2 to conduct a purge of officials of the former regime, but had warned that haste could cause a breakdown of both services and justice. The state-controlled television network issued repeated warnings against "mini-revolutions" May 3, asserting they could hinder economic development.

The junta issued a communique May 5 ordering workers in publicly owned enterprises to stop holding meetings during office hours to force removal of their superiors. The Communist Party issued an appeal the same day against unauthorized seizures of institutions, city councils and property associated with the former regime, calling such actions "counterrevolutionary" and a "adventurist."

Workers had also taken over from their old leaders the official labor unions to which workers were forced to belong under the old government.

Military amnesty. The junta May 2 declared an amnesty for the thousands of men who had deserted the armed forces or evaded the draft to avoid fighting in the colonies.

The amnesty applied only to those who promptly reported for military service. Soldiers in army jails for desertion were returned to active duty, and deserters and draft dodgers who had taken refuge in foreign countries were given 15 days to return to Portugal and report for duty.

An estimated 1,000 leftists described by the junta as "Maoists" invaded the Lisbon military airport late May 3 and reportedly kidnapped 10 soldiers about to embark for the colonies. Another 10 soldiers reportedly refused to embark and were allowed to remain in Portugal.

Secret police arrested. About 900 members of the ousted government's secret police had been arrested since the military coup, a junta spokesman reported May 11.

Inspector Jose Sachetti, second in command of the political police force, had been reported arrested April 30 while trying to flee across the Spanish border.

'3 Marias' acquitted. Three women writers were acquitted in a Lisbon court May 7 of charges that they had offended public morals in a book attacking the suppression of women's rights in Portugal. The authors, known as the "Three Marias," were Maria Velho de Costa, Maria Teresa Horta and Maria Isabel Barreno. Immediately after the verdict, they announced they would start a women's liberation movement in Portugal with the first aim of legalizing abortion.

In arresting them in 1973, the Caetano government had charged that their book, "New Portuguese Letters," contained obscene passages. Nearly 3,000 copies had been sold before it was banned. The case had aroused international protests.

Portugal Under Spinola

Spinola heads new government. Gen. Antonio de Spinola was proclaimed provisional president of Portugal May 15. He announced a 15-man Cabinet which included three Socialists, two Communists and other representatives of the left and the center.

Spinola said he would give up the office within a year, after elections were held for a new president and a constituent national assembly. "Having fulfilled this mission," he pledged, ". . . I will withdraw again to the armed forces, from which I never separated myself . . ."

Spinola warned that "democracy does not mean anarchy." As for the nation's African territories, the general said their "final choice" in a free and peaceful election would be "scrupulously respected."

Spinola was proclaimed president by Gen. Francisco da Costa Gomes, chief of the general staff, who said Spinola would rule with the powers of the current authoritarian Constitution. Costa Gomes praised the young officers who apparently organized the April 25 military coup, chose Spinola as interim president and selected the Cabinet ministers. He said they had carried out the "most dignified revolution in contemporary history."

After his investiture, Spinola announced a Cabinet headed by Premier Adelino da Palma Carlos, a liberal law professor whose moderate opposition under the ousted regime had caused him to be banned from teaching and public office for several years by the late dictator Antonio Salazar.

Socialist Party leader Mario Soares became minister of foreign affairs, and Communist Party chief Alvaro Cunhal was named minister without portfolio. The Cabinet included two other Socialists (Francisco Salgado Zenha, justice minister, and Raul Rego, social communications [information] minister) and one other Communist (Avelino Pacheco Goncalves, labor minister).

Lt. Col. Mario Firmino Miguel, a member of the young officers' group, was named defense minister. The key Interior Ministry, which controlled the police, was given to a centrist, Joaquim Magalhaes Motta.

Twenty-two deputy ministers were also named, representing a wide variety of political views and technical skills. Many had been imprisoned or exiled under the ousted dictatorship.

Before Spinola's investiture, 42 military officers who had supported the former regime had been retired to insure discipline in the armed forces. Twenty-four generals and admirals who had backed the dictatorship had been retired April 30, including Gen. Joaquim da Luz Cunha, who had been named chief of the general staff shortly before the coup.

Widespread strikes. A wave of strikes swept Portugal in late May and subsided after the demands of many strikers were met and the government appealed to workers to prevent labor anarchy.

More than 8,000 workers at the Lisnave shipyard in Lisbon, the nation's largest employer, struck May 15 for a 50% wage increase, profit-sharing and better working conditions. They returned to work May 23, after their demands were granted.

Bus and train conductors throughout the country refused to accept fares from passengers May 15–16, to protest their working conditions. Thousands of textile workers in Oporto and more then 5,000 members of the National Federation of Wool Industries in Lisbon began wildcat strikes May 16.

More than 60,000 Portuguese industrial workers were reported on strike May 20. The Organization for Economic Cooperation and Development announced that day that Portuguese inflation for the 12 months ending in March had reached 30%.

Several industries were reported returning to normal May 21, and 2,000 workers at the Goncalves auto plant ended a strike May 22 after winning large pay increases and a 40-hour workweek. But the stoppages picked up again May 24, when Lisbon's subway workers walked out for three hours and won a 50% wage hike. (The government later determined that the subway system could not afford the raise, and fired the entire subway board May 30.)

Officials announced a wage-price freeze May 25. The next day government and union leaders appealed to workers to refrain from strikes pending further labor-management talks, and the Communist Party condemned "strikes for strikes' sake."

Streetcar and bus workers in the capital struck May 27 for wage increases similar to the subway workers'. They were joined the next day by bakery workers and employes of the central post office.

After the subway workers' strike, members of the military junta and the provisional government were in almost permanent session to resolve the labor disputes. Government efforts were led by Labor Minister Avelino Pacheco Goncalves and Minister without Portfolio Alvaro Cunhal, both Communists. They persuaded many of the striking textile workers to return to their jobs May 27.

Gen. Carlos Galvao de Melo, appearing on television May 27, charged that strikers were misusing the freedom they gained after the April military coup. He said the armed forces were "disgusted and almost frightened by the ingratitude" they had shown. The leftist Portuguese Democratic Movement warned the strikers that the nation could not afford their stoppages.

The national radio network broadcast warnings to the strikers from government junta and civilian leaders several times May 28. The Communist Party issued a stern declaration the next day urging workers to "unmask demagogues and adventurers" who were pushing the country toward anarchy.

Spinola warned May 29 that economic disruption played into the hands of "reactionaries and counterrevolutionaries." He appealed to the people to "choose between democratic freedom and anarchy," and asserted; "It is not by way of anarchy, economic chaos, disorder and unemployment that we build the Portugal of the future."

Bakery and transit workers were persuaded to return to work May 30 while labor-management talks continued. Workers at the Electrolux shipyard in the north returned to work the same day after a two-day stoppage.

Spinola warned in a second speech May 31 that the country could not "distribute wealth before we produce it," and urged citizens to build "a democratic Portugal, truly free and with more social justice."

Caetano, Thomaz exiled to Brazil. Former Premier Marcello Caetano and ex-President Americo Thomaz were flown May 20 to Brazil, which granted them asylum on condition that they abstain from political activity.

The decision to exile the former leaders was made by the military junta over the objections of leftist members of the provisional government, who wanted Caetano and Thomaz tried for crimes laid to the secret police and other agencies during their dictatorship. The junta apparently believed their trial would deeply divide the country.

The Communist Party issued a strong statement May 21 claiming the deportation of Thomaz and Caetano "cannot but profoundly shock the working class and all those who suffered during almost 50 years of Fascist repression and tyranny." The party said it did not seek a "vindictive policy," but thought that "decisions of great political importance [should] be taken only after consultations."

The Socialist Party also expressed displeasure at the deportations, but its leader, Foreign Minister Mario Soares, stressed that the decision had been taken before the provisional government was formed. The leftist Portuguese Democratic Movement "energetically" protested the deportations.

In an apparent move to appease critics of the deportations, officials announced May 24 that two former Cabinet ministers, a vice admiral, an army general and colonel and a former National Assembly deputy would be tried for crimes committed under the dictatorship. The Cabinet officials were former Interior Minister Cesar Moreira Baptista and ex-Defense Minister Joaquim da Silva Cunha, who were transferred back to Lisbon from Madeira May 23.

Rios arrested. Manuel Rios, leader of the Free Portugal Front, was arrested in Lisbon May 22, less than two weeks after he returned to Portugal from exile in France. The newspaper Diario de Noticias reported his arrest was motivated by "strong assumptions" that he had belonged to PIDE, the now abolished secret police.

Post-Coup Developments in Africa

Angola. Gen. Francisco da Costa Gomes, chief of the general staff, visited Angola May 4–6 and dismissed a number of military officers whom the junta suspected of preparing a right-wing counter-coup. About 1,200 political prisoners had been released from a detention camp in the south May 3.

The several rebel independence movements rejected the junta's May 5 cease-fire offer and vowed to continue their struggle. Agostinho Neto, leader of the Popular Movement for the Liberation of Angola (MPLA), had started on a European tour April 25 in an effort to secure support for his movement. Neto met with Portuguese Socialist leader Mario Soares in Brussels, and he also paid visits to leaders in Copenhagen and in East Berlin. In a statement reported by the French newspaper Le Monde May 12–13, Neto specified that "a cease-fire would be meaningless without Portugal's acknowledgement in an official and public pact" of Angola's right to "complete and immediate independence. Then the negotiations can begin."

The MPLA and the two other principal independence groups in Angola, the National Front for the Liberation of Angola (FNLA) and the National Union for the Total Independence of Angola (UNITA), were competing for leadership and power in the evolving chain of events since the April 25 coup in Lisbon.

After Soares had said May 22 that he would negotiate with all three groups, each sought to establish itself as the sole legitimate agent of the Angolan liberation movement and, by virtue of protracted inter-group conflicts, had thus far failed to engage in any official negotiations with Portugal as had Portuguese Guinea and Mozambique.

A May 26 meeting between FNLA leader Holden Roberto and Neto failed to reconcile them. Neto said May 30 that he saw "no immediate possibility of unification" for the MPLA and the FNLA. In a May 27 interview reported in the Algiers newspaper Al Moudjahid, Neto rejected the Lisbon referendum proposal, saying that Portugal must "purely and simply" leave Angola.

The French newspaper Le Monde reported June 6 that the FNLA, with the aid of Zaire President Mobutu Sese Seko, was maneuvering to weaken support for the MPLA. (FNLA headquarters were located in Kinshasa.) The Zaire press agency reported June 2 that the first contingent of Chinese military instructors had arrived in Kinshasa to train FNLA troops in guerrilla warfare.

Political meetings and demonstrations had been banned in Angola May 27 following racial violence in Luanda May 26–27.

Political tensions were further strained by the emergence of a group in Cabinda, the oil-rich Angolan exclave surrounded by Zaire and the Congo, which was seeking independence of Angola and federation with Portugal, the New York Times reported June 3.

Military sources in Angola said that they had ceased offensive military operations, it was reported May 18. Lt. Gen. Joaquim Antonio Franco Pinheiro, commander in chief of Portuguese forces in Angola, said June 1: "There is no more defoliation, no more destruction of crops. All that is finished."

Military reports, noted by the New York Times June 3 and the London Times June 8, claimed that 21 Portuguese soldiers had been killed in May and that 265 rebels and civilian sympathizers had been captured. A June 1 New York Times report quoted the Portuguese army commander in Angola as saying that troops had seized about 300 men, women, and children a month and put them into "resettlement villages" under government control to remove them from rebel influences.

Gen. Silvino Silverio Marques was sworn in as governor of Angola June 11 in Lisbon. Known for his rightist views, Marques was apparently appointed to placate the territory's uneasy white population; about 500,000 of Angola's 6 million people were Portuguese, according to the French newspaper Le Monde May 29.

Lisbon reached agreement June 17 to end hostilities with UNITA "as soon as possible." Although neither of the other two groups was willing to enter into any such agreement until Lisbon first gave assurances of total independence, Portuguese military headquarters in Luanda reported July 7 that guerrilla activities in Angola had diminished in June.

A military council was put in control of Angola July 23 after a week of violence that had erupted in Luanda when black workers went on strike July 15. In demonstrations that followed through July 23, at least 43 people were killed and 160 injured. Rear Adm. Antonio Rosa Coutinho, a member of the Lisbon military junta, arrived in Luanda July 24 to head the military council. (Angola's governor had been recalled to Lisbon.)

Coutinho called on the three Angolan liberation movements July 26 to join in a coalition government and not jeopardize plans for a referendum to be held in March 1975.

According to a July 29 report, Agostinho Neto had quit as head of the Popular Movement for the Liberation of Angola [MPLA] following a factional dispute. The MPLA and the National Front for the Liberation of Angola had agreed, the report said, to join their forces in a "common front."

According to an Argus Africa News Service report Aug. 8, blacks and whites were fleeing Luanda's outer suburbs at a rate of more than 1,000 a day in the wake of persisting racial strife and guerrilla clashes. Eighteen were reported dead and 122 wounded in clashes Aug. 5-8. The report further said that the military leadership was being criticized for the handling of the situation.

Portuguese Guinea (Guinea-Bissau). Lt. Col. Sa Gouveia, newly appointed chief of the Portuguese military high command in Portuguese Guinea, announced May 1 that the territory's governor had been dismissed and that a military triumvirate had been placed in control. All African political chiefs appointed by the governor had been dismissed and replaced by military personnel. It was also reported May 1 that all political prisoners had been released and that the army had arrested members of the former political police.

In a statement reported May 9 from Dakar, Senegal, Francisco Mendes, an official of the self-proclaimed government of Guinea-Bissau, rejected the junta's May 6 cease-fire offer. However, he later noted that he expected further clarifications from Lisbon "because the situation in Portugal isn't very clear." Spokesmen for the rebel government issued a statement May 12 from Algiers calling for negotiations.

Diplomatic support of the Guinea-Bissau government was expressed May 12 when envoys from the Soviet Union, Yugoslavia, Rumania, Algeria and Guinea presented their credentials in Conakry to Luis Cabral, head of the rebel government.

Portuguese Foreign Minister Mario Soares opened peace talks with representatives of the African Party for the Independence of (Portuguese) Guinea and Cape Verde (PAIGC) in London May 25. Soares had announced the talks May 17 following a meeting with PAIGC leader Aristides Pereira in Senegal.

Interviewed May 22, Soares had said the scenario anticipated by Portugal for the political future of the African territories was "a cease-fire, self-determination [through a referendum] and independence," with the London talks to focus on the cease-fire. The negotiations bogged down, however, for the PAIGC had, according to the London Times May 27, established preconditions, including the recognition by Portugal of the "state" of Guinea-Bissau, a step which would effectively rule out the need for a referendum.

A PAIGC announcement May 25 stated that it had ceased all guerrilla operations.

Luis Cabral said in a May 25 radio broadcast that the guerrillas would resume combat if Portugal did not "respect our conquests." (According to the London Times May 28, the rebels controlled three-quarters of the territory.)

Another snag was encountered over the issue of the Cape Verde Islands. Because of the strategic air and naval bases located there, Portugal was seeking to keep the islands' status distinct from that of Portuguese Guinea. The PAIGC, however, was pressing for Portuguese recognition of "the unity of Guinea-Bissau and the Cape Verde Islands."

(Cape Verde's governor, ousted May 1, was replaced by Rear Admiral Pedro Fragoso Matos, commander in chief of the territory's armed forces. Political prisoners from Cape Verde, Angola and Portuguese Guinea were released from the islands' prison complex May 2. A May 13 report noted demonstrations by pro- as well as anti-independence groups.

(Eight people were injured May 19 when opposing groups demonstrated in Praia, the capital of Cape Verde. Supporters of the independence movement staged sympathy demonstrations in Lisbon May 21.)

Soares returned to Lisbon May 28, but negotiations continued with Antonio de Almeida Santos, minister of interterritorial coordination, heading Lisbon's delegation. The London negotiations ended after a major compromise was offered by the PAIGC May 31 "to discuss Cape Verde issue separately."

Mozambique. After a post-coup combat lull, the Front for the Liberation of Mozambique (FRELIMO) attacked a bus in northern Mozambique May 8, killing at least six passengers. One person was killed when the insurgents blew up a train on the Beira-Malawi line May 9.

FRELIMO announced May 8 that its forces had shot down two Rhodesian aircraft and captured the pilots April 20. Gen. Francisco da Costa Gomes said May 13 that the rebels had used Soviet-made surface-to-air missiles.

Costa Gomes had made informal contacts with FRELIMO during a May 10–13 "fact-finding mission." Speaking May 11 in Laurenco Marques, he urged the rebels to transfer their headquarters from Tanzania to Mozambique and operate as a political party in forthcoming elections. He proposed immediate negotiations with FRELIMO, "without preconditions, without a symbolic surrender of arms . . . We would like to receive them with the respect due them for their bravery and courage."

(In televised remarks on his return to Lisbon May 14, the general expressed fears that Portugal would not be able to hold Mozambique because of the deteriorating conditions there. The general had observed in comments reported in the New York Times May 13 that Portuguese forces in Mozambique were "heavy" in mind. He contrasted the situation there with that in Angola where, Costa Gomes said, "there are many people whose thinking is close to ours in metropolitan Portugal.")

The conciliatory tone of Costa Gomes' May 11 appeal spurred the momentum of a mounting "white backlash" movement that found its chief political expression in a new party calling itself the Independent

Front for Western Continuity, whose Portuguese acronym, FICO, means "I stay." FICO supporters demonstrated in the capital May 4-5 against Portuguese abandonment of Mozambique. Violent demonstrations between blacks and whites broke out in Lourenco Marques May 11 and in Beira May 12.

FRELIMO issued a statement May 10, stressing that it was not waging a racial war, but was "struggling against Portuguese colonialism for Mozambique's independence." Rebel leader Samora Moises Machel called May 8 for a "general offensive" until the territory's right to independence was acknowledged.

A major group emerging was the United Group of Mozambique, GUMO, a multi-racial party seeking "gradual autonomy" for the territory and presenting itself as "FRELIMO without the violence." In remarks reported May 11, GUMO Vice President Joanna Simiao, a black African, stressed that FRELIMO was the most important element in Mozambique's political future.

Mozambique military authorities had taken moves May 6 which seemed aimed at placating both left- and right-wing factions of the population: a new "information service" was established whose primary purpose would be to avert any attempt at a counter-coup waged by the extreme right; at the same time, military officers were named to supervise the publication of four Mozambique newspapers.

Portuguese Interterritorial Coordination Minister Antonio de Almeida Santos announced May 21 that a referendum would be held in Mozambique within a year. He saw "no doubt that the majority of the people . . . will choose independence." Almeida was accompanied on a May 20-23 visit to Mozambique by Lt. Col. Sausa Belchior, the junta member responsible for African territories, and had been empowered to make political decisions without referring back to Lisbon.

Almeida, a native of Mozambique, reiterated the promise of independence May 22 in an address to thousands of dock and cashew plant workers, on strike since May 17, who were demanding more pay and better working conditions. Work was resumed May 23 after a compromise wage increase was agreed to in negotiations between Almeida and workers' representatives. Strikes had been illegal and real labor negotiations unknown in Mozambique prior to the April 25 coup.

Lisbon held "preliminary and exploratory" talks with FRELIMO in Lusaka, Zambia June 5-6 in the first formal contacts between Portugal and the rebel movement since its emergence as an anticolonial force in 1962.

Portuguese Foreign Minister Mario Soares headed Lisbon's delegation and greeted FRELIMO president Samora Machel June 5 with great warmth and emotion, saying: "We were and are objectively allied . . . We two have enemies common to us both."

The talks failed to achieve a hoped-for cease-fire and ended sooner than expected because, the final communique issued June 6 said, "the Portuguese delegation considered it necessary to consult its government." The communique also stated that "the two delegations recognized that the establishment of a cease-fire depends on prior global agreement related to fundamental political principles"—an apparent reference to FRELIMO's insistence that Portugal acknowledge Mozambique's right to independence before meaningful negotiations could progress.

(Zambian President Kenneth Kaunda had been instrumental in organizing the talks, having called on Portugal as early as May 1 to undertake negotiations with the African rebel movements. Tanzania and Zaire had also taken an active role; Kaunda, Tanzania President Julius Nyerere and Zaire President Mobutu Sese Seko had held meetings in Lusaka with rebel leaders May 23-26 to help chart plans for the peaceful attainment of independence by the Portuguese territories.)

Gen. Basto Machado, commander in chief of Portuguese forces in Mozambique, was replaced by Gen. Orlando Barbosa May 23.

A June 8 military report stated that several hundred members of the recently disbanded Directorate General of Security (DGS) had been arrested and jailed "following reports of alleged atrocities committed during the rule of former Premier Marcello Caetano." It was reported June 10 that a number of DGS members had fled across the border to South Africa and Rhodesia. A white liberal, Pereira Leite, was attacked by a group of whites in Lourenco Marques June 26 after complaining to Lisbon authorities that almost all of the 500 members of the Directorate General of Security who had been arrested since the coup had been released.

Henrique Soares de Melo, a Mozambique lawyer, had been sworn in as governor of Mozambique June 11 in Lisbon.

Massacres reported—Dutch missionaries reported May 9 that Portuguese security forces in Mozambique had massacred 113 black Africans Feb. 18–23 in reprisal for guerrilla activities in the Inhaminga area. It was reported that 22 more had been executed April 26, the day after the Lisbon coup. The missionaries also accused the security forces of torturing prisoners and children and charged that Portuguese troops had used napalm in large-scale operations since March 8.

First reports of the massacres had come from Portuguese officers in Mozambique who claimed that Rhodesian parachutists conducting raids in Mozambique, with the consent of the Portuguese authorities, were "under orders not to take civilian or military prisoners, but to kill everyone they found." The report was first printed in the British newspaper The Guardian April 23.

A five-member United Nations commission established in 1973 to investigate reports of atrocities in Mozambique concluded in its final report June 27 that "many hundreds" of unarmed villagers had been killed by Portuguese troops.

The panel reported that the most recent mass slayings had occurred near Inhaminga in March. The commission criticized the new Portuguese government for not cooperating with the inquiry. Despite a May 30 assurance of cooperation, Portuguese officials had not permitted the commission to enter Mozambique or to interview military authorities, the panel said.

Spinola cites independence options. Gen. Antonio de Spinola, provisional president of Portugal, in a major policy statement June 11 offered the nation's African territories a choice of "federation, confederation, community or the mere existence of totally independent states." It was the first time he had noted the option of independence; previously he had spoken of "self-determination." However, Spinola continued to maintain that such a decision would be made in a referendum to be held following a gradual program of decolonization.

A number of military officers doubted that his proposals would be accepted by the African nationalists and criticized the absence of a timetable and the diffusion of economic development funds when Portugal itself was in need of such financing, according to a New York Times report June 11.

(Talks were resumed in Algiers June 13 by representatives of Lisbon and of the African Party for the Independence of [Portuguese] Guinea & Cape Verde [PAIGC], but the negotiations collapsed June 14, reportedly because PAIGC leaders were angered by Spinola's speech.)

OAU action. The heads of state of the Organization of African Unity (OAU) held their 11th annual summit meeting June 12–16 in Mogadishu, Somalia. In resolutions and statements adopted June 16, the heads of the OAU states declared that they were ready to open diplomatic relations with Portugal if Lisbon recognized Guinea-Bissau as an independent state and negotiated with guerrilla leaders for the total independence of Angola and Mozambique.

Guinea-Bissau was admitted as the OAU's 42nd member at the Mogadishu conference and rebel leader Luis Cabral was elected a deputy chairman of the organization June 13. The OAU authorized a meeting between its newly elected secretary general and Portuguese Foreign Minister Mario Soares to discuss future relations. (Outgoing Secretary General Nzo Ekanghaki said June 7 that a Brazilian government delegation had assured him of Brazil's support for the independence of Portuguese colonies in Africa.)

Portugal & Malawi cut ties. Portugal announced July 24 that it had broken diplomatic relations with Malawi following President Hastings Kamuzu Banda's "unacceptable" refusal to expel Jorge Jardim, a right-wing Mozambique white separatist, for directing terrorist activities from a protected base in Malawi. Banda announced later that day that he had, in turn, severed his country's relations with Portugal. He rejected Lisbon's charge and defended Jardim.

(Portugal had also recalled its ambassador from Malawi in 1972, accusing the government of harboring guerrillas.)

According to Agence France-Presse reports July 14 and 21, white mercenaries were infiltrating Mozambique's borders in growing numbers, suggesting that Jardim's strength was a significant force. The forces Jardim had included more than 1,000 paratroopers, mainly FRELIMO deserters, the reports said.

Colonies to Be Freed

Guinea-Bissau to be independent first. Portuguese Provisional President Spinola announced July 27 that Lisbon would start an immediate transfer of power in its African colonies, beginning with Guinea-Bissau.

The government had asked the liberation movements of Angola and Mozambique to participate in provisional coalition governments being formed in the two territories that would eventually cede power to Africans, it was reported August 2. The coalitions would be run by military-dominated juntas, headed by members of the seven-man Lisbon military junta.

The Council of State issued a constitutional law July 17 abolishing an article of the old Constitution that made the overseas territories integral parts of Portugal.

United Nations Secretary General Kurt Waldheim visited Lisbon Aug. 2-4 for talks with the Portuguese leaders. It was announced after the meetings that the Portuguese government:

- was "prepared to sign agreements at once with the Republic of Guinea-Bissau for the immediate transfer of power" and would give its "full support" to the African nation's request for admission to the U.N. (The self-proclaimed government of Guineau-Bissau [Portuguese Guinea] had applied for full membership status in the U.N. July 29. A total of 84 countries had already recognized it, including Brazil July 18 and Japan July 24.)

- recognized the rights of Mozambique, Angola, Sao Tome e Principe and the Cape Verde Islands to independence and expressed willingness to implement U.N. decisions on decolonization.

- undertook "fully to insure the unity and integrity of each of the territories" and declared itself "against any separatist attempts to divide them, whatever the source." (This was seen as a warning to white-ruled South Africa and Rhodesia and the conservative black government of Malawi, all of which were deemed hostile to the emergence of revolutionary black rule in Mozambique.)

Guinea-Bissau independence pact. Portugal signed an agreement with the African Party for the Independence of Guinea-Bissau and the Cape Verde Islands (PAIGC) Aug. 26 which set Sept. 10 as the date upon which the Portuguese colony would become independent. The agreement was signed in Algiers by Portuguese Foreign Minister Mario Soares and Guinea-Bissau Vice Minister of Defense Pedro Pires.

Under the agreement, which formally ended 11 years of guerrilla warfare and signaled the close of five centuries of colonial rule, Lisbon agreed to withdraw all of its armed forces from the territory by Oct. 31. (A de facto cease-fire had gone into effect in May.) The pact specified that Cape Verde's political future would be decided later by a referendum in the islands. (Henrique da Silva Horta was named governor of the Cape Verde Islands Aug. 7.)

The United Nations Security Council had unanimously recommended Aug. 12

that Guinea-Bissau be admitted to the U.N.; Portugal lent its support to the recommendation. Official recognition of Guinea-Bissau was extended that day by the nine member nations of the European Community.

Guinea-Bissau free. Portugal formally recognized the independence of the Republic of Guinea-Bissau Sept. 10, as Provisional President Spinola gave the documents ending Portugal's rule to Maj. Pedro Pires, who headed the new African state's delegation to Lisbon.

Pires said Aug. 29 that Guinea-Bissau would follow a policy of nonalignment. The new nation's President was Luis de Almeida Cabral, leader of the nation's liberation movement.

The new Guinea-Bissau government shifted the capital from Bissau to the rural village of Madina do Boe, where in September 1973 the former rebel movement had declared the republic's independence.

The U.S. recognized Guinea-Bissau and offered to establish diplomatic relations, the State Department announced Sept. 10. The U.N. General Assembly admitted Guinea-Bissau to U.N. membership Sept. 17.

Mozambique liberation advances. As the time for Mozambique's independence grew shorter, the French news agency Agence France-Presse reported July 22 that Portuguese army troops had abandoned a number of camps and in many instances were refusing to fight with the rebels.

Three members of the Lisbon junta arrived in Lourenco Marques July 25 to set up a new military administration which would lead to self-rule in Mozambique. Governor Henrique Soares de Melo resigned his post that day to make way for the new government.

The Front for the Liberation of Mozambique (FRELIMO) then announced Aug. 3 that a de facto cease-fire between rebel and Portuguese troops was in effect in several regions in Mozambique. Ac-

cording to an Aug. 5 report, many communities were making their own contacts with FRELIMO and arranging local agreements.

Some racial violence took place: serious confrontations disrupted the northern port of Antonio Enes Aug. 10 and a right-wing group attacked the Lourenco Marques office of the daily newspaper Noticias Aug. 15. Whites were continuing to leave Mozambique at the rate of 1,000 a week, it was reported Aug. 11.

Some 3,000 civil servants in Lourenco Marques struck Aug. 20 to demand higher wages and the immediate turnover of the government to FRELIMO.

The British news agency Reuters reported that five political groups had merged Aug. 24 to form the National Coalition of Mozambique as a challenge to FRELIMO.

Independence pact sets FRELIMO rule. Samora Moises Machel, leader of the Front for the Liberation of Mozambique (FRELIMO), and Portuguese Foreign Minister Mario Soares signed an agreement in Lusaka, Zambia Sept. 7, under which Mozambique would be ruled by a transitional joint Portuguese-FRELIMO government until June 25, 1975 when independence would be granted and a government formed by FRELIMO. An abortive white backlash movement in Mozambique was mounted in response, seeking unsuccessfully to abrogate or modify the pact's terms.

The agreement, which ended 10 years of guerrilla warfare, was concluded after a final round of talks begun Sept. 5 in the Zambian capital resolved details of the decolonization procedure.

In addition to declaring a cease-fire and setting a date for independence, the pact provided for appointment of a Portuguese high commissioner to supervise the transitional phase (Adm. Vitor Crespo was sworn into the post Sept. 10.); a transitional government with a premier appointed by FRELIMO and nine ministers, six of whom would be appointed by FRELIMO; joint defense of Mozambique's borders; a multiracial society; creation of a central bank with funds to be transferred

by Portugal; and acceptance by FRE-
LIMO of financial obligations undertaken
by Portugal if deemed in the territory's
interests. (This was an apparent reference
to the Cabora Bassa hydroelectric project
being built in Mozambique with South
African funds.

(South African Prime Minister John
Vorster told the Parliament in Cape Town
Aug. 30 that creation of a black government in Mozambique was inevitable and
said he would "take the earliest opportunity to establish contact with it and
to come to an understanding with it." He
also said that South Africa would neither
interfere in nor invade Mozambique unless attacks against South Africa were
mounted from Mozambique.)

White rebel movement collapses—A
white rebel movement sought unsuccessfully to seize control in Lourenco Marques
Sept. 7, hours after Lisbon and FRE-
LIMO had signed a pact which provided
for Mozambique to become independent
under black nationalist rule.

The white backlash movement was defused Sept. 10 by police and Portuguese
troops after three days of violence had disrupted the Mozambiquan capital. According to a Portuguese government communique Sept. 11, 100 persons, most of
them black, had been killed and 250 injured in street riots.

(An attempt by whites to seize control
of Beira, a major port in central Mozambique, was put down Sept. 9 by Portuguese
troops. Several deaths were reported.

(Fresh disturbances broke out in
Lourenco Marques Sept. 10 and a black
backlash had reportedly begun as rioting
took place in the shanty towns surrounding the capital.)

Calling themselves the "Dragons of
Death," the whites had seized control of
Mozambique's main radio station and
broadcast a call for independence without
FRELIMO participation, demanding the
abrogation of the pact signed in Lusaka.
For two days, several thousand whites
and some blacks gathered outside the
radio station forming a human wall to
deter Portuguese troops. The group also
freed some 200 jailed members of the disbanded secret police from a Lourenco
Marques prison.

Gen. Francisco Costa Gomes, Portuguese chief of the general staff, Sept. 8
directed Portuguese troops in the capital
to restore order. Reinforcements from
northern Mozambique were flown in.
(Portugal had imposed a news blackout
on the Mozambique developments, broadcasting only official bulletins.

(FRELIMO leader Samora Machel had
warned Sept. 9 that FRELIMO would
take up arms against the movement if it
weren't put down by Portuguese troops
FRELIMO took no active role in quelling
the uprising. Machel also reiterated FRE-
LIMO's advocacy of a multiracial society,
urging white Mozambiquans to remain
in the country as government control
shifted.)

Two representatives of Portuguese Provisional President Antonio de Spinola
were sent to Lourenco Marques Sept. 9
for talks with the white rebel leaders who
subsequently announced their readiness to
negotiate with FRELIMO in the hope of
forming a coalition government. The
whites withdrew from the radio station
Sept. 10. Three of the movement's leaders
were arrested, it was reported Sept. 11.

According to Sept. 11 reports, the white
resistance movement had collapsed amid
fears of a nationwide bloodbath resulting
from overt racial conflicts. With the Portuguese government's strong affirmation
of its FRELIMO pact, hopes for substantial troop defections and aid from Lisbon were destroyed, rendering the movement impotent. The "Dragons of Death"'
had been joined by the Independent Front
for Western Continuity [FICO], a white
nationalist party, and the black National
Coalition Party to form an association
dubbed Movement for a Free Mozambique.
The racial composition of the population—one white to about 40 blacks—and
lack of broad-based support for the National Coalition further undercut possibility of the movement gaining strength.
(The United Group of Mozambique
[GUMO] had joined forces with FRE-
LIMO July 6, according to the French
newspaper Le Monde Aug. 23.)

Violence continues in Angola. Racial
violence that broke out in July continued

through August with 20 people reported dead in Luanda and its suburbs Aug. 9–11. Fighting broke out again after whites demonstrated Aug. 12 to demand the return of arms confiscated by the army. Angola's military junta appointed a special military unit Aug. 16 to restore order in the capital.

According to a London Times report Aug. 20, the National Front for the Liberation of Angola (FNLA) was the only one of the three major independence movements continuing to engage in warfare; it announced Aug. 13 that it was launching a new offensive in the North, the French newspaper Le Monde reported Aug. 15. The Popular Movement for the Liberation of Angola (MPLA) and the National Union for the Total Independence of Angola had reportedly agreed to unofficial cease-fires.

An Aug. 10 announcement from Lisbon setting a two-year "blueprint" for Angola's independence was rejected by the FNLA Aug. 11 as an attempt to cause "secession and chaos" in the territory. The MPLA followed suit Aug. 16. (One of several movements in Cabinda, the Front for the Liberation of Cabinda, demanded direct independence negotiations with Portugal Aug. 21, denouncing Angolan claims to jurisdiction over the oil-rich exclave.)

New rule in Macao. Gen. Francisco Rebelo Goncalves was named acting military commander of Macao June 3, replacing Col. Manuel Mesquita Borges who, with his deputy, had been dismissed that day. About half of the 500 Portuguese troops stationed in Macao, a small colony on the southern coast of China, had demonstrated in their barracks June 1–2, denouncing senior officers and shouting, "We want to go home." The hasty dismissal of Mesquita Borges was apparently aimed at quelling the disturbances, although government sources said that the decision to replace him had been made earlier in Lisbon.

Rebelo Goncalves lifted press censorship in Macao June 5.

A new interim governor, Lt. Col. Manuel Maia Goncalves, was installed in Macao Oct. 14.

Domestic Problems

News media curbed. The provisional government instituted severe restrictions on all news media June 22 in an apparent effort to still criticism of its management of the economy and of Portugal's wars in Africa.

A committee of seven military officers was established to administer new regulations for newspapers, radio, television, the theater and movies until a permanent press law was enacted. The committee's decisions could be appealed to the courts.

Fines of up to $20,000, suspension for 60 days and possible further prosecution were decreed for the following offenses:

Incitement to military disobedience, strikes or unauthorized demonstrations; insult to the provisional president, members of the Council of State or the Cabinet, foreign heads of state, or diplomats accredited to Portugal; "ideological aggression" against execution of the program of the Armed Forces Movement; and unauthorized divulgence of military operations.

The news media also were required to publish the entire texts of declarations by Provisional President Antonio de Spinola, without headlines or omissions that could change their meaning.

The government declared it would not return to the prepublication censorship of the ousted civilian dictatorship. It guaranteed effective freedom of expression and the planned transition to democracy, but "without internal convulsions that could affect the peace, progress and well-being of the nation."

The press restrictions apparently had been demanded by Spinola, who reportedly told military leaders June 13 that he would resign unless he was given powers to stop the extreme left from subverting the program of the Armed Forces Movement. Spinola regularly had attacked the extreme left in emotional speeches during the wave of strikes which recently swept Portugal.

The government took over the state-subsidized television network for an indefinite period June 14, and took full control of the state-run radio network June 19. Information Minister Raul Rego said June 15 that some restraints on the press were in order because, "after all, the country is still at war."

The military junta's representative to the television network June 10 had cut off a satirical television program which showed the Roman Catholic patriarch of Lisbon blessing a member of the hated and now disbanded secret police.

The government June 7 had arrested Jose Luis Saldanha Sanches, editor of the weekly newspaper Luta Popular and leader of the extreme leftist Movement to Reorganize the Portuguese Proletariat, after an article in Luta Popular urged soldiers in Portugal and its colonies to "desert with their weapons." The arrest, protested by demonstrators in Lisbon June 8 and 12, was approved by Spinola and the Communist Party leadership.

In another press development June 7, the editorial staff of the newspaper Diario de Noticias took over the paper and forced the resignations of its director, Fernando Fragoso, and its editor in chief, Joao Coito.

In the first action under the junta's new press curbs, the Lisbon newspapers A Capital and Republica were fined July 3 for publishing news of a demonstration against the arrest of two officers who had refused to accept a plan to assume military control of Lisbon's strikebound post office.

A Capital was fined $4,000 and Republica $1,200. The Republica fine was considered embarrassing to Information Minister Raul Rego, who was the newspaper's publisher.

Postal workers strike. Postal workers struck for higher wages June 17, but returned to work June 20 in the face of government intransigence and growing public hostility to their action.

The strike, which tied up mail and telecommunications, supported demands for a 50% wage increase. The government offered a 25% raise, and refused to increase this in extensive negotiations with strike leaders. Negotiations between postal service management and staff had begun at the end of May, after workers at Lisbon's central post office struck for 24 hours.

The Communist Party rallied public opposition to the strike, calling it "unrealistic" and warning that such disruption played into the hands of "reactionary forces." Other leftists also applied pressure, asserting the nation could not afford the strikers' wage demands.

Economy falters. The Portuguese economy was said to have deteriorated since the April coup. The inflation rate was among the highest in all of Europe. Industrial production had fallen, with workers spending much of their time either on strike or in organizational meetings of various kinds. Remittances from Portuguese workers abroad, the nation's largest source of foreign currency, were said to have dropped by 80%, and tourism, the second biggest money earner, had also declined.

Utility take-over set. The provisional government bowed to pressure from workers June 25 and said it would take "control" of Companhia das Aguas de Lisboa, the utility which supplied water to the Lisbon district.

The government said it would assume the administration of all works and waters of the company "without prejudice to the legitimate interests of the shareholders." It added that an inquiry was being ordered into the administration of the utility.

Economic program planned. The provisional government announced an extensive economic and social program July 6 to reassure alarmed businessmen and to curb labor unrest, soaring inflation and deficits in public finances.

The program, embodied in a series of decrees, was drafted by Economic Coordination Minister Vasco Vieira de Almeida, who warned at a news conference July 5 that citizens would have to exercise discipline in order "to meet the challenge of building a new country." Vieira noted that Portugal had to simultaneously contain "the highest rate of inflation in Europe"—some 30% annually—and expand its economy.

The new measures included:

Incentives for expanding bank credit for investment instead of for consumption through increasing interest rates for savings accounts and lowering reserve requirements for banks.

More effective control of prices of raw materials and food at production levels rather than at retail levels, and incentives for greater farm production to replace high-priced imports.

Incentives for construction of low-rent housing to relieve the housing shortage, lower rents and provide work for the unemployed.

An increase in taxes on higher incomes, on farm land not being cultivated and on urban building sites kept idle for speculative purposes. Taxes on luxury goods would also be increased.

An increase in wages for low-paid government civil and military employes.

Limitations on the right to strike, principally to eliminate wildcat walkouts, and on employer lockouts. Procedures for collective bargaining would be set up.

Establishment of categories by industry in which the state would exercise either majority control, in the case of defense plants, or production supervision, in the case of basic industries such as mining, energy, transport, petrochemicals and steel.

Establishment of a special institute to encourage mergers by small and medium-sized industries and another agency to promote new industries where private investment is lacking.

Encouragement of foreign investment that supported national needs and simplification of administrative procedures.

Vieira acknowledged that many Portuguese had lost their jobs since April, particularly in the small industries in the North. He also admitted that the country faced serious balance of payments problems; tourism and remittances from Portuguese workers abroad—two of the nation's major money-earners—had decreased, while the cost of importing oil, food and raw materials had increased.

Tourism had been adversely affected by recent outbreaks of cholera in different parts of the country, which had caused eight deaths, and by the economic downturn in Europe, according to the New York Times July 8. Unemployment had been aggravated by West Germany's decision in 1973 to cut off immigration of foreign workers, many of whom were Portuguese.

The new program suffered a major blow July 8 when thousands of civil servants demonstrated against it in Lisbon. The demonstrators were in the civil services' lowest paid categories, and had received proportionately the lowest pay increases granted under the program.

Bishops under attack. More than 500 Roman Catholics meeting in Oporto issued a statement urging all bishops to resign for allegedly having collaborated with the ousted civilian dictatorship, it was reported June 3.

The declaration accused the church hierarchy of remaining silent about repression, police tortures and colonial wars under the former regime, and demanded public denunciation of all members of the clergy who had cooperated with the now abolished secret police.

"With rare exceptions, the present Portuguese bishops have collaborated with the former regime, both by carrying out its orders or defending its ideology, and by deciding not to denounce its many insults to human dignity, which ranged from providing moral cover for war to open protection of capitalist exploitation," the declaration stated.

The statement was drawn up in three sessions held in Oporto in May. One of the meetings was attended by the city's bishop, Antonio Ferreira Gomes, an outspoken opponent of the late dictator Antonio Salazar, who exiled him for 10 years.

Delgado slayers seized. Foreign Minister Mario Soares announced July 3 that two men under arrest had confessed participating in Portugal's most notorious political assassination—the murder in 1965 of Gen. Humberto Delgado, a prominent leader of opposition to the ousted civilian dictatorship.

The two were among hundreds of members of the ousted regime's secret police who were arrested after the April military coup. A third suspect in the case, a political official in the colony of Angola, was also under arrest, the New York Times reported July 7.

Lawyers in Lisbon who had followed the case said the inquiry into Delgado's death was just beginning, and complained that criminal police were not pursuing it diligently enough, the Times reported. A young police inspector was said to be working on the case virtually alone.

The judicial police announced July 30 that it had completed its inquiry into the case.

Ten members of the abolished secret police, including the force's leader, Fernando da Silva Pais, were charged in the case. Seven were under arrest and the other three, including Casimiro Monteiro, who allegedly executed Delgado, were still at large.

Foreign Affairs

Communist-world ties. The provisional government agreed to exchange ambassadors with Rumania June 1 and with the Soviet Union June 9. Portugal had not enjoyed normal diplomatic relations with Rumania for 25 years, nor with Russia since 1917.

Foreign Minister Mario Soares, who negotiated the renewal of relations with both countries, said June 1 that Portugal sought ties with "all socialist countries, all Arab countries and all African countries." Lisbon's opening to Eastern Europe was seen as part of an economic strategy to widen the market for exports from both Portugal and its African colonies, the Washington Post reported June 10.

Observers in Moscow said June 9 that re-establishment of relations between Portugal and the Soviet Union followed a favorable assessment by the Kremlin of Lisbon's intentions in Africa, the London Times reported.

The renewal of relations was facilitated by the Portuguese Communist Party's faithful adherence to the Moscow political line, according to most reports. Portuguese party leader Alvaro Cunhal, minister without portfolio in the provisional government, had lived in Moscow during part of his exile under the ousted civilian dictatorship.

The provisional government also established diplomatic relations with Yugoslavia and East Germany (reported June 20) and with Czechoslovakia (June 27).

U.S. intentions questioned. Despite indications that the U.S. approved the goals of the provisional government, some young officers who carried out the April military coup were suspicious of Washington's long-term intentions regarding Portugal, the Washington Post reported May 23.

One unidentified officer, a founder of the Armed Forces Movement that led the coup, charged that large numbers of U.S. Central Intelligence Agency (CIA) agents had been active in the northern industrial center of Oporto, the Post reported. He added that the CIA maintained a communications vessel called "Apollo" off Lisbon. Similar allegations had been made by the Central Committee of the Portuguese Communist Party.

U.S. officials said the allegations were merely leftist propaganda, according to the Post. They cited a number of friendly moves by the U.S., including notes from President Nixon to Provisional President Antonio de Spinola and Premier Adelino da Palma Carlos.

Nixon, ending a Middle East tour, flew June 18 to the U.S. air base at Lajes in the Azores and conferred with Spinola June 19. Nixon said he had assured Spinola of U.S. support in coping with the problems of his country. "An independent, free, prosperous Portugal is vital not only to the Atlantic alliance [NATO] but vital also to the interests of the United States," Nixon said.

Spinola said he and Nixon had discussed Portugal's technical, economic and financial requirements to enable it "to be economically on a par with the other countries of Europe."

The Portuguese Foreign Ministry Aug. 22 denied a U.S. intelligence report that Arab nations had offered Lisbon a large sum of money to refuse the U.S. permission to use the base. U.S. aircraft transporting military supplies to Israel during the October 1973 Middle East war had refueled on the Azores. The U.S. report said the Arabs had also offered to end an oil embargo against Portugal if U.S. use of the Azores was prohibited.

Mitterrand visits. French Socialist leader Francois Mitterrand visited Portugal July 2–5. He spent most of his time at Socialist Party meetings, but he met July 3 with Adelino da Palma Carlos, then premier, and with Provisional President Antonio de Spinola.

Mitterrand's visit reflected concern on the part of Portuguese Socialists about the growing popular support of the Communist Party, their principal rival on the left, the New York Times reported July 3. Shortly before Mitterrand's arrival, the Socialist Party issued a radical, anti-capitalist declaration in an apparent effort to draw more support from workers.

The declaration, which contrasted with the generally moderate Communist statements, called for a "classless society" in which the means of production were collectivized. It criticized the provisional government's "disorderly" economic performance and demanded immediate steps to establish state control of the economy and of basic industries, banking, energy and transport.

Party leader Mario Soares acknowledged July 1 that, like its French counterpart, the Portuguese Socialist Party must form an alliance with the Communists for the left to win in national elections. However, he sought first to build up the Socialists' power so they could deal with the Communists on equal terms, according to the Times.

Foreign loans & aid. First National City Bank of New York said Sept. 16 that a five-year, $150 million standby credit had been arranged for Portugal by a group of international banks headed by Citicorp International Bank Ltd. and Morgan Guaranty Trust Co. It was the largest Eurocredit ever organized for Portugal and the first international loan arranged for Lisbon since the civilian dictatorship was overthrown.

The Consultative Assembly of the Council of Europe unanimously approved a resolution Sept. 28 calling on all democratic nations of Europe to give economic and technological aid to the new Portuguese regime, to facilitate a return to "democratic and stable institutions."

It authorized the Committee of Ministers to discuss with Portuguese leaders activities in which they wanted to participate, pending fulfillment of conditions for full membership in the Council of Europe.

India ties set. Portugal and India reestablished diplomatic relations Sept. 24, after Lisbon recognized India's full sovereignty over Goa, Damao and Diu, the small, formerly Portuguese enclaves near Bombay. Relations between the two countries had been suspended in 1961 when Indian troops occupied Goa.

Government Changes & Other Developments

Premier, centrist ministers quit. Premier Adelino da Palma Carlos and four centrist Cabinet ministers resigned July 9 after the Council of State denied a request by Palma Carlos for additional powers.

The resignations were not immediately accepted by Provisional President Antonio de Spinola, who attempted unsuccessfully July 10 to persuade Palma Carlos to remain in office. Spinola too had been rebuffed by the Council of State in an attempt to increase his own personal powers.

The moves by Spinola and Palma Carlos followed increasing disputes between leftists and more conservative members of the provisional government and the armed forces, aggravated by the recent wave of economic and social unrest. Both leaders were considered moderates.

Palma Carlos appealed to the Council of State July 8 to make Cabinet ministers directly responsible to him, rather than to Spinola, and to grant him other powers he deemed necessary to effectively carry out his duties. Among other reasons for making the appeal, Palma Carlos sought authority to enact a strict labor law which the Cabinet had failed to pass after heated debate, the Washington Post reported July 11. The law, which a liberal army officer described as tougher than the one prevailing under the ousted civilian dictatorship, would be an addition to the economic stimulation program announced by the government July 6.

The Council reportedly granted Palma Carlos some of the powers he asked, but not enough to satisfy him.

Spinola reportedly asked the Council to approve a series of proposals including a presidential election Oct. 31 (instead of in the spring of 1975, as pledged earlier by the Armed Forces Movement); a referendum on continuing the present Constitution, and postponement of general elections for a constituent assembly from the spring of 1975 until a year later. Spinola's chances of being elected president would be enhanced if the election were updated, according to most press reports.

The Council rejected Spinola's package by a 15–3 vote with three abstentions, according to sources cited by the Washington Post July 10. Since 14 of the Council's 21 members were military officers, the vote indicated that at least eight officers opposed Spinola. They apparently were not swayed when Spinola gathered loyal troops around him in Lisbon before the Council's vote, in an effort to demonstrate his power.

Palma Carlos resigned after the Council's vote. Three other centrist civilian Cabinet ministers quit in sympathy with him, and the defense minister, Lt. Col. Mario Firmino Miguel, also resigned. The civilians were Deputy Premier Francisco Sa Carneiro, Economic Coordination Minister Vasco Vieira de Almeida and Interior Minister Joaquim Magalhaes Motta.

The resignations left the Cabinet dominated by Socialists, Communists and other leftists brought into the governing coalition after the April military coup.

Communists and Socialists in the Cabinet generally had cooperated with

government moderates, helping to curb strikes, contain wage demands and even to restrict the press. However, both the Communist and Socialist Parties had opposed Spinola's attempt to consolidate his power, and in a direct challenge to the president, had denounced the appointment of one of his advisers, Jose Veiga Simao, as Portugal's chief representative to the United Nations.

Veiga Simao had served as education minister under the ousted dictatorship. A Communist statement issued July 8 charged his appointment to the U.N. post "internationally discredits the new Portuguese government and hinders the realization of a new policy," and warned that "fascists and reactionaries" were moving back into positions of responsibility and endangering the revolution. A Socialist statement proposed that "in connection with certain nominations that have just been made," persons associated with the old regime be declared temporarily ineligible for public office.

Cabinet dismissed; colonel named premier. Provisional President Antonio de Spinola dismissed the Cabinet July 11 and named army Col. Vasco dos Santos Goncalves as the new premier July 13

Goncalves, 53, was considered a leftist and the senior ideologist of the Armed Forces Movement, which overthrew the civilian dictatorship in April and set up the existing government. He belonged to the movement's coordinating committee and to the Council of State, the highest constitutional body.

Goncalves said July 12, when his designation was reported, that he would retain as many members of the old Cabinet as possible. He conferred July 13 and 14 with Alvaro Cunhal, head of the Communist Party, and with leaders of other political groups. The Communist newspaper Avante reaffirmed its support for the Armed Forces Movement July 12 and blamed the recent Cabinet crisis on Adelino da Palma Carlos, who resigned as premier after a clash with the Council of State.

Spinola's first choice to succeed Palma Carlos had been Lt. Col. Mario Firmino Miguel, who had resigned along with the premier. However, Miguel apparently was rejected by the Armed Forces Movement's coordinating committee; according to one report, he was vetoed because he insisted on denying the labor portfolio to the Communists, causing them to protest.

The coordinating committee reportedly pressed its own choice, Goncalves, on Spinola, and he acceded after meeting with Goncalves for two hours. Goncalves was the first committee member to emerge from the background since the military coup. Until his designation as premier, attention had been focused on Spinola, who was not only provisional president but chairman of the military junta and chief of the Council of State.

Goncalves was considered an architect of the Armed Forces Movement's program to bring democracy to Portugal by the spring of 1975 and to end the wars in its African territories as quickly as possible. He was a veteran of military campaigns in Angola and Mozambique.

Goncalves said July 13 that his government's most important tasks would include formulation of new laws on the press, labor unions and the electoral system.

New Cabinet. Premier Vasco Goncalves named a military-dominated Cabinet July 17, and Provisional President Spinola swore in the ministers July 18.

Military men received six of the 16 posts, including the key ministries of defense, interior, labor and information. The other portfolios went to civilians of varying political views, including the leaders of the Socialist and Communist Parties.

Goncalves and three of the new ministers—Capt. Jose da Costa Martins, labor minister, and Majors Vitor Alves and Eduardo de Melo Antunes, ministers without portfolio—were members of the 12-man coordinating committee of the Armed Forces Movement, which led the

April military coup and now openly asserted its power.

The other military men in the Cabinet were Lt. Col. Mario Firmino Miguel, defense minister; Lt. Col. Manuel da Costa Braz, interior minister; and Maj. Jose Sanches Osorio, information minister.

Socialist Party leader Mario Soares was confirmed as foreign minister and two other Socialists also retained their posts: Francisco Salgado Zenha as justice minister and Antonio de Almeida Santos as overseas territories minister. Communist Party leader Alvaro Cunhal was confirmed as minister without portfolio, but his party gave up the labor ministry to Capt. Costa Martins. The small Popular Democratic party was reduced to one post, with Joaquim Magalhaes Motta moving from interior minister to minister without portfolio.

Emilio Rui Vilar, a centrist, was named economy minister. The other Cabinet officials were: Jose Augusto Fernandes, environment; Jose da Silva Lopes, finance; Vitorino Magalhaes Godinho, education; and Maria de Lourdes Pintassilgo, the first woman to serve in a Portuguese Cabinet, social affairs.

On swearing in the ministers, Spinola warned the nation that "any attempt to subvert discipline will be regarded . . . as treason against freedom and democracy." "This climate of anarchy cannot continue," he said, in apparent reference to recent labor and social unrest. "We did not stage the revolution to allow the situation to go from one extreme to the other."

Goncalves warned that "we all have to live now in a true period of austerity." Without "hard work by all the Portuguese at all levels," he asserted, "the development of the nation will never be accomplished."

Goncalves said Portugal recognized the right of its African territories to self-determination "with all its consequences, including independence. But we must have a just process of decolonization that does not lead to neo-colonialism." He said "considerable progress" had already been achieved by the first provisional government in negotiations with African liberation movement leaders.

Goncalves, Alves and Melo Antunes

were considered the top leaders of the Armed Forces Movement, and their presence in the Cabinet was seen as a sign that Spinola and the provisional government would faithfully follow the movement's program to end the wars in Africa and hold democratic elections in 1975, the Washington Post reported July 18. Spinola appeared to have been reduced to the position of figurehead.

Internal security decree. The Joint Defense Staff July 13 issued a tough new internal security decree and established a Continental Operations Command to enforce it.

The command, which would include marines, paratroopers and commando units, would guarantee "peace and tranquility" in Portugal, intervening "directly in the maintenance and re-establishment of order" when normal police forces were inadequate, the decree stated. Officials said the command would be used to avert strikes in private and state-owned institutions, services and factories which were essential to the nation, the Washington Post reported July 14.

The command would be directed by Gen. Francisco da Costa Gomes, chief of the joint staff, who would be independent of government direction and have rank equivalent to the premier. His deputy chief would be Otelo de Carvalho, 37, a leader of the Armed Forces Movement, who was promoted from major to brigadier general July 13 and appointed military governor of Lisbon.

Newspapers' suspension rescinded. In its harshest move against the press since the April military coup, the military junta Aug. 2 temporarily suspended publication of three Lisbon newspapers. It rescinded the measure the next day in the face of strong protests from other newspapers and from junior army officers.

The evening dailies A Capital and Diario de Lisboa were suspended for two days and Republica for one day for publishing in their Aug. 1 editions reports of a rally the day before by the Movement to

Reorganize the Portuguese Proletariat (MRPP), an extreme leftist group. Speakers at the rally had denounced the government's policy in Portugal's African colonies. The suspension order also cited a report in Diario de Lisboa which said Luanda, the capital of the colony of Angola, was gripped by fear.

The evening newspaper Diario Popular refused to publish Aug. 2 to protest the suspensions, and Republica, which was suspended only for Aug. 2, refused to publish Aug. 3. Two weeklies, Expresso and Sempre Fixe, also protested by withholding their Aug. 3 editions.

A spokesman for the Communications Ministry said Aug. 2 that the suspensions had not been ordered by the Ad Hoc Commission, the group of junior officers appointed by the junta to enforce the government's press regulations. Press reports said the seven-man junta itself ordered the suspensions. The commission reportedly resigned in protest Aug. 2.

Premier Vasco Goncalves called in newspaper publishers Aug. 3, as the protests mounted, and rescinded the suspensions. However, the junta warned Aug. 5 that those who criticized the armed forces would be "severely punished," and it indefinitely suspended publication of the MRPP's organ, Luta Popular. The newspaper's publisher, Luis Saldanha Sanches, had been in jail since June.

The indefinite suspension of Luta Popular appeared to violate the government's press restrictions, which limited suspensions to 60 days. It was criticized Aug. 6 by the Socialist Party.

(Soldiers prevented an MRPP rally from taking place in Lisbon Aug. 7, according to the French newspaper Le Monde Aug. 9.)

In a move to ease tension with the press, the government announced Aug. 6 that a joint committee of newspaper management and journalists would draw up the final version of the new press law, which had been completed in its basic form after three weeks of preparation.

Strike law issued; TAP stoppage broken. The government published a law Aug. 28

establishing the right to strike within severe limits. It simultaneously broke a stoppage by ground employes of TAP, the national airline, by placing the strikers under military orders.

The new law allowed strikes for the first time in more than 40 years, but it forbade stoppages for political and religious reasons, and for the purpose of upsetting the terms of a collective bargaining agreement. Strikes by policemen, firemen, military personnel and magistrates were illegal, as were strikes to show solidarity with striking workers in another profession. A separate law would deal with stoppages by civil servants.

Strikes that were allowed could not be called until after 30 days of negotiation and a further seven days' notice for the employer. Picketing was allowed, but not occupation of plants. Partial strikes by some workers in key sections of a plant were forbidden if they tied up total production.

Lockouts were allowed after seven days' notice to workers, except in companies performing a public service.

The TAP strike was called to demand higher wages and changes in top management, according to press reports. It had cost the airline $40,000 a day and interfered with the repatriation of soldiers from Portuguese Guinea, which was being granted its independence, according to Information Minister Maj. Jose Sanches Osorio. TAP had been losing money steadily before the strike.

The 17 foreign airlines operating in Portugal were paralyzed Sept. 6–7 when the 650 Portuguese workers on their staffs struck to demand a clause in their contracts concerning unfair dismissal. The strikers did not give the seven days' notice required by the new strike law.

Wage freeze partly discarded. The government partly lifted the three-month wage freeze Aug. 31, but took measures to prevent salary increases from aggravating inflation. Half of most future wage increases would have to be paid in treasury bonds which would pay no interest for five years. Premier Vasco Goncalves had announced new price increases Aug. 19.

Bank takeover. The regime Aug. 28 said it would nationalize three issuing banks: the Banco de Portugal, the Banco Nacional Ultramarino and the Banco de Angola. Private shareholders in the banks would be compensated.

Secret police prisoners mutiny. An estimated 600 jailed members of the abolished secret police occupied a cell block of Lisbon's Caxias prison for 12 hours Aug. 12 to demand better medical care for themselves and greater financial support for their families. They ended the revolt peacefully after they were allowed to send representatives to air their grievances before Gen. Carlos Galvao de Melo, a member of the military junta.

A spokesman for the prisoners, who charged a prisoner had died recently for lack of adequate medical care, said Galvao de Melo had agreed to study the complaints.

Leftists denounced the mutiny Aug. 13. The Communist Party called the prisoners' claims "a real insult to the Portuguese people, who were martyred for half a century by the fascist dictatorship and by its greatest instrument of terror," the secret police. The newspaper Diario de Noticias, which generally reflected Socialist Party opinion, condemned the mutiny as a scandal.

Spinola's Departure

Spinola resigns, Costa Gomes becomes president. Gen. Antonio de Spinola resigned as provisional president of Portugal and head of the military junta Sept. 30, 1976, leaving power almost exclusively in the hands of leftist military officers and civilians.

Three other members of the seven-man junta, including air force commander Manoel Diogo Neto and Defense Minister Mario Firmino Miguel, also resigned. All were conservative supporters of Spinola and were linked by leftists to an alleged right-wing plot against the provisional government.

Seventy-seven persons had been arrested and awaited trial in connection with the plot, according to the Washington Post Oct. 2. The government charged the plot was conceived by organizers of a giant pro-Spinola rally to have taken place in Lisbon Sept. 28. Spinola had openly sympathized with the rally, but he was forced to ban it under pressure from Premier Vasco Goncalves and other leftists in the armed forces, the government and civilian political groups, who asserted the rally would provoke a major armed confrontation between leftists and rightists.

Spinola was replaced Sept. 30 by Gen. Francisco da Costa Gomes, chief of the joint military staff. Costa Gomes' first act in office was to reappoint Goncalves as premier. Goncalves, who had been promoted from army colonel to brigadier general Sept. 14, now appeared to be the strongest figure in the government.

Spinola delivered an emotional farewell address on radio and television Sept. 30, denouncing what he called the betrayal both in Portugal and its African colonies of the program of the Armed Forces Movement, which overthrew the civilian dictatorship in April.

In a clear attack on the left, particularly the Communist Party, which had representatives in the Cabinet, Spinola charged that creation of democracy in Portugal—a major objective of the armed forces—was impossible when it was based on a systematic assault on the nation's institutions by political groups "whose ideology offends the most elemental concept of liberty." The country was heading toward "new forms of slavery," he warned.

Spinola said the armed forces had sought harmony among all political beliefs, but civilian political activists were indulging in "psychological coercion" by using the press and radio and television to slander all who opposed them. He urged Portuguese to reject this coercion and "trust in the secret ballot," which he called the "great democratic weapon of free and orderly men."

Spinola noted that Portugal was beset "by an economic crisis to which we are fast heading, by unemployment, by un-controlled inflation, by business recession, by the retraction of investments and by the ineffectiveness of central powers." In this general climate of anarchy, he said, "everyone dictates his own law," and "crisis and chaos are inevitable in flagrant contradiction with the aims" of the Armed Forces Movement.

Spinola denounced the rapid granting of independence to Portugal's African territories, referring to "antidemocratic measures" which he said violated the real interest of the colonies' inhabitants. In an apparent reference to white Portuguese, he charged the government's African policies did not protect "Portuguese of all races and creeds."

The nation was calm after Spinola's resignation, but the armed forces were alerted to thwart any move by supporters of the general. A broad purge of army and navy officers had taken place during the previous few weeks, with the forced retirement of some 200 army officers between the ranks of lieutenant and colonel and about 130 naval officers, the New York Times reported Oct. 2.

Goncalves made an impassioned public rebuttal of Spinola's speech Sept. 30, defending the provisional government and rejecting what he called Spinola's "catastrophic and apocalyptic view of Portuguese society at this moment." He asserted elections would be held as scheduled in March 1975, although he admitted that some unexpected occurrence could prevent them from taking place.

Goncalves said the nation's economic, social and political problems were inherited from the ousted dictatorship, but he denied Portugal was heading toward "economic chaos." After 50 years of authoritarian rule, he asked, "What other people has undergone as much change in five months and practically without a shot being fired?"

In his swearing-in speech, Costa Gomes vowed that he would help build a just, democratic future for Portugal. He was highly regarded by young military officers and was said to be more flexible and a better politician than Spinola, the Washington Post reported Oct. 2.

Spinola's resignation followed a week-long buildup of tension between rightists and leftists within and outside the government. Rightists and leftists had clashed Sept. 27 outside a bullfight arena in Lisbon, where hundreds of conservatives had massed to cheer Spinola and denounce Goncalves, both of whom attended a charity bullfight inside. After the clashes, in which several persons were reported arrested, leftists began preparations to disrupt the pro-Spinola "silent majority" rally scheduled for the next day, leading to its cancellation.

The government Sept. 18 had banned the extreme rightist Portuguese National Party, composed of members of the Portuguese Legion—the force which fought alongside Generalissimo Francisco Franco's troops in the Spanish Civil War—and former agents of the abolished secret police. The government ordered an investigation to determine whether members of the party should be prosecuted for trying to "destroy democratic institutions."

A new right-wing newspaper, Bandarra, appeared in Lisbon Sept. 18 with a violent attack on the Communist Party and other leftist groups. A new right-wing political group called the Portuguese Alliance for Social Progress had been formed several days earlier, according to the Lisbon newspaper Expresso Sept. 14.

Foreign Minister Mario Soares reportedly told foreign diplomats in Lisbon Oct. 1 that rightists had planned to assassinate Spinola before his resignation, to bring down the provisional government. The government implicated six conservative groups in the plot, including the Progressive Party, whose Lisbon head-quarters were raided by troops Oct. 2. Arms and subversive propaganda reportedly were found.

New junta members named. The Council of State appointed five new members to the Junta of National Salvation Oct. 15, two weeks after the resignation of Provisional President Antonio de Spinola.

The new junta members from the army were Brig. Gen. Carlos Soares Fabiao, the last governor of Portuguese Guinea (now Guinea-Bissau), and Lt. Col. Fisher Lopes Pires, a prominent member of the Armed Forces Movement. The new air force members were Cols. Pinheiro Freire and Mendes Dias, and the new navy member was Capt. Silvano Pereira.

Spinola was retired Nov. 17 under a new military policy designed to "rejuvenate ranks and create new posts." Top generals, admirals and rear admirals would henceforth retire at 62 (Spinola was 64), brigadier generals and commodores at 60, and colonels and navy captains at 57. The policy apparently was aimed at restricting the influence of certain prominent military leaders, according to the London Times Nov. 18. There also was a plan to completely restructure the army, the Times reported Nov. 19.

Premier Brig. Gen. Vasco Goncalves took over the Defense Ministry Oct. 3 and made the Information Ministry directly responsible to his office. Education Minister Vitorino Magalhaes Godinho resigned Nov. 29, ostensibly for health reasons, and Goncalves said he would be replaced by a member of the Armed Forces Movement.

Left Seeks Power

Western Nations Fear Communist Takeover

The presence of Communists in the Portuguese Cabinet and the apparent growth of leftist influence in the provisional government roused fears in Western capitals that Portugal, a NATO member, might go Communist. Portugal's recently chosen provisional president, Francisco da Costa Gomes, tried to quell these fears during meetings with the U.S.' new president, Gerald R. Ford, and other U.S. leaders in October 1974. But leftist gains in Portugal during 1975 caused many Western leaders to doubt his assurances.

U.S. mission. Costa Gomes visited the U.S. Oct. 16–20, 1974, addressing the United Nations General Assembly in New York and conferring with President Ford and Secretary of State Henry Kissinger in Washington.

The purpose of the trip was to reaffirm Portuguese ties with the U.S. and the North Atlantic Treaty Organization (NATO), and to secure U.S. and international aid for the troubled Portuguese economy, according to most press reports. Costa Gomes was accompanied by Foreign Minister Mario Soares and by Vitor Constancio, secretary of state for economic planning.

At the General Assembly Oct. 17, Costa Gomes asked financial aid for Portugal's "peaceful revolution" and urged the U.N. to lift the embargoes and restrictions it imposed on Lisbon under the ousted civilian dictatorship.

"The predemocratic situation in which we are living contains considerable economic and financial difficulties which will best be overcome if the democratic countries of the world show a material and moral solidarity which is rapid, brotherly and fair in its financial and political price," he declared.

Costa Gomes asked Assembly members to ignore reports of widespread unrest in Portugal, calling the reports "alarmist generalizations based on minor social disturbances which the provisional government has always healed and overcome." He asserted the government would "restore to the Portuguese people their lost dignity by creating more just conditions of life through pluralistic democratic institutions legitimized by the freely expressed will of the people."

Costa Gomes departed from his prepared text to ask African nations to believe in the "honesty and sincerity" of Portugal's vow to free its African colonies. After Costa Gomes had finished, Foreign Minister Soares conferred with

African delegates and urged them to establish diplomatic relations with Lisbon as soon as possible.

(Soares had said Sept. 13 that Portugal was unable to enforce the U.N.'s trade sanctions against Rhodesia—which African nations did enforce—because the results would be disastrous for the economy of Mozambique, a Portuguese African territory that would gain full independence in June 1975. He asserted the Mozambique Liberation Front, the black rebel movement which headed a transitional government in the territory, agreed. Many Rhodesian exports were shipped through Mozambique ports.)

Costa Gomes met with Ford at the White House and with Kissinger at the State Department Oct. 18. Soares told the press after the meetings that Costa Gomes had requested U.S. economic aid in five areas—railways, highways, education, energy and geothermal power.

On his return to Lisbon Oct. 20, Costa Gomes called his U.S. talks "extraordinarily important" because they paved the way for negotiations "in which both countries are interested, especially us, since the help that we will be able to get from the great country will be of the kind that we desire."

He stressed Portuguese membership in NATO, asserting: "We have a geostrategic position that obliges us to make a choice." He said the government's continuing support for NATO corresponded with "the wishes of the Portuguese people."

Costa Gomes and diplomatic sources indicated the visit to Washington helped allay U.S. fears that Portugal would be taken over by Communists, the New York Times reported Oct. 21. Kissinger was reported concerned over the power of the Portuguese Communist Party, fearing it would gain full control in Lisbon and help precipitate Communist take-overs in Spain, Italy and Greece.

Despite favorable reports from the U.S. embassy in Lisbon, Kissinger had recently sent high-level intelligence and diplomatic missions to Portugal to evaluate the situation, the Washington Post reported Oct. 27. He also sent a mission to Spain, which was equally concerned

over leftist tendencies in Portugal, according to the Post.

Lt. Gen. Vernon Walters, deputy director of the Central Intelligence Agency, had been sent to Lisbon Aug. 9-12 for a "personal appraisal," the Post reported. He held 12 meetings with senior U.S. embassy staffers and with high Portuguese officials including Gen. Antonio de Spinola, then provisional president, and Costa Gomes, who subsequently replaced Spinola.

In early October, Kissinger sent a second mission to Lisbon headed by Alan Lukens, director of the State Department's Iberian section, and including experts on monetary affairs and on Portugal's African territories, the Post reported.

Walters' visit was reported in the Portuguese press in August and September, aggravating fears by Portuguese leftists of a U.S.-supported, right-wing coup against the reformist provisional government. The special Continental Operations Command, headed by Brig. Gen. Otelo de Carvalho, the military governor of Lisbon, began to track foreigners arriving in the country, particularly anti-Communist Cuban exiles, Chileans, Spaniards and U.S. citizens, the Post reported.

Carvalho said in a magazine interview Oct. 11 that the CIA had "focused [its] attention" on Portugal and posed a "grave threat" to the country. "The Americans have a morbid terror of communism and as you know they have a series of specific organs to fight against it," he asserted. "The CIA, which uses the most incredible methods—and you have only to look at the example of Chile—is probably the most dangerous, but it is not the only one: NATO is another example of an organization created specifically to fight communism."

Soviets pledge aid. The Soviet Union Nov. 2, 1974 promised economic assistance to Portugal "with regard for available resources."

Soviet President Nikolai Podgorny made the pledge at a meeting with members of a Portuguese delegation which visited Moscow Oct. 29–Nov. 3. The group was headed by Minister Without Portfolio Alvaro Cunhal, head of the Portuguese Communist Party.

The qualification in Podgorny's offer suggested the Soviet Union might not be able to meet Portuguese requests for food, the New York Times reported Nov. 3. Moscow recently had purchased grain and meat from abroad, apparently for its own needs.

While he was in the Soviet Union, Cunhal met with Foreign Trade Minister Nikolai S. Patolichev and with Boris N. Ponomarev, who headed the Kremlin's relations with non-ruling Communist parties in the West.

Matio Vicoso Neves, the new Portuguese ambassador in Moscow, had presented his credentials to Soviet authorities the day before Cunhal arrived.

NATO exercises scored. Thousands of Portuguese workers defied a ban on demonstrations in Lisbon Feb. 7, 1975 to protest NATO naval and air exercises off the Portuguese coast and the mooring of 19 NATO warships in Lisbon's harbor to give their sailors shore leave.

The exercises, held Jan. 31–Feb. 7, had been criticized by leaders of most Portuguese political parties. Foreign Minister Mario Soares, the Socialist leader, called the maneuvers "inopportune" Jan. 31, noting that most Portuguese felt they were designed to intimidate the leftist provisional government.

NATO member nations reportedly were wary of Portugal because the provisional government contained Communist officials. U.S. pressure had kept Portugal out of a recent NATO nuclear planning group meeting, the Washington Post reported Feb. 1.

The exercises controversy followed official Portuguese denials Feb. 1 that the Soviet Union had asked for port facilities in Portugal for its Atlantic fishing fleet. Reports of the request, attributed to reliable Portuguese officials Jan. 31, had caused concern among NATO members who noted that Soviet fishing trawlers could carry electronic surveillance equipment.

Foreign Minister Soares charged Feb. 3 that the reports were a "trial balloon" floated by the Portuguese Communist Party. The Soviet news agency Tass Feb. 4 called the reports a "provocative fuss clearly calculated . . . to confuse Portuguese public opinion."

Despite these controversies Portugal expressed a desire to continue in NATO. Gen. Alexander Haig, commander of NATO forces, visited Lisbon Feb. 19 and conferred with Provisional President Gen. Francisco da Costa Gomes, Premier Gen. Vasco Goncalves, and Soares.

African ties. Congolese and Portuguese delegations to the U.N. announced Feb. 13, 1975 that their two countries would establish diplomatic relations at the ambassadorial level. Government authorities in Brazzaville had said Jan. 25 they considered the process of decolonization in Portugal's African territories irreversible.

Portugal and Zambia agreed on closer ties and technological, scientific, cultural and trade relations, according to a communique issued May 8 at the conclusion of a visit May 6–8 to Portugal by President Kenneth D. Kaunda. During a press conference in Lisbon, Kaunda emphasized that Portuguese Provisional President Francisco da Costa Gomes had "stretched out to us the hand of friendship," adding that "from now on Zambia is ready to cooperate fully with this revolutionary government."

Political-Economic Conflict

Tight parties law. The provisional government Oct. 31, 1974 published a law requiring political parties to register at least 5,000 members to earn the right to run candidates in elections. The law empowered courts to disband parties which "systematically use methods which are illicit and against public morality or order, or which disrupt the discipline of the armed forces."

The centrist Progressive Democratic Party (PPD) withdrew from the Portuguese Democratic Movement Nov. 5

after the latter decided to register as a party and run in the scheduled 1975 elections. The PPD charged the movement was controlled by the Portuguese Communist Party.

(The Communists held a national congress in Lisbon Oct. 20, attended by an estimated 4,000-6,000 persons. For the first time the party published the names of members of its Central Committee, which included two women.)

In another political development, police clashed Nov. 4 with hundreds of leftists who tried to storm a Lisbon rally of the right-wing Social Democratic Center (CDS). Premier Goncalves apologized to the CDS for the incident, in which 30-40 persons were injured. The Communists and the PPD denounced the leftist action as counterrevolutionary.

Government split widens. Political differences among members of the provisional government and the Armed Forces Movement (MFA) were exacerbated in January 1975 by a new government economic program and new labor law.

The widening split caused fear that the provisional government might break down and be replaced by a full military dictatorship. However, the government remained intact and it announced Jan. 29 that the campaign for constituent assembly elections would begin March 4.

The new labor law, approved by the Cabinet Jan. 22, provided for the establishment of a single national labor union if more than half the nation's workers desired one. The measure was supported by the Communist Party and by leftist military officers led by Premier Vasco Goncalves; it was opposed by the Socialist Party, the Popular Democratic Party (PPD) and the Social Democratic Center.

The new economic program, reported by the New York Times Jan. 27, was opposed by Goncalves and the Communists and supported by moderates, including Maj. Eduardo de Melo Antunes, minister without portfolio. Leftists believed the program, which stressed help to private business, did not go far enough in dismantling capitalist monopolies, the Times reported.

The Socialists, Centrists and the PPD criticized the labor law sharply, charging the Communists sought to create a single, compulsory labor union under their control as a step toward creating a single political party to rule Portugal. They were joined by Roman Catholic priests who declared in sermons Jan. 19 that workers should have the right to choose their own labor unions without state interference.

The Socialists and Centrists succeeded in amending the law before it was approved, insuring that confederation would not be compulsory and the law would be reviewed in a year. The Socialists planned a demonstration in Lisbon Jan. 31, but they were thwarted when the Communists called a rival rally, forcing the MFA to cancel both marches Jan. 29 in fear of violence.

The Socialists and the PPD reportedly were concerned by indications that the Communists had grown less enthusiastic about holding free elections after an MFA public opinion poll revealed a decline in the Communists' popularity. The poll, reported by the New York Times Jan. 20, showed 20% of those questioned would vote for the Socialists, 10% for the PPD, 10% for the Communists and 5% each for extreme leftists and conservatives. The other 50% refused to express a preference.

In a clear attack on the Communists and their supporters in the MFA, Foreign Minister Mario Soares, the Socialist leader, charged Jan. 27 that "totalitarians" were threatening the Portuguese democratic process and risking a civil war. Soares called on civilian political leaders to meet with the so-called Council of 20, the MFA's steering committee, to draft a political plaform "so we can tell the people what road we are taking."

Socialist sources said Soares had been negotiating secretly with retired Gen. Antonio de Spinola, the former provisional president, to enlist the aid of his conservative supporters against the leftward drift of the provisional government, the Washington Post reported Jan. 28. Spinola had said in a magazine interview earlier that there was "danger of a dictatorship of the left" in Portugal, it was reported Jan. 5.

The informal alliance between the Socialists, moderates and centrists in the government had caused the Socialist radical wing to break away and form a new leftist group, the Socialist Popular Front. The Front was established Jan. 9 under the leadership of Manuel Serra, who charged the Socialist Party had "compromised itself with the ruling class, European social democracy and extreme right-wing adventurism."

Centrist congress attacked—Hundreds of leftist rioters surrounded a Social Democratic Center congress in Oporto Jan. 25–26, preventing delegates from leaving the meeting hall for 14 hours. Police finally escorted the delegates away, after clashing with demonstrators who burned four automobiles and reportedly wounded five policemen with gunfire.

A Centrist statement Jan. 28 indirectly criticized authorities for allowing the leftist siege to last so long. "Under what revolutionary law do we live?" the Centrists asked. "That of the Armed Forces Movement, or that of the street?"

Leaders of many European Christian Democratic and conservative parties attended the congress and were trapped in the siege. Among them was Geoffrey Rippon, foreign affairs spokesman for the British opposition Conservative Party, who received a formal apology Jan. 27 from Provisional President Gen. Francisco da Costa Gomes.

Military sets post-election role. The Armed Forces Movement announced Feb. 18, 1975 that it would continue to play an active role in politics after the election of a president and a legislative assembly later in 1975.

The decision, reversing an earlier pledge to withdraw from politics after the elections, was made at a meeting of the MFA's 200-member assembly Feb. 17. The MFA withheld details of its new strategy, but said it would discuss them with the political parties.

The strategy reportedly was welcomed by the Communist Party but not by the other two major political groups, the Socialist and Popular Democratic Parties. All three had asked the MFA to take a formal stand on the matter, according to Capt. Vasco Lourenco, an MFA spokesman.

The armed forces currently exercised great power through military ministers in the provisional government, and the all-military Junta of National Salvation and Council of State. All three units were supposed to disappear after the president and legislative assembly were elected, presumably in the fall.

The junta's powers had been widely expanded Feb. 8. The junta was given authority to abolish all organs of the ousted civilian dictatorship, to take measures "to purge and give morality" to the nation's way of life, to fight any actions against the economy, national defense or public order, and to organize trials for persons held responsible for the political policies and abuses of the ousted regime.

The weekly magazine O Expresso warned against the institutionalization of military power Feb. 8, saying it feared "revolutionary legislation" that would "interfere arbitrarily in the life of every citizen." Although the MFA was said to be divided, leftist officers were reported in control.

(In an apparent effort to end its internal divisions, the MFA established a special agency Feb. 11 to report on the spirit of military units and to "enlighten and increase the consciousness of army personnel" about the MFA's national program. The official military publication Movimento said the army was "not easily accepting" the consequences of the April 1974 coup, and that many soldiers were gathering in "closed, slanderous circles" to discuss their complaints.)

Capt. Duarte Pinto Soares, an MFA leader, said Feb. 19 that politicians who warned of a possible civil war should be prosecuted. Foreign Minister Mario Soares had made such a warning Jan. 27 in an attack on the Communist Party and its supporters in the MFA.

Parties organize. Among political organization developments of February 1975:

The Christian Democratic Party, not yet legally recognized, held its first national congress in Lisbon Feb. 2 under the leadership of Maj. Jose Sanches Osorio,

who served as information minister under
Gen. Antonio de Spinola, the former provisional president. The party declared that
"trade union freedom is a basis of the
democratic system," implicitly criticizing
the new labor law which provided for establishment of a single national workers'
federation. The congress closed early
after the MFA said it could not protect
the delegates from threatened violence by
leftist groups, reportedly including the
Maoist MRPP.

The Popular Democratic Union, a
coalition of three Marxist-Leninist
parties, presented a petition to the Supreme Court Feb. 11 with the 5,000 signa-
tures required for legal recognition as a
political party. The People's Monarchist
Party submitted its petition Feb. 18.

Economic plan. Premier Goncalves Feb.
20, 1975 announced a three-year program
aimed at modernizing the economy and
creating a "more just and equal society."

The plan, set out in a 184-page document titled "Program for Economic and
Social Policy," was devised under the
direction of Maj. Eduardo de Melo
Antunes, minister without portfolio. It
was praised Feb. 21 by leaders of the
Socialist, Communist and Popular Democratic Parties, the three civilian political
groups in the provisional government.

The plan's provisions included a land
reform program to break up large family
estates and increase agrarian productivity
and employment; state intervention in key
industries; foreign investment in certain
sectors; and measures to cut inflation
and unemployment and to redistribute the
nation's wealth.

Western economic specialists considered the plan a moderate document that
should bring Portuguese society into
line with other Western European countries and the U.S., according to the Associated Press Feb. 20. (The plan's text
said that although its provisions were
"revolutionary," it was "necessary to
begin pragmatically, taking into account
the existing realities and giving ourselves
time to carry out certain experiments before definitely consecrating far-reaching
institutionalized schemes.")

Under the plan, irrigated farms would

be limited to about 125 acres, and un-
cultivated land on large holdings would
be either expropriated or forcibly leased
to small holders. Some farms totaling
thousands of acres had been left fallow
by their owners while farm workers were
out of jobs.

The government would take 51% interest in key industries such as coal, iron ore,
copper, oil and gas, petrochemicals,
steel, tobacco, munitions and electricity,
compensating their current owners. In big
industries not brought under state control, antitrust action would be brought
against conglomerates. Medium and small
firms would receive government aid.

Foreign investment was welcomed, but
not in land, financial institutions, insurance companies, the news media, production and distribution of electricity, or
activities related to national defense. Foreign investors were also barred from gaining control of existing Portuguese firms
and from investing in goods and services
already glutting the market.

Other measures in the plan included a
national employment policy, moves
against speculation and hoarding, redistribution of the tax burden and heavy
penalties for tax evasion, a cut in imports
of non-essential goods, government food
subsidies, and austerity in government
spending.

The plan's preamble predicted "heavy
sacrifices" in the near future and called
for "hard work and total devotion to the
cause of national reconstruction." It
stressed that private enterprise would be
allowed to operate freely so long as it did
not prejudice the true interests of the
nation, according to a London Times report Feb. 21.

A secret report prepared by the government before the plan's announcement,
and reported by the Journal of Commerce Feb. 5, said Portugal's economic
crisis would last at least through 1975
because of structural problems in the
economy and because of the general
European recession.

The report noted that the Portuguese
gross national product had increased by
only 2%–3% in 1974, falling at least 4%
below the 1973 increase. Growth in
industrial production fell from 9% in 1973

to 5% in 1974, while the increase in investment dropped by 3%–5%.

"In purely economic terms there is no reason to expect any improvement in 1975," the report said.

U.S. aid program—The U.S. and Portugal signed the first part of a $30 million program under which the U.S. would help finance Portuguese housing, educational, health and agricultural programs, the Washington Post reported March 2 .

Military Revolt Fails

Regime crushes rebellion. Troops backing the provisional government suppressed a military revolt March 11, 1975 by conservative followers of Gen. Antonio de Spinola, the former provisional president. Spinola fled to Spain.

The Armed Forces Movement (MFA) decided after the coup attempt to take permanent political control of Portugal through a "revolutionary council" that would retain executive and legislative powers after the election of a president and a legislative assembly later in 1975.

As the revolt began, rebel paratroopers from the Tancos air base north of Lisbon seized the military airfield next to the capital's Portela Airport early in the morning and sent up planes to strafe the barracks of the 1st Light Artillery Regiment, killing at least one person and wounding 18 others. Loyal troops broke the revolt shortly after the air raid by seizing in the Tancos base. Members of the paramilitary Republican National Guard in Lisbon attempted to join the revolt, but they were quickly put down by the Guard's commander.

More than 60 persons were arrested, including several bank directors and two key aides to Spinola. The former president, who had visited the Tancos base before dawn March 11, fled across the Spanish border in a military helicopter with 18 other officers and his wife. Four rebel Republican National Guard officers took asylum in the West German embassy in Lisbon, but they were handed over to Portuguese authorities March 12.

(Spinola soon left Spain and then traveled to Brazil, where he was granted asylum March 15 on condition that he not make any political statements. Officers who had fled Portugal with Spinola issued a statement March 15, before arriving in Brazil, asserting they had rebelled to prevent the armed forces from replacing the old right-wing dictatorship with a new leftist one. However, friends of Spinola quoted by the New York Times March 19 said the former general was denying any connection to the abortive coup. Spinola, deprived of his Portuguese citizenship, was given a Brazilian passport May 23.)

Provisional President Gen. Francisco da Costa Gomes and Premier Brig. Gen. Vasco Goncalves made radio broadcasts March 11 denouncing the rebels as "reactionaries" and asserting everything was under control. Supporters of the MFA staged demonstrations in Lisbon and Oporto, attacking headquarters of the Social Democratic Center, a conservative political party, in both cities.

Brig. Gen. Otelo de Carvalho, governor of Lisbon and head of the military security command, told reporters late March 11 that he could not guarantee the safety of U.S. Ambassador Frank Carlucci. He said Carlucci "had better leave" Portugal "after what happened today," hinting the U.S. was somehow involved in the abortive coup. The U.S. State Department denied any involvement. Soldiers were placed on guard outside the U.S. embassy in Lisbon, where demonstrators gathered to shout slogans against the U.S. Central Intelligence Agency.

(Despite Carvalho's statement, Carlucci was declared acceptable to Portugal March 12 by navy Cmdr. Jorge Correia Jesuino, the new information minister.)

The 200-member MFA assembly met all night March 11–12, deciding to expel Spinola from the army and to establish the revolutionary council. Cmdr. Jesuino said March 12 that the elections for a constituent assembly would be held as scheduled April 12, with the campaign opening March 20.

The council, whose duty would be to "direct the revolution," would have power to initiate legislation, examine and veto bills passed by the elected civilian assembly, and pass revolutionary laws even against the wishes of parliament. One of its first tasks would be to outlaw some "fringe parties" on the extreme right and left, Jesuino said.

(The council was officially sworn into office March 17 by President Francisco da Costa Gomes. It consisted of 24 military officers including Costa Gomes and Goncalves [both army generals], seven members of the MFA's coordinating committee and other representatives of the three armed services.)

Meanwhile, Jesuino added, the MFA would be purged of rebels and the provisional government would be "remodeled" by Premier Goncalves. Various individual service councils would be abolished if any members were linked to the failed coup attempt, he asserted. (The councils had been elected by the three armed services to give voice to military grass-roots opinion, according to the Washington Post March 13. In recent council elections followers of Gen. Spinola had defeated several left-wing officers.)

Though officially in retirement, Spinola had been gaining favor among conservative and centrist officers in the weeks before the coup attempt, according to press reports. There were reports that the Socialist Party, which was represented in the provisional government, had made contact with Spinola in an apparent attempt to form a coalition against a possible dictatorship by leftist military officers and members of the Portuguese Communist Party, who maintained close contact with Goncalves.

Fears of such a dictatorship were fueled by recent attacks by leftist demonstrators on rallies of the Popular Democratic Party (PPD), a center-left group represented in the provisional government, and the Christian Democratic Party, a new conservative movement.

The worst of the attacks took place late March 7 in the port of Setubal, south of Lisbon, where an estimated 400 leftists stoned a PPD rally. Police used gunfire to disperse the rioters, killing three persons and wounding 26. PPD leaders March 9 accused the Communist Party of taking part in the disturbance— Setubal was a Communist stronghold, according to press reports—but the Communists joined the PPD and the Socialists in denouncing the rioters.

The PPD and the Socialists had also been apprehensive over the MFA's plan to retain some power after the elections. The plan, discussed by officers with civilian political leaders in late February and early March, was denounced as "a blueprint for military dictatorship" by one political source quoted by United Press International Feb. 22. The revolutionary council approved after the March 11 coup attempt would have many of the powers sought in the MFA plan, including control over the decrees and legislation of future civilian governments.

In another move that increased military power, Premier Goncalves Feb. 20 had named Cmdr. Jesuino information minister and navy Capt. Silvano Ribeiro defense minister, creating a military majority in the Cabinet for the first time since the April 1974 military coup. The revised Cabinet now had nine military officers and eight civilians.

Banking, commercial and industrial executives were among 49 civilians arrested in connection with the coup attempt, according to an official list released March 15. (Fifty-two military officers also were arrested.) The civilian detainees included six members of the Espirito Santo banking family, led by Manuel and Jose Espirito Santo, and Jose Carlos Champalimaud, son of the industrialist Antonio Champalimaud. The Espirito Santos were reported released March 17. Other businessmen reportedly went into hiding or fled the country.

The government issued a list of other "reactionaries" to be arrested for subversion, and civilian leftists cooperated in turning the men in. Members of the Portuguese Democratic Movement, a small leftist group closely identified with the Communist Party, joined security forces in arresting suspects, according to a Manchester Guardian report printed by the Washington Post March 18.

Rightist rebel 'army' reported in Spain. Military authorities asserted March 23 that a right-wing subversive organization calling itself the Portuguese Liberation Army (ELP) was operating in Spain under the cover of two commercial firms. The armed group allegedly sought to overthrow the current Portuguese government and the African nationalist regimes which were scheduled to take control of Mozambique and Angola, the Portuguese colonies.

The ELP's leaders allegedly included men who had helped overthrow democratic governments in Latin America and who had close ties to white mercenary groups in Africa. Lisbon newspapers March 24 carried a photograph of two of the alleged leaders, one identified as Hugh C. Franklin, a Guatemalan engineer, and the other identified only as Morgan.

Spanish officials March 24 denied any knowledge of the ELP. Antonio Martinez Feal, owner of Tecnomotor S.A., one of the ELP's alleged cover firms, said he had never heard of the Portuguese group. The other alleged cover firm, Sociedad Mariano, had only a post office box in Madrid.

Government Suppresses Parties, Revises Regime's Leadership

Cabinet resigns. The Cabinet resigned March 16 to allow Premier Goncalves to name new ministers after the attempted coup.

3 parties banned. The regime March 18, 1975 banned three political parties until after the elections for a constituent assembly, which were postponed until April 25.

The banned parties were the right-wing Christian Democrats and two leftist groups—the Maoist MRPP and the Alliance of Workers and Peasants (AOC). The Christian Democrats' leader, Maj. Jose Sanches Osorio, fled to Spain, according to reports March 16.

The bans left only one conservative party in the April elections—the Social Democratic Center (CDS)—and strengthened the hand of the Communist Party, of which the MRPP and AOC were bitter rivals. In an apparent further move to reduce its competition, the Communist Central Committee issued a statement March 20 expressing its "reservations" about having the center-left People's Democratic Party (PPD) in the Cabinet. The PPD had accused the Communists of having totalitarian designs, and the Communists had implied the PPD might have been involved in planning the abortive coup attempt.

The government's reason for postponing the elections was technical. Officials said the CDS must be given time to present new lists of candidates since it had previously presented joint lists with the Christian Democrats, now banned. In addition, three leftist parties and the Communists had used the hammer and sickle as an emblem, which was considered confusing to the partly illiterate and politically inexperienced electorate.

The PPD decided to remain in the April elections despite continuing harassment from leftist youths, reportedly including Communists, who attacked a PPD rally in Oporto March 21. PPD youths retaliated by attacking Communist headquarters in the city, and later two PPD offices were burned down in an apparent counterattack.

A CDS decision to remain was made March 22 despite harassment that included threats on the lives of party leaders, who reportedly slept at different places each night to avoid expected attacks from leftists.

Meanwhile, the Maoist MRPP, banned from the April elections, asserted March 21 that it would not accept its proscription "without a fight." Party leader Jose Luis Saldanha Sanches said he believed in mass violence, and that the Portuguese "revolution is fast approaching the violent phase."

Executive council expanded. Moderate leftist military officers led by Adm. Vitor Crespo, Portuguese high commissioner in Mozambique, forced the adoption of major changes in the Supreme Revolutionary Council, Portugal's new executive body, at a secret showdown March 21–22, 1975, the Washington Post reported March 23.

Under the changes, the council's membership would be expanded from 24 to 28—to include Crespo and two other reputed moderates—and the 200-member MFA Assembly would be empowered to review council decisions and to expel council members who appeared to diverge from the MFA's political aims, the Post reported.

The other new council members were Maj. Vitor Alves, Capt. Jose da Costa Martins and Maj. Ernesto de Melo Antunes. Melo Antunes, appointed foreign minister March 25, had drawn up the relatively moderate government economic plan from which the council had diverted in nationalizing the banks and insurance companies March 14–15.

The changes in the council reportedly mollified the Socialists and the PPD, which had been considering withdrawing from the government and from the constituent assembly elections in April to protest the increasing dominance of leftist military officers and their civilian allies, the Communists and the MDP. The moderates newly admitted to the council reportedly sought cooperation between the military and most civilian political parties.

Mario Soares, the Socialist leader, attacked the Communists March 28 in an interview in the French Socialist organ L'Unite, asserting the Communists had "never made a declaration which manifested their acceptance of the free play of democracy with all it implies, particularly the principle of alternation in power, respect for the right of minorities to express themselves freely, and respect for the principles of liberty and political democracy."

Soares harshly criticized Communist leader Alvaro Cunhal for saying March 21 that there would be "no bourgeois democracy in Portugal." "Could it be the intention of the Communist Party to set up a people's republic in Portugal?" Soares asked. "We do not accept this prospect."

(According to an Algeria Press Service correspondent, Cunhal had said: "The fundamental point of [the Communist] disagreement with the Socialist Party lies in the fact that the Socialists think that democratic freedom of the Western European type is possible in Portugal, whereas, in our opinion, a democratic regime is incompatible with the power of the monopolists and big landowners.")

New Cabinet sworn. A new leftist Cabinet was named March 25 and sworn in March 26. It was the fourth since the provisional government was established in May 1974.

The Cabinet, which would implement decisions of the Supreme Revolutionary Council of the Armed Forces Movement (MFA), was expanded from 17 to 21 members. It comprised eight military officers, five independent leftists, and two representatives each from the Popular Democratic Party (PPD), the Communist and Socialist Parties and the Popular Democratic Movement (MDP).

The major changes in the Cabinet were the creation of a ministry to coordinate planning and economic activities, the appointment of independent leftist technocrats to key economic posts, the transfer of Foreign Minister Mario Soares, a Socialist, to minister without portfolio, and the inclusion of the MDP, which was brought into the government by the Communists over the objections of the Socialists and the PPD.

The new economic coordination post was given to Mario Murteira, a former MDP member and director of the Bank of Portugal. Other independent leftists were named to the industry, agriculture and foreign trade portfolios.

The Communists, the most influential party in the provisional government, gained a portfolio with the appointment of Alvaro Veiga de Oliveira as transport and communications minister. Party leader Alvaro Cunhal, a close adviser of Premier Vasco Goncalves, remained minister without portfolio.

Two major departures from the Cabinet were those of Maj. Vitor Alves, minister without portfolio, and Lt. Col.

Manuel da Costa Braz, interior minister. The latter was considered a blow to the Socialists, who reportedly trusted Costa Braz and wished to see him remain in office to supervise the April elections for a constituent assembly. Costa Braz' replacement was Maj. Antonio Metelo, an associate of Premier Goncalves.

The new Cabinet:

Premier—Brig. Gen. Vasco Goncalves; foreign affairs—Maj. Ernesto de Melo Antunes (not Eduardo de Melo Antunes, as reported earlier); interior—Maj. Antonio Metelo; defense—Capt. Silvano Ribeiro; labor—Capt. Jose da Costa Martins; information—Capt. Jorge Correia Jesuino; planning & economic coordination—Mario Murteira (Independent); finance—Jose Joaquim Fragoso (MDP); industry—Joao Gomes Cravinho (Ind.); agriculture—Fernando Oliveira Batista (Ind.); foreign trade—Jose da Silva Lopes (Ind.); social affairs—Jorge Carvalho Sa Borges (PPD); justice—Francisco Salgado Zenha (Socialist); social infrastructure & environment—Col. Jose Augusto Fernandes; transport & communications—Alvaro Veiga de Oliveira (Communist); overseas territories—Antonio de Almeida Santos (Ind.); education—Maj. Jose da Silva; ministers without portfolio—Alvaro Cunhal (Communist), Mario Soares (Socialist), Joaquim Magalhaes Mota (PPD), Francisco Pereira de Moura (MDP).

At the swearing-in ceremony March 26, Premier Goncalves predicted a period of "total austerity" for Portugal and vowed that the government would "proceed with the nationalization of the basic economic sectors." He did not say which nationalizations would come next, but he pledged a "clear demarcation of the sectors in which private enterprise can expect to continue operating.'

Goncalves said the new government would have the task of "dynamizing the economy and consolidating the advances already made through the nationalization of the banks and insurance companies." He said it would have to reorganize certain enterprises which had come under state control as a result of the bank nationalizations, presumably including Portugal's newspapers, almost all of which were owned by banks.

Goncalves asserted Portugal's foreign policy would continue to be based on national independence, adherence to existing commitments and mutual respect among nations. Observers expected the new foreign minister, Maj. Melo Antunes, to give more attention to African and Asian countries than his predecessor, Soares, according to the London Times March 27.

(The Times reported that it was Soares' own choice to leave the Foreign Ministry. His new post as minister without portfolio gave him a key position in the government while allowing him more time, as leader of the Socialists, to campaign for the constituent assembly elections.)

Leftist Trend Gains Momentum

Banks, insurance firms seized. The Supreme Revolutionary Council, Portugal's new executive body, ordered the nationalization of most banks March 14, 1975 and of the most important insurance firms March 15.

Premier Vasco Goncalves said the banks' nationalization was the "first firm, irreversible step in the antimonopolistic campaign" of the Armed Forces Movement (MFA).

The banks' nationalization gave the state control over a vast complex of bank-owned industries. Compensation for bank owners was not mentioned, but individual accounts were guaranteed. Only foreign banks and savings and agricultural credit institutions were not nationalized.

Bank employes had pressured the military leadership toward nationalization, going on strike immediately after the abortive coup attempt and guarding bank buildings to keep owners from retrieving important documents. Banks reopened March 15 with $200 limits on withdrawals from individual accounts.

Goncalves said in announcing the nationalization that now "the people's money will be used for the real needs of the people." The nationalization was hailed by the Socialist, Communist and other leftist parties and by thousands of demonstrators who marched through Lisbon's streets March 12-15 to celebrate the defeat of the rightist revolt.

NATO nations fear left drift. The spurt of nationalization and general leftward drift of the Portuguese government reportedly alarmed leaders of the North Atlantic Treaty Organization (NATO), to which Portugal was considered strategically important. In an apparent effort to reassure NATO members, the revolutionary council declared March 14 that Portugal would honor all its international commitments.

(NATO members, led by the U.S., were particularly concerned over disclosure by the Portuguese Information Ministry March 15 that an unnamed private transport company had asked authorization to provide requested refueling facilities on Madeira Island for the Soviet merchant fleet. The ministry said it was considering the request.)

The U.S. warned Portugal's military leaders March 25 that their turn to the left was hostile to the interests of the U.S. and of NATO.

The message was delivered to Provisional President Gen. Francisco da Costa Gomes by U.S. Ambassador Frank Carlucci.

In a similar warning, U.S. Secretary of State Henry Kissinger said in Washington March 26 that the U.S. was "disquieted by an evolution in which there is a danger that the democratic process [in Portugal] may become a sham, and in which parties are getting into a dominant position whose interests we would not have thought were necessarily friendly to the United States."

"What seems to be happening now in Portugal," Kissinger declared, "is that the Armed Forces Movement, which is substantially dominated by officers of leftist tendencies, has now appointed a new Cabinet in which Communists and parties closely associated with the Communists have many of the chief portfolios."

This "will of course raise questions for the United States in relation to its NATO policy and to its policy toward Portugal," Kissinger said. He added that the U.S. was "in close contact" with NATO's other members about Portuguese developments.

U.S. Senator James Buckley (Cons.-R, N.Y.) told a press conference in Washington March 21 that military action against Portugal would be one option for NATO should the Communists take full power in Lisbon. "There is nothing else now going on in the world—not in Southeast Asia, not even in the Middle East—half so important and so ominous

as the Communist drive to power in Portugal," Buckley said.

Despite these warnings, U.S. Ambassador Carlucci said in his first public speech in Portugal March 26 that the U.S. had confidence in Lisbon and would continue to aid the government. Nevertheless, attacks against Carlucci continued in the Portuguese press.

The Lisbon newspaper A Capital charged March 26 that the abortive right-wing military revolt two weeks before had been fomented by the U.S. Central Intelligence Agency and by Carlucci, whom it called a prominent figure in "agitation, sabotage and the overthrow of governments." The CIA, A Capital added, was behind the Portuguese Liberation Army (ELP), a rightist subversive organization which, according to military leaders, operated in Spain.

Carlucci officially protested the A Capital article March 28. The Information Ministry issued a statement the same day repeating that Carlucci was "persona grata" in Portugal and chiding the newspaper for "irresponsible and unfounded speculation" about him.

Premier Vasco dos Santos Goncalves later affirmed April 8 Portugal's intention to fulfill its commitments to NATO and to permit U.S. use of the Azores air bases. However, Goncalves said, the Azores facilities would not be available for U.S. use against Arab countries. (The New York Times reported April 30 that Portuguese officials had signalled to their U.S. counterparts a willingness to resume talks on use of the Azores base.)

The head of the military security police, Brig. Gen. Otelo de Carvalho, complained April 28 that the U.S. had brought economic pressure against Portugal by canceling orders for Portuguese goods and rejecting loan applications. According to the New York Times May 29, the U.S. had set aside $15 million during the current year for loans and grants to Portugal and $20 million in mortgage guarantees but Portuguese officials had not submitted the necessary contracts. The Times reported May 18 that Information Minister Jorge Correia Jesuino and Labor Minister Jose da Costa Martins had been in the U.S.

that week for goodwill visits and that Martins had expressed confidence that the U.S. intended "to give us help."

Reds in media posts. A shake-up in the state-run radio and television networks had placed Communist Party members in most executive positions, according to Alvaro Guerra, head of the networks' news department, who announced his resignation April 9 to protest the shake-up.

Guerra told the newspaper Republica that there was "an effort to divide public life into Communists and Fascists," with the latter including all who opposed Communist policies. Guerra called this "an extremely worrisome and dangerous phenomenon [which] is becoming general in Portugal."

Arrests & dismissals. The armed forces April 9 announced the arrests of 28 military men and three civilians on charges of participating in the attempted military coup March 11.

The arrested soldiers included officers and non-commissioned officers. The civilians included Nuno Rocha, a prominent business executive who had been trying unsuccessfully to publish a new newspaper in the wake of the nationalization of Portugal's banks, which put most papers in the hands of the government. Rocha said April 10 that he was held only a few hours for questioning.

The arrests coincided with reliable reports of a purge of military personnel opposed to the radical policies of the Supreme Revolutionary Council, according to the New York Times April 10. The second and fifth divisions of the general staff, which dealt with intelligence and public information respectively, were among the units undergoing purges, the Times reported.

The MFA Assembly had been purged and enlarged from 200 to 240 members, with new members carefully selected by the Revolutionary Council, the Times reported. The new assembly met for the first time April 11.

Extreme leftists were also being arrested, according to the London Times April 12.

Some 50–100 members of the Maoist MRPP and leaders of the Alliance of Workers and Peasants (AOC) had been seized in the past few weeks, the Times reported. Independent Portuguese sources estimated there were at least 1,700 political prisoners in Portugal, the majority of them former members of the ousted dictatorship's secret police and other fascist organizations, according to the Times. The provisional government claimed there were no political prisoners, only persons accused of committing crimes under the old dictatorship and others connected to abortive plots against the current regime.

Party Heads Accept Junta, Voters Elect Moderates

Civilian leaders endorse military rule. Leaders of Portugal's six major political parties signed an agreement with the armed forces April 11, 1975 providing for at least three more years of military rule.

The pact set the essential terms of a new constitution to be written by the constituent assembly which would be elected April 25. The agreement was signed enthusiastically by the Communist Party and its two allies, the Portuguese Democratic Movement and the Popular Socialist Front, and reluctantly by the Socialist and Popular Democratic Parties and the Social Democratic Center. The last three said they signed because there was no other way to retain any influence in the government.

The pact virtually eliminated civilians from decision-making roles during a three-to-five year "transitional period" in which the ruling Armed Forces Movement (MFA) would put the nation "irreversibly on the road to Portuguese socialism." Provisional President Gen. Francisco da Costa Gomes said such a period was necessary to insure political stability and to educate "politically ignorant" Portuguese against reactionary, autocratic or extreme leftist movements.

(Five minor leftist parties and the Popular Monarchist Party refused to sign the agreement. The leftist parties, described by the New York Times as extremist, felt

the armed forces were not being revolutionary enough and were merely per-
petuating "bourgeois power," the Times
reported April 12. The Monarchists refused to sign to avoid associating themselves with the moderate leftist parties
which did sign, according to the London
Times April 12.)

Under the new constitution, government policy would essentially be formulated by the Supreme Revolutionary
Council, the 28-member executive body
elected by the MFA. The president of the
republic would be a military man and he
would chair the Revolutionary Council.
He would be elected not by universal suffrage, as the MFA had pledged when it
seized power in 1974, but by an electoral
college comprising members of the MFA
and of a civilian legislative assembly to be
elected after the constitution was enacted.

The Revolutionary Council would have
authority to approve or veto legislation
passed by the government or the civilian
assembly; to dissolve the assembly; to
amend the constitution, and to direct the
president to declare war. The assembly
could override the Council by a two-thirds
vote, but the Council could declare
legislation unconstitutional.

Before signing the agreement, the
Socialists, Popular Democrats and Centrists had tried for several days to negotiate major changes in its terms. However, they achieved only minor changes,
such as reducing the assembly vote needed
to override a Council veto from three-
fourths to two-thirds.

In an apparent response to these efforts
and to continuing strife among civilian
political parties, Information Minister
Jorge Correia Jesuino had expressed the
MFA's "dissatisfaction" with civilian
parties April 10, accusing them of being
more interested in their own power than in
the welfare of Portugal. He said "it was
probably a mistake to allow parties to be
formed after April 25," 1974, the day the
MFA overthrew the civilian dictatorship
of Premier Marcello Caetano.

Jesuino said only the Communist Party
was cooperating fully with the MFA, jus-
tifying the Communists' growing power in
the regime. He added that in order not

to be accused of complicity with the Communists, he would do all his work in the
future without the aid of any political
party.

Rear Adm. Antonio Rosa Coutinho, a
top MFA leader, said April 14 that he
would like to see the MFA aided by a
coalition of existing Marxist parties such
as the Portuguese Democratic Movement,
the Socialist Left Movement, the Popular
Socialist Front and "parts" of the Socialist and Communist Parties. He said
some Socialist leaders, notably Minister
Without Portfolio Mario Soares, were too
conservative, and some Communist leaders
were too radical.

Meanwhile, the 12 political parties approved by the MFA campaigned for the
April 25 constituent assembly elections.
Each party would be allotted 90 minutes
of television time and 12½ hours of radio
time during the campaign, which officially
began at midnight April 1.

In an unexpected development April 13,
Roman Catholic priests throughout Portugal delivered sermons forbidding Catholics "to vote for parties which by their
ideology, objectives, prejudices and history, have shown themselves to be incompatible with the Christian concept of man
and his life in society." The directives,
apparently aimed against the Communists
and other Marxists, were expected to help
the Centrists, who had emphasized their
support for Christian principles.

Priests also warned their flock against
abstaining in the election or casting blank
ballots. The MFA had urged voters who
were confused or undecided to cast blank
ballots rather than abstain, and moderate
politicians had protested that the armed
forces might use a high total of blank
ballots to justify forming their own political party and excluding the other parties
from power.

**Moderates win constituent assembly
vote.** Moderate left-wing and centrist
candidates won a majority of seats in the
projected constituent assembly April 25,
in the first free Portuguese elections in
nearly 50 years.

The moderate Socialist Party led the

vote with 37.82% of the ballots and 115 seats in the 247-seat assembly, which would write a new constitution according to guidelines dictated by the ruling Armed Forces Movement (MFA). The center-left Popular Democratic Party (PPD) was second with 26.41% of the votes and 80 assembly seats, and the Communist Party followed with 12.54% and 30 seats. The conservative Social Democratic Center (CDS) was fourth with 7.6% and 16 seats, and several small leftist parties and a monarchist group trailed.

91.74% of the 6.17 million eligible voters went to the polls, and only 6.97% cast blank or spoiled ballots. The voting and the campaign that preceded it were relatively peaceful, with only occasional outbreaks of violence reported.

MFA leaders emphasized after the vote that government policy would not change despite the victory by the Socialists and the PPD, who opposed certain measures taken by the Supreme Revolutionary Council, the MFA executive body dominated by radical army officers and influenced by the Communist Party.

Information Minister Jorge Correia Jesuino reminded the parties April 26 that they had signed an agreement before the vote accepting military rule for three to five years and endorsing military guidelines for the constitution. Premier Vasco Goncalves said the vote would not "decisively influence the revolutionary process," declaring that "the constituent assembly is one thing, the provisional government and the revolution are another."

In a stronger statement April 28, Brig. Gen. Otelo de Carvalho, an outspoken MFA leader, accused the victorious parties of representing only their own interests, and not the Portuguese people. He said the constitution drawn up by the assembly would reflect "what we [the MFA] consider to be the will of the people."

Radical MFA leaders had minimized the importance of the elections before April 25, encouraging voters to cast blank ballots to show their confusion and indecision. However, Provisional President Gen. Francisco da Costa Gomes urged voters April 24 to vote for "socialism" and "pluralism of parties," reportedly giving a boost to Socialist Party candidates.

The Socialists decisively defeated their major rivals, the Communists, winning 46% of the vote in Lisbon (to 19% for the Communists) and doing well in normally Communist strongholds. The Socialists and Communists attacked each other bitterly during the three-week campaign, but Socialist leader Mario Soares made a conciliatory statement after the voting April 26, asserting his party was "not anticommunist" and that Socialists considered Communists "essential to democracy in this country."

The Communists charged during the campaign that the Socialists favored "bourgeois democracy" and that they had played a role, directly or indirectly, in the unsuccessful March 11 attempted coup. The Socialists denied both charges, asserting they wanted to build "an inde-

Portuguese Election Results

Party	Vote Total*	Vote Percentage*	Assembly Seats**
Socialist Party	2,052,937	37.82%	115
Popular Democratic Party	1,433,392	26.41%	80
Portuguese Communist Party	680,678	12.54%	30
Social Democratic Center	412,692	7.60%	16
Portuguese Democratic Movement	223,723	4.12%	5
Popular Socialist Front	68,838	1.18%	
Socialist Left Movement	55,706	1.03%	
Popular Democratic Union	42,798	0.79%	1
Communist Electoral Front	30,828	0.57%	
Popular Monarchist Party	30,396	0.56%	
Popular Unity Party	12,263	0.23%	
International Communist League	10,356	0.19%	

*Source: Le Monde, April 29, 1975
**London Times, April 30, 1975

pendent Portuguese socialism" in full collaboration with the MFA.

(The Communists were supported in the second charge by a government report, issued April 22, which accused "certain responsible politicians" of helping create the unstable climate which preceded the coup attempt by conducting an "alarmist campaign" which warned of a possible civil war in Portugal. Both Soares and PPD leader Francisco Sa Carneiro had warned of the possibility before the abortive uprising.)

The campaign was marked by occasional clashes between Communists and CDS members, particularly in northern Portugal. Twenty persons were injured, three by gunfire, when leftist youths attacked a CDS rally in the town of Guimaraes April 20. In neighboring Oporto, Communist youths attacked a CDS motorcade the same evening.

Seven persons were injured April 21 when leftist youths broke up a CDS march and besieged CDS headquarters in Braga, north of Oporto. CDS members disrupted a Communist rally in neighboring Trofa April 22, causing injuries to about 10 persons.

Foreign reaction—The Soviet Communist Party newspaper Pravda said April 27 that the constituent assembly vote was "an important phase" in Portugal's "free, independent and democratic development." A Soviet national television news program reported April 27 that leftist parties had won 55% of the Portuguese vote and extreme rightists had won only 8%. Neither Pravda nor the television program cited the Communist Party's low vote total.

In London, the Daily Telegraph reported April 27 that voters seemed to have "decidedly weakened" the MFA's prospects for turning Portugal into "an Iberian Cuba." The Sunday Times said the election results should be seen as "an expression of the voters' opinion of the radical fashion in which the Armed Forces Movement has carried out its program."

In Rome, newspapers interpreted the vote results in the light of Italian politics. The Christian Democratic paper Il Popolo reported April 27 that the Portuguese had rejected an "historic com-

promise" between the Communists and the military. (Italy's Communists sought a "compromise" with other political parties. By contrast, the Communist paper L'Unita said the Portuguese left had established the importance of "unity among all the forces that support progress and the democratic transformation of Portuguese society."

The New York Times said in an editorial April 27 that Portuguese voters had "delivered a humiliating defeat for Communism, an emphatic endorsement of democratic reform rather than Marxist revolution, and a solid vote of confidence for the country's strong ties with Western Europe and the United States. If the ruling armed forces movement will recognize these results and act accordingly, Portugal will have passed an historic milestone on the road to becoming a modern, Western democratic nation."

Nationalization pressed. Take-over of five concerns by the government May 16 was the latest in a series of nationalization moves.

The government announced April 16 it was taking over control of companies that produced and distributed electricity and oil and of four transport companies—the railway system, the national airlines and two shipping firms.

The cement, cellulose and tobacco industries were nationalized May 14, and wage controls were laid down. No citizen was allowed to earn more than $1,458 a month after taxes. All wages above $500 a month were frozen, and the national monthly minimum wage was increased from $137 to $167. Companies that had received government credits were forbidden either to declare bankruptcy or to distribute dividends without state approval.

The government also froze prices until the end of 1975 on bread, meat, milk, sugar, flour, oil, margarine and codfish.

The five companies nationalized May 16 were not identified, although news reports said takeovers that day brought to 48 the number of such acquisitions by the government within the previous 10 days.

In other industrial developments, the port wine industry, which employed some

4,000 persons and was a major source of foreign exchange, was struck April 16 when workers in Oporto walked off the job demanding higher pay.

In a move that appeared to stop short of outright nationalization, the government May 24 put state officials and workers in charge of Companhia Unjao Fabril (CUF), a conglomerate listed as one of the largest companies in the world, employing 30,000 workers in a range of industrial fields including tobacco and steel. CUF reportedly accounted for more than 10% of the country's industrial production.

Leftist Trend Opposed

Socialists boycott cabinet. The Socialist Party, which had led the vote in elections for the constituent assembly, announced May 22, 1975 a boycott of cabinet meetings because of what it termed disproportionate Communist influence in the nation's political life. The move occurred amid increasing signs that the military government was losing patience with partisan disagreement.

At a press conference May 22, Socialist Party leader Mario Soares demanded an end to Communist take-overs in the communications field, the holding of union elections to test Communist power in labor organizations and local elections to replace Communists who had seized municipal power illegally. No deadline for meeting these terms was reported.

A meeting of the armed forces General Assembly May 27 condemned the Socialist refusal to attend cabinet meetings and promoted to major general two military figures the Socialists had accused of supporting Communist positions—Brig. Gen. Vasco dos Santos Goncalves, the premier, and Brig. Gen. Otelo de Carvalho, head of security.

The Socialists participated in a cabinet meeting called May 28 to discuss Angola, and they ended their boycott May 30.

May Day disturbance, Republica seizure—One of the events leading to the boycott took place May 1 when the Supreme Revolutionary Council, the executive body of the ruling Armed Forces Movement, promulgated a law establishing the Communist-dominated Intersyndical Congress as the nation's only legal labor union. At a May Day rally in Lisbon later that day, several Intersyndical guards attempted unsuccessfully to prevent Soares from entering the stadium, although the Socialist Party had been officially invited to the event. Members of the center-left Popular Democratic Party (PPD), a Socialist ally not invited to the gathering, were turned away. The confrontation led to meetings between Soares, Provisional President Gen. Francisco da Costa Gomes and Alvaro Cunhal, head of the Communist Party. A tentative reconciliation between the two parties was announced May 6.

In another pre-boycott incident, Information Minister Capt. Jorge Correia Jesuino May 20 closed the newspaper Republica, a journal owned by private shareholders but considered sympathetic to the Socialist cause, after several days of disturbances. He charged that some 3,000 Socialist demonstrators at the Republica office were a threat to public order. The demonstrators were protesting seizure of the paper the previous day by Communist printers, who were objecting to the appointment in April of two Socialist journalists. (The Italian Communist Party Newspaper L'Unita said May 20 that the take-over of Republica had been a "counterrevolutionary coup" brought about by "extremist agitators.")

The New York Times May 21 reported the government argued that its only lawful recourse was to close Republica when Communist printers took it over and contended the matter would have to be settled in the courts. Jesuino was said to have described control of communications by a single group as "a grave problem." According to the Times May 27, Jesuino had reminded the printers the night they took over the newspaper that "Republica belongs to its shareholders. These are represented by the management, which has the legal right to run the paper. I repeat, the newspaper has the right to publish the kind of information it chooses. Nor do I think it is as one-sided as you gentlemen insist. If any of you disagree with its policies, you should work somewhere else. I only wish there were more newspapers like it."

Other political action—The Revolutionary Council announced May 27 it would set up a group to study formation of alliances between the government and "popular structures," or workers' committees, which would act as "unified blocs to overcome any political diversions and guarantee a correct sequence of the revolutionary process." Soares declared May 27 that he was "extremely worried" about the proposal, which he described as "only one step short of outlawing all democratic rights and creating a dictatorship." (Soares had accused the government May 23 of bypassing the ordinary political process. "We are often surprised," he had declared, "by newspapers announcing decisions which were never discussed in the cabinet and of which we were not even informed." In a May 19 speech Alvaro Cunhal, head of the Communist Party, had said: "We believe the general condemnation of the political parties by the military is a grave error.")

The military government dismissed the city council of Oporto May 26 and replaced it with officials from the armed forces after continued disagreement among representatives of political parties there.

In related party developments, authorities in Lisbon May 28 arrested dozens of members of the Movement for Reorganization of the Proletarian Party (MRPP), a Maoist group banned from the April elections.

The Popular Democratic Party declared May 6 its objection to monopoly of local council seats held by the Popular Democratic Movement (MDP), a Communist ally, which had won only 4% of the April vote. The statement called the MDP "a minority party considered increasingly by the people an appendage of another party, without either an ideology or a life of its own."

(As the Socialists and Communists continued to feud, the army moved against the Maoist MRPP organization, arresting an estimated 300–600 Maoists May 28–29 and charging June 5 that the MRPP had planned to assassinate important military leaders. The Maoists took most of their members from the universities and high schools, where the traditional political parties had little support, according to press reports.)

Ford cites danger to NATO. In a repetition of warnings made by U.S. officials in March, President Gerald Ford declared May 23 that he intended to inquire formally at the coming NATO ministerial conference in Brussels whether Portugal ought to remain a member of the alliance.

Ford remarked in a White House interview with foreign correspondents: "I don't see how you can have a Communist element significant in an organization that was put together and formed for the purpose of meeting a challenge by Communist elements from the East." He said he was concerned about the Communist "influence in Portugal and, therefore, Portugal's relationship with NATO. This is a matter that I will certainly bring up when we meet in Brussels."

Secretary of State Henry A. Kissinger explained May 24 that President Ford had not meant to imply that the Lisbon government was under Communist control but was referring to "trends" in the country's political development. He added: "We wish Portugal well. We hope Portugal will have a democratic evolution, in conformity with its own national aspirations." Kissinger conceded, however, that "an alliance that is designed to prevent a Communist attack on Western Europe acquires unique features when it includes in its deliberations a government of which many members are Communists."

Ford arrived in Brussels May 28, and later he met May 29 with Portuguese Premier Vasco dos Santos Goncalves, who asserted that Portugal was "a loyal NATO member." Seeking to rebut U.S. statements that Lisbon's leftist government threatened NATO, Goncalves denied that Portugal represented a "Trojan horse" in the alliance. Nonetheless, Ford reiterated his concern in a May 30 press conference, saying he had "pointed out the contradiction that would arise if Communist elements came to dominate the political life of Portugal."

Portuguese aid request deferred. The nine EEC foreign ministers June 24 rejected a proposal by the European Commission for "immediate and substantial" aid to Portugal.

In addition to a large sum of financial aid, the Commission had proposed June 12 improving the EEC's free trade accord with Portugal, in effect since January 1973, to facilitate access to the EEC of Portuguese agricultural and industrial goods and offer better benefits for Portuguese migrant workers living in the EEC nations.

The Commission proposals were in response to a decision by the EEC foreign ministers in Dublin May 26 to intensify their trade and aid relations with Portugal in an apparent effort to stem the leftist orientation of the country's ruling military council. Some EEC members, particularly West German Foreign Minister Hans-Dietrich Genscher, were reported to have argued that any aid should be linked to the maintenance of democracy in Portugal.

Irish Foreign Minister Garret FitzGerald, current president of the EEC Council of Ministers, visited Lisbon June 1–3 to discuss with Portuguese officials the scope and form of a new trade and aid agreement.

Meanwhile, the European Free Trade Association had agreed to aid the Portuguese economy, it was reported May 22. Portugal was an EFTA member. Among the measures approved in principle were tariff concessions for infant industries and a relaxation of the timetable for Portuguese tariff cuts on other products; concessions on imports into EFTA nations of certain Portuguese agricultural products; establishment of an industrial development fund; and technical assistance.

Radio Renascenca & Republica seizures. The MFA Supreme Revolutionary Council July 3 named an administrative committee to manage the Roman Catholic radio station Radio Renascenca, which the government had ordered returned to its owners two days earlier. The council said all radio stations eventually would be nationalized.

Radio Renascenca had been seized earlier by some 20 employes who claimed the station's owners, the Roman Catholic hierarchy, were reactionary. The military security force, Copcon, had refused to remove the workers from the station, even after the government ordered the station returned to its owners. The station's occupation occasioned bitter demonstrations by supporters and opponents of the employes, including an incident June 18–19 in which leftists attacked some 300 Roman Catholics outside the archbishop's palace in Lisbon, forcing troops to intervene to protect the Catholics. The nation's bishops declared July 4 that they would not accept government management of the station, charging the armed forces weakly gave in to disruptive minorities.

A similar conflict continued over the occupation of the Socialist newspaper Republica, begun May 19 by Communist printers ostensibly demanding improved working conditions and a say in editorial policy.

The Supreme Revolutionary Council ruled June 6 that Republica should be returned to its director, the Socialist Raul Rego, but the council praised the printers for what it called "correct initiatives." Copcon was instructed to remove the seals placed by the government on the Republica building. However, Rego demanded certain conditions to resume the newspaper's management, including the removal of 12 leaders of the printers, which Copcon refused to approve June 16. Copcon officers than gave the keys to the building to the printers, who immediately reoccupied it. This occasioned a new sealing of the building, and when the seals were removed again June 18, presumably to allow both printers and editorial staffers to enter, Copcon officers gave the keys to printers two hours before the appointed time, leading to a new occupation.

The Republica controversy was aggravated by the publication in Paris June 23 of a Republica supplement including an alleged Soviet document instructing Communist parties in Western European nations on methods of gaining full political power. The document, allegedly signed by Boris Ponomarev, a Soviet Communist Party secretary for relations with non-ruling Communist parties in Western European nations, was called fabricated by both Portugal's Communists and by the Soviet news agency Tass, which charged June 24 that its publication amounted to "police provocation" on the part of Portuguese Socialists. The Republica supplement appeared in the leftist newspaper Le Quotidien de Paris.

The Republica controversy exacerbated the feud between Portugal's Socialists and Communists, leading the Socialists to threaten a new boycott of the military-civilian cabinet June 4 (their first boycott ended May 30) and leading Communist leader Alvaro Cunhal to charge June 28 that the Socialists were merely a front for "a dictatorship of capitalism and the right."

Regime Presses Program, Moderates Quit Cabinet

'Direct democracy' planned. The General Assembly of the Armed Forces Movement approved a plan July 9, 1975 to create workers' control of production and government at the local, regional and national levels, with ultimate authority resting indefinitely in the MFA's executive body, the Supreme Revolutionary Council.

The plan, described as a system of "direct democracy," was announced at the end of an 18-hour meeting, the last of a series of marathon conferences by military leaders seeking a unified approach to the nation's deepening economic crisis, labor unrest and political strife.

The plan would initially create local industrial, agricultural and neighborhood committees which would choose their leaders and legislate by show of hands. Municipal, district and regional assemblies would follow, culminating in a National People's Assembly. Under an "alliance of the people and the Armed Forces' Movement," the Supreme Revolutionary Council would be the "maximum organ of national sovereignty."

Workers would control the means of production in both state and private enterprises, and they would run the government machinery from transport to public

health, according to the plan. "People's tribunals" would be established to deal with "non-criminal problems."

In addition to the plan, the MFA Assembly approved a report by Premier Vasco Goncalves which, according to the Washington Post July 10, outlined an international conspiracy against the military-civilian government which had harmed the Portuguese economy and created an atmosphere of counterrevolution.

(The government's apparent inability to halt the nation's economic decline and labor and political unrest had led recently to rumors that Goncalves would be removed from office. Approval of his report showed that he still had the confidence of other military leaders, according to the state press agency ANI.)

The MFA plan received the immediate support of the Communist Party, which stood to gain from the plan through its superior national organization and its locally organized "committees for the defense of the revolution." Other parties objected that the plan would deny them any power, with some Socialists talking of a "putsch" and the Popular Democrats charging the armed forces had violated the pact they made with the political parties before the April elections for a Constituent Assembly, according to the New York Times July 10.

(The pact provided for eventual creation of a democratic state with a political party system, after transitional military rule from three to five years. The Assembly, dominated by moderates, opened as scheduled June 2, but it immediately ran afoul of the military by allowing itself daily periods of debate on important national issues, which the armed forces banned.)

The MFA plan appeared to abrogate not only the political pact but a more recent MFA policy statement, issued June 21, which envisioned workers' control of production but also rejected "dictatorial means" of government. The statement had been hailed by Socialists and centrists as a "victory" over military and civilian leaders who sought to do away with the political parties altogether.

The statement gave a grim assessment of the Portuguese economy, citing a foreign payments deficit that would surpass $1 billion in 1975; "practically exhausted foreign reserves" with the exception of gold holdings; an 8% unemployment rate; and an expected 6% drop in the gross national product in 1975. The MFA said the gravity of the economic and financial situation obliged the military-civilian government "to overcome its differences and arrive at a common solution to the problem of economic development." However, following the July 9 MFA plan and other military actions in economic and labor matters, the role of the government in devising a solution was held in doubt.

The regime June 1 had decreed surcharges of up to 30% on an extensive range of imports, including most raw materials and consumer goods but not oil. The surcharges, part of an attempt to stem the drain on gold and foreign reserves, would hit ordinary workers particularly hard, according to the Financial Times of London June 4.

The government June 14 decreed the nationalization of 54 bus companies.

The government recently had ordered a 50% increase in public transport fares, but the Supreme Revolutionary Council had revoked it July 3, allowing "working class" commuters to buy season tickets at the old price.

The government announced July 5 that it would expropriate agricultural holdings larger than 700 hectares and all private hunting estates.

The government July 10 formally nationalized the Companhia Uniao Fabril, the nation's largest industrial conglomerate, which had important interests in shipbuilding, cement, tobacco, textiles and chemicals, in addition to previously nationalized banking interests.

Socialists, PPD leave government. Portugal's political crisis deepened as the two moderate groups in the provisional government, the Socialists and the Popular Democratic Party (PPD), withdrew in July in protest against allegedly dictatorial actions of the ruling Armed Forces Movement (MFA).

Their departure left only two political parties—the Communists and their ally, the Portuguese Democratic Movement—in the cabinet. It also cast doubts on the future of the Constituent Assembly, in which the Socialists and the PPD held a majority.

The Socialists withdrew July 11, accusing the provisional president, Gen. Francisco da Costa Gomes, and the MFA's executive body, the Supreme Revolutionary Council, of going back on a decision to return the newspaper Republica to its Socialist staff. The Revolutionary Council had appointed a military commission to run the newspaper after it was occupied by Communist printers, but the commission had effectively handed the paper over to the printers. Republica had resumed publication July 10, and its first issue had attacked the Socialists as the most reactionary party in Portugal.

The Socialists' two ministers and five deputy ministers left the cabinet, and party leader Mario Soares, who resigned as minister without portfolio, denounced the seizure of Republica. Soares noted that, on the basis of elections for the Constituent Assembly, the Socialists were "the majority party in the country."

The PPD, which ran second to the Socialists in the elections, issued an ultimatum to President Costa Gomes July 11, asserting it would also leave the government unless it was assured by July 16 that the MFA would guarantee freedom of the press, prompt municipal elections, firm exercise of public authority, continued movement toward representative democracy, and urgent measures to resolve the current economic crisis.

The PPD leadership met with Costa Gomes July 14 and 16, but it received insufficient assurances, and withdrew from the government early July 17. Two independent cabinet officials, Foreign Trade Minister Jose da Silva Lopes and Overseas Territories Minister Antonio de Almeida Santos, also resigned.

Opposition to regime grows. Increasing opposition to the policies of the Armed Forces Movement (MFA) was reported.

The PPD and the Socialists had worked together in the cabinet and the Constituent Assembly against the radical policies of the Supreme Revolutionary Council, which were unfailingly supported by the Communists. They joined July 10 in attacking the MFA's plan for "direct democracy," with the Socialists asserting: "This reduction of the country to a hybrid organizational blueprint serves, fundamentally and only, to cover up the installation of a dictatorship."

Opposition to MFA policies was also expressed by Roman Catholics and businessmen. More than 10,000 Roman Catholics demonstrated in the northern town of Aveiro July 13 against the military takeover of a Catholic radio station, Radio Renascenca. In Rio Maior the same day, about 200 angry farmers and Catholics destroyed the headquarters of the Communist Party and another leftist group, the Popular Socialist Front.

Representatives of private industry began a three-day meeting July 10 to decide ways to protect private enterprise and reverse the nation's economic decline. They suspended their conference at the end of the next day, reportedly under military pressure. Small shopkeepers had scheduled a similar meeting for July 13, but they too canceled under pressure.

The Supreme Revolutionary Council and its supporters severely criticized the Socialists and other moderates. The council asserted July 12 that the Socialists had opened "a wider field of maneuver for counterrevolutionary acts when ... the enemies of the transformation of Portuguese society" were trying to divide "the political parties, the people and the Armed Forces Movement." Thousands of Socialists replied with a march in Lisbon July 15 at which they chanted, "The people are not with the Armed Forces Movement." (The chant inserted a negative into a popular jingle backing the Armed Forces Movement.) Mario Soares declared the demonstration was preparatory to a general strike against the MFA.

Middle-class Portuguese were continuing to emigrate at an accelerated rate, the New York Times reported July 17. Canadian Pacific Airlines reported heavy bookings from Lisbon to Canada by Portuguese scouting job opportunities in Canadian cities, according to the Times.

Meanwhile, there were varying reports of division within the Supreme Revolu-

tionary Council. The Financial Times of London reported July 14 that adoption of the MFA's "direct democracy" plan had followed an attempt within the council to oust Premier Vasco Goncalves, who was closely identified with the Communists. Goncalves reportedly escaped dismissal by moderates in the council by delivering a convincing report on an alleged international conspiracy against the Portuguese revolution.

Press reports speculated that, following the withdrawal of the Socialists and the PPD, Goncalves would form a cabinet of military men and independent civilian technocrats, excluding all political parties. Capt. Vasco Lourenco, an MFA spokesman, had told the newspaper O Seculo July 16 that he favored "a non-party government led by the Armed Forces Movement and containing civilian elements of recognized merits. There will always have to be representatives of the Armed Forces Movement because at present I see no way that the military could be left out of the government."

Triumvirate Takes Power, Attack on Left Grows

Military junta established. The Supreme Revolutionary Council, the executive body of the ruling Armed Forces Movement (MFA), transferred its legislative and executive powers July 1, 1975 to a three-man military junta headed by Provisional President Francisco da Costa Gomes.

In addition to Costa Gomes, who was considered a moderate, the members of the junta were Gen. Vasco Goncalves, the Communist-oriented premier, and Gen. Otelo de Carvalho, the security chief, who many observers thought to be an extreme leftist. The Supreme Revolutionary Council would act as an advisory board to the junta, which would be called the Directorate.

Creation of the junta had been approved July 25 by the MFA Assembly, following an unsuccessful attempt by moderate officers to unseat Goncalves, whom they considered incompetent and too close to the Communist Party. The Assembly meeting was boycotted by seven moderate leaders including Maj. Ernesto de Melo Antunes, the former foreign minister; Adm. Vitor Crespo, former high commissioner of Mozambique, and Capt. Rodrigo Sousa e Castro, who reportedly resigned from the Supreme Revolutionary Council in protest July 24. His resignation was reportedly rejected.

Goncalves & left under continued attack—Opposition to Goncalves within the MFA continued after the junta was established, according to press reports. The Washington Post reported Aug. 1 that Costa Gomes was leading a move to ease out the premier because he represented a radical political and military minority that had antagonized and frightened the majority of the Portuguese people as well as the Western world. Senior military sources told the Post that Costa Gomes sought not to depose Goncalves but to let him die a "natural political death" over his inability to form a new government of "people of stature" able to deal with Portugal's serious economic, political and diplomatic problems.

Goncalves had failed to form a new cabinet following the withdrawal from the government of the Socialist and Popular Democratic Parties, which had commanded a majority of the votes in the April elections for the Constituent Assembly. The Socialists and Popular Democrats had refused to re-enter the government and had denounced formation of the military junta as unconstitutional and as violating the pact between the MFA and Portugal's political parties, signed before the Constituent Assembly vote.

The Socialists and Popular Democrats held protest rallies in various cities July 27. At the major Socialist rally in Figueira da Foz, on the coast north of Lisbon, party leader Mario Soares called on Costa Gomes to leave the junta and form a "government of national salvation," presumably including members of the democratic parties. Of the junta members, Soares asked: "Who chose these men? Little by little our revolution has been stolen from us."

"The Portuguese people are fed up with ideology, political debate and calls to fight this or that battle," Soares declared. "What the people want is answers to their problems." He urged the MFA to sit down with the democratic parties and "plan concrete and realistic policies to save the country and the revolution."

The Socialists had held several large rallies before creation of the junta to demand Goncalves' resignation. At a rally of more than 50,000 persons in Lisbon July 19, Soares had called for a government headed by a military man "who gives better guarantees of political neutrality" than Goncalves. The MFA issued a communique the next day denouncing Soares for attacking the premier.

(Communists had attempted July 18 to set up barricades to block a Socialist rally in Oporto that evening and the rally in Lisbon the next day. However, Socialists had torn down the Oporto barricades and the military security force, Copcon, had ordered the Communists to dismantle the Lisbon barricades.)

Meanwhile, attacks on Communist Party offices continued throughout the country. A total of 14 party headquarters were reported destroyed by July 22. In one incident, in the town of Aveiro July 19, a soldier was killed accidentally by a fellow soldier as troops fired into the air to disperse anticommunist demonstrators.

Several hundred persons attacked Communist headquarters in Alcobaca July 22, severely beating two Communist organizers, one of whom shot and wounded an attacker. Portuguese in Sao Joao de Madeira, south of Oporto, besieged Communist headquarters July 29 and sacked offices of the party's Electoral Front.

Responding to the violence July 30, Gen. Carvalho, head of Copcon, said the MFA might find it necessary to "take up the very hard path of repression" and turn Lisbon's main bullring into a concentration camp for reactionaries. "It's becoming impossible to carry out a socialist revolution by completely peaceful means," he asserted.

Carvalho described Mario Soares as the greatest enemy of the Portuguese left. "At the moment," he said, "Soares is the hope of the right wing ... not only the right wing, but all reactionaries."

Carvalho spoke on his return from a

nine-day visit to Cuba, where he and Cuban Premier Fidel Castro expressed firm support for each other's governments. "We are going to see now what we can use here of what we learned in Cuba," Carvalho told a group of supporters including Communist Party chief Alvaro Cunhal. "I have just come back from a socialist country and I can tell you it is worth the sacrifice."

In contrast to Carvalho, Gen. Costa Gomes had appealed July 25 for a deceleration of the Portuguese revolution, asserting its pace had "accelerated to a point that the people have not been able to match." "Let us put aside for the moment the ideologies which inspire us and take note with humility that nearly all the people used to be with the revolution and today we have to recognize that this is no longer the case."

Costa Gomes noted that although Portugal sought national independence, it depended on Western nations for trade and it had three million emigrants and settlers abroad. "It seems to me that ... independence cannot be attained in the short run by any way that involves hostility to the West," he said. "A concerted maneuver by the West, with a reduction in trade and the return of the emigrants, is a threat to which we have no valid response."

Costa Gomes' statement was interpreted as an attempt to reassure Portugal's trade partners and its fellow members of the North Atlantic Treaty Organization on the eve of the European security conference in Helsinki.

New cabinet named; MFA split widens. Premier Vasco Goncalves named a new cabinet Aug. 8, but divisions within the ruling Armed Forces Movement (MFA) deepened with the emergence of a strong moderate faction and a smaller leftist group opposed to his Communist-influenced policies.

The two factions pressed President Francisco da Costa Gomes to dismiss Goncalves, as did the Socialist and Popular Democratic Parties and an increasing number of Roman Catholic Church officials. Opponents of the premier staged large demonstrations and destroyed Communist Party offices in a number of cities and towns.

Goncalves announced a cabinet of radical military officers and civilian technocrats Aug. 8. He named two deputy premiers, Lt. Col. Arnao Metelo and Jose Teixeira Ribeiro, a finance and taxation specialist and rector of Coimbra University. Only one cabinet minister was considered allied with a civilian political party—Economic Coordination Minister Mario Murteira, who was identified with the Popular Democratic Movement (MPD), a Communist Party ally.

The new cabinet:

Foreign affairs—Mario Ruivo; interior—Maj. Alfredo Candido de Moura; justice—Joaquim Rocha e Cunha.; information—Cmdr. Jorge Correia Jesuino; defense—Capt. Silvano Ribeiro; industry & technology—Capt. Fernando Quiteiro de Brito; economic coordination—Mario Murteira; agriculture—Fernando Oliveira Batista; foreign trade—Domingo Lopes; internal trade—Manuel Macaista Malheiros; social affairs—Francisco Pereira de Moura; social infrastructure & environment—Henrique Oliveira Sa; labor—Capt. Jose da Costa Martins; finance—Jose Joaquim Fragosa; education—Maj. Emilio da Silva.

The swearing-in ceremony for cabinet officials was boycotted by nine moderate members of the Supreme Revolutionary Council, the former executive body of the MFA, who had issued a manifesto the previous day denouncing the "fascist spirit" of attempts by a radical minority in the MFA to impose a "bureaucratic dictatorship" in Portugal along "Eastern European" Communist lines.

The moderates, who included Maj. Ernesto de Melo Antunes, the former foreign minister, Adm. Vitor Crespo, the former high commissioner of Mozambique, and Capt. Vasco Lourenco, a frequent MFA spokesman, were all leaders of the April 1974 military coup which ousted Portugal's civilian dictatorship.

They asserted the nationalization policies adopted by Goncalves had caused economic chaos and hurt small businessmen. They proposed instead a slow and orderly evolution toward a "classless" Portuguese society.

The ruling triumvirate of Goncalves, Costa Gomes and Gen. Otelo de Carvalho denounced the moderate manifesto as "divisive" Aug. 8, although Costa Gomes and Carvalho were later reported to sympathize with the moderates, objecting only to the timing of the manifesto's release. Costa Gomes was widely described as a moderate, but Carvalho's position was more confusing, linked alternately to the moderates and to extreme leftists within Copcon, the security force under his command.

(Costa Gomes had declared on his return from the European security conference in Finland Aug. 2 that Portugal should seek to establish a "pluralistic socialism in which there is respect for the individual rights accepted by the United Nations." The moderate manifesto, while endorsing a gradual evolution toward socialism, rejected the Western European-style social democracy Costa Gomes was presumed to favor.)

The triumvirate expelled the nine moderate leaders from the Supreme Revolutionary Council Aug. 9 and forbade any mention of the manifesto in the information media. However, the moderates continued to circulate the manifesto in military barracks, claiming Aug. 11 that 85% of officers and soldiers were signing it.

The Washington Post reported Aug. 13 that a majority of officers were signing a second petition demanding the dismissal of Goncalves and appointment of Adm. Crespo as premier to form a new government. Costa Gomes continued to resist pressure to fire the premier, reportedly calling in Socialist leader Mario Soares Aug. 13 and asking him to call off demonstrations against Goncalves for 45 days. Soares reportedly refused.

Another group of military officers, reportedly numbering around 100 and all belonging to Copcon, issued a manifesto Aug. 13 calling for establishment of a political system based on neighborhood and worker associations after a period of transitional rule by "the Armed Forces Movement and all revolutionary political organizations which demand and defend power for the workers." The plan, similar to the MFA's blueprint for "direct democracy," was reported to be endorsed by Carvalho.

The Copcon document accused Portugal's civilian political parties, particularly the Communist Party, of trying to dominate the state apparatus. The Communists and the MPD had shown themselves incapable of solving problems at the level of local councils, it added. The document called for eventual establishment of a "national popular assembly" of representatives from neighborhood councils with no party allegiance.

(Issuance of the document followed reports of political divisions within Copcon similar to those within the MFA at large. One controversy centered around the dismissal by Carvalho July 30 of Col. Jaime Neves, chief of a commando unit outside Lisbon, who was described in a majority of press reports as a moderate. Neves charged publicly that his dismissal had been secured by the Communist Party, and the soldiers in his regiment voted him back into command Aug. 4, occasioning an apology by Carvalho, who claimed he was misled about Neves by associates.)

Anticommunist riots—Foes of Goncalves and the Communists continued to demonstrate throughout Portugal and to attack Communist Party headquarters in cities and towns, in some cases routing troops that tried to defend the Communist buildings. Two persons were killed Aug. 3 when troops opened fire on a crowd of several hundred that was storming Communist offices in Vila Nova de Famalicao, outside Oporto. Thousands of anticommunists rioted in Famalicao Aug. 5, ransacking Communist headquarters and wrecking the homes of Communist leaders.

At least 43 persons were injured in Braga Aug. 10–11 as hundreds of Roman Catholics and other anticommunists rioted for 18 hours, burning down Communist headquarters and wrecking offices of the MPD and the Intersindical, the Communist-dominated labor union. Twenty of the injuries were caused when Communists fired into a crowd stoning their headquarters Aug. 10.

The Braga demonstrators heard a sharply anticommunist address Aug. 10 from the local Catholic archbishop, Most

Rev. Francisco Maria da Silva. "The Portuguese problem," Da Silva declared, "is this and only this: On one side a minority, against the will of the people, is imposing communism on the nation in which there would be room for neither an independent fatherland nor for religion; on the other hand, an overwhelming majority says 'no' to communism."

In Lisbon, thousands of Socialists marched Aug. 14 chanting, "Out with Vasco," a reference to Goncalves. A similar demonstration was held that day by Popular Democrats in Cascais, near the capital. In Arcos de Valdevez and in Amarante, near Oporto, angry crowds sacked Communist Party headquarters.

One person was killed and well more than 100 injured in anti-Communist riots Aug. 18 in the northern town of Ponte de Lima. Many injuries occurred when police fired over a crowd of 5,000 storming the Communist headquarters. Two persons were reported killed Aug. 25 in Leiria, in central Portugal, when Communists opened fire on a crowd attacking their headquarters. The night before, anti-Communists had sacked the local offices of the MPD.

The anti-Communist violence was decried by Goncalves, who charged at a rally in the Lisbon suburb of Almada Aug. 18 that his opponents were opponents of a socialist revolution and supporters of a return to the ousted civilian fascist dictatorship. Goncalves steadfastly refused to abandon the premiership even after it was clear that a majority of the armed forces opposed him.

Azores anticommunists riot. Anticommunist farmers rioted Aug. 17 in Angra do Heroismo, on Terceira Island in the Azores, destroying local offices of the Communist Party and its ally, the Portuguese Democratic Movement (MPD), and beating leftists in the streets.

The leftist mayor of Angra do Heroismo had resigned July 23 after farmers attacked Communist and MPD offices and threatened to occupy municipal buildings. The governor of Sao Miguel Island, the largest of the Azores, had resigned June 6 after farmers blocked the runway of the local airport and oc-cupied the radio station in Ponta Delgada, the island's capital.

The rioting farmers were conservative Roman Catholics who opposed the leftist military government in Lisbon and who favored close ties to the U.S., which maintained an Air Force base at Lajes on Terceira Island. In the April elections for the Portuguese Constituent Assembly, Azoreans had voted overwhelmingly for the Popular Democratic and Socialist Parties, giving the Communists only 2% of their ballots. The Socialists and Popular Democrats, who subsequently had withdrawn from the Lisbon government, were not represented among Azorean officials.

A small, clandestine independence movement called the Azores Liberation Front (FLA) had begun operating recently, distributing pamphlets and making radio broadcasts every other night from a hidden transmitter outside Angra do Heroismo. The FLA warned that if the Communist Party took full power in Lisbon, as many Azoreans feared, Azoreans would never again see relatives who had emigrated to the U.S. and Canada, it was reported Aug. 9.

(There were an estimated 700,000 persons of Azorean descent in the U.S. and Canada, more than double the islands population of 335,000. Azoreans abroad sent money back to the islands, providing an important source of income.)

The FLA also denounced the Lisbon government for taking most of the money paid by the U.S. to rent the Lajes air base and returning very little of it to the Azores for schools, roads and other services, it was reported Aug. 9.

In an attempt to placate the restive Azoreans, the Lisbon government Aug. 12 announced a $12.5 million investment credit for the islands and established a governing commission, called the General Junta, for the entire archipelago. Previously Lisbon had ruled through three separate administrative regions which kept the nine Azores islands apart but tightly tied to the mainland.

U.S. warns against Soviet intervention. U.S. Secretary of State Henry Kissinger warned the Soviet Union Aug. 14 against interfering in the internal affairs of Portugal.

In a major policy speech delivered in Birmingham, Ala., Kissinger asserted Moscow "shouldn't assume that it has the option, either directly or indirectly, to influence events contrary to the right of the Portuguese people to determine their own future." However, he added that the U.S. would do whatever it could to prevent a Portuguese "antidemocratic and doctrinaire minority" from seizing power in Lisbon.

Kissinger's warning came amid violent demonstrations in Portugal against Premier Vasco Goncalves and his ally, the Portuguese Communist Party, accused by moderate and conservative civilians and soldiers of trying to impose a Communist dictatorship against the will of a majority of Portuguese.

In an apparent reference to the recent European security conference in Helsinki, which had endorsed the principle of nonintervention, Kissinger declared: "The involvement of external powers . . . in a country which is an old friend of [the U.S.] and ally of ours is inconsistent with any principle of European security." He added that if a "major Communist influence" persisted in the Portuguese government, Lisbon might be expelled from the North Atlantic Treaty Organization.

President Ford had said in an interview Aug. 3 with U.S. News & World Report that it was "very tragic" that the U.S. could not help moderate forces in Portugal "because of the [Congressional investigation of the Central Intelligence Agency] and all the limitations placed on us in the area of covert operations." He noted, however, that some Western European nations were "helping their Social Democratic friends in Portugal."

British Prime Minister Harold Wilson had conferred in Helsinki Aug. 1 with Portuguese President Francisco da Costa Gomes, reiterating the recent decision of the European Economic Community (EEC) not to grant financial aid to Portugal until Lisbon established a "pluralistic democracy."

The Soviet Communist Party newspaper Pravda had denounced the EEC decision Aug. 8, calling it a "gross interference in the affairs of the [Portuguese] state" and a violation of the Helsinki accord.

Swedish Premier Olof Palme had announced Aug. 2, at the end of a conference of Western European Social Democratic party leaders in Stockholm, that a committee had been formed to support democratic socialism in Portugal. The European leaders reportedly pledged to Portuguese Socialist leader Mario Soares, who attended the meeting, that they would contribute to the Portuguese Socialists as much money as the Eastern European Communist parties were giving the Portuguese Communists. (The Soviet contribution was estimated between $2 million and $10 million per month, according to varying press reports.)

Pravda denounced the Portuguese Socialists Aug. 19, asserting they and the centrist Popular Democratic Party sought to divide Portugal's ruling Armed Forces Movement and separate it from the Portuguese people. The Socialists had "declared war on the truly progressive forces, rallying all the reactionary forces in Portugal," Pravda asserted.

The leaders of the Italian Socialist and Communist parties published a joint statement in Rome Aug. 15 calling for recognition of democratic rights in Portugal and for unity among Portuguese Socialists, Communists and military officers. They urged Portugal's democratic forces to reach an agreement "based on the recognition of popular representation . . . in proportion to the results of the elections for the Constituent Assembly," won in April by the Socialists and the Popular Democrats.

Goncalves Removed, Left's Power Wanes

The growth of Communist power in Portugal apparently came to a halt in late August 1975 with the removal of Vasco Goncalves as premier. His descent from power came in two stages, and he surrendered all authority in early September.

New premier named, Goncalves chief of staff. President Francisco da Costa

Gomes yielded to intense pressure from moderate leftists and conservatives Aug. 29 and dismissed Gen. Vasco Goncalves as premier. However, he prolonged the acute military and political crisis by appointing Goncalves chief of staff of the armed forces.

Costa Gomes named as the new premier Vice Adm. Jose Pinheiro de Azevedo, the naval chief of staff and vice president in the provisional government. Pinheiro de Azevedo was not linked to any political faction, but the navy was considered the most radical of the armed forces and the most sympathetic to Goncalves.

Goncalves' appointment to armed forces chief of staff, a position heretofore held by Costa Gomes, was immediately protested by top military leaders, notably the nine moderate officers who had led the campaign for his dismissal as premier. The promotion was also denounced by the Socialist Party and other moderate and conservative civilian groups.

As chief of staff, Goncalves could purge his opponents from the armed forces and distribute arms to civilian groups backing him.

The military moderates, led by Maj. Ernesto de Melo Antunes and by Brig. Gen. Carlos Charais, commander of the central military region, rejected Goncalves' promotion Aug. 30. The same day Costa Gomes assumed personal command of Copcon, the military security force, reportedly at the request of its regular commander, Gen. Otelo de Carvalho, who had barred Goncalves from all Copcon garrisons and suggested that Goncalves take a long vacation.

The air force chief of staff, Gen. Jose Morais da Silva, added his rejection of Goncalves Sept. 1. Referring to the great influence exerted on Goncalves by the relatively small Communist Party, Morais da Silva asserted: "A revolution made by 80% of the Portuguese cannot be transformed into a dictatorship by 20% of the Portuguese over the other 80%."

The army staff chief, Gen. Carlos Fabiao, denounced Goncalves Sept. 3, asserting there was "no doubt whatsoever that Gen. Vasco Goncalves will not contribute in any way to the unity of the army. Quite the contrary." Fabiao

presided over a general assembly of army officers and men which voted overwhelmingly Sept. 3 to ask Costa Gomes to rescind Goncalves' appointment and to postpone a meeting of the General Assembly of the Armed Forces Movement (MFA), scheduled for Sept. 5, until the army could elect new representatives to the assembly.

The army's current delegation to the assembly was dominated by supporters of Goncalves, mostly from Lisbon and southern Portugal, while the army itself was dominated by moderate leftists, many from the more conservative North. Although the army was 10 times as large as either the navy or the air force, it held only half of the assembly's 240 seats.

The navy was the only service to endorse Goncalves' promotion, at a general assembly Sept. 4. The navy was more radical than the army and air force because it took its recruits mostly from the universities, where leftist political activity was traditional.

Several army garrisons in the North rebelled against Goncalves' promotion Aug. 30, rejecting their commander, Brig. Gen. Eurico Corvacho, a supporter of Goncalves, and placing themselves under the command of Brig. Gen. Carlos Charais of the central region. Charais had declared two days earlier that his troops were prepared to resist imposition of a Communist dictatorship in Portugal. Some rebel garrisons returned to their normal command channels Aug. 31, according to press reports, but others maintained their shift in allegiance to Charais.

Meanwhile, Vice Adm. Pinheiro de Azevedo began talks with civilian political leaders Aug. 31 to form a new cabinet, which he hoped would include members of the three leading parties—the Socialists, Popular Democrats and Communists. However, the Socialists, the largest party, refused to participate in the government until Goncalves' promotion was rescinded and the Socialist newspaper Republica and the Roman Catholic radio station Radio Renascenca were returned to their owners by the Communist workers who had occupied them.

Socialist leader Mario Soares sent a letter to Costa Gomes Sept. 3 urging him to abandon Goncalves. "This is not the time for paralyzing compromises," Soares asserted. "Exercise your authority. You will see that the country will follow it without hesitation."

Soares supported Pinheiro de Azevedo's plan for a coalition government of Socialists, Popular Democrats and Communists, and he called for municipal elections to be held in January and for trade unions to be run democratically.

Throughout the crisis, Costa Gomes' position remained unclear. Numerous press sources reported that the president, who had been seen as a moderate, was attempting to ease out the premier without provoking an armed conflict between pro- and anti-Communists in the MFA. However, the moderate majority increasingly lost faith in him as he allowed Goncalves to cling to office in the face of overwhelming opposition, according to reports.

In elections Aug. 30 for control of the bank and office employes' unions, the Communists had been decisively defeated by a coalition of Socialists and extreme leftists. However, the Communists had refused to give up their positions, occupying union offices under the pretext of protecting a computer which served the Intersindical, the single state-approved labor federation. Several hundred extreme leftists tried to take control of the union offices Aug. 31, but they were repelled by Copcon troops. Copcon escorted 53 Communists from the offices, but refused to let in the newly elected union officials.

Goncalves out, triumvirate ends. Vasco Goncalves abandoned all positions of authority Sept. 5-6, declining an appointment as armed forces chief of staff, resigning as head of the caretaker cabinet and being removed from the Supreme Revolutionary Council, executive body of the ruling Armed Forces Movement (MFA).

The Supreme Council effectively resumed leadership of the Portuguese revolution with the dissolution of the triumvirate of Goncalves, President Francisco da Costa Gomes and security chief Gen. Otelo de Carvalho. Costa Gomes and Carvalho remained in office and on the Council, now dominated by moderate

leftists who opposed Goncalves' Communist-influenced policies.

Goncalves resigned his appointment as military chief Sept. 5 in the face of overwhelming opposition within the MFA and the civilian political parties. He was abandoned by the Communist Party, which agreed to cooperate with more moderate civilian and military forces, and by Costa Gomes, who was reportedly told by moderate officers that he would lose the presidency if he continued to support Goncalves.

Costa Gomes called a meeting of the MFA General Assembly Sept. 5 despite a boycott by most delegates from the army and air force, who demanded that Goncalves' appointment be rescinded and that the Assembly be reorganized along more representative political and regional lines. After Goncalves resigned the appointment, a rump assembly of 107 of the 240 delegates voted to reorganize the Supreme Revolutionary Council, reducing its membership from 30 to 21.

Adm. Vitor Crespo, a moderate and former high commissioner of Mozambique, was purged from the Council, as were Brig. Gen. Eurico Corvacho and Capts. Luis Macedo and Manuel Ferreira de Sousa, considered supporters of Goncalves or the Communist Party. Two moderates, Majs. Ernesto de Melo Antunes and Vitor Alves, and a supporter of Goncalves, Capt. Jose da Costa Martins, were added to the Council when it held its first meeting Sept. 8.

Goncalves resigned as premier along with the caretaker cabinet Sept. 6, as Costa Gomes and Premier-designate Vice Adm. Jose Pinheiro de Azevedo began discussions with six civilian political parties on formation of a broadly based government with strong civilian participation. The parties were the Socialists, Communists and Popular Democrats, the Social Democratic Center, the Portuguese Democratic Movement and the Socialist Left Movement.

The Socialists and Popular Democrats demanded that the new cabinet reflect the results of the April elections for the Constituent Assembly, in which the two parties won 64% of the votes, it was reported Sept. 8. The Socialists also demanded that elections for a legislative assembly and for municipal governments be held shortly, and that the Socialist newspaper Republica and the Roman Catholic radio station Radio Renascenca be returned to their owners by the Communist workers who had occupied them.

The Supreme Revolutionary Council met Sept. 8 and voted to reorganize the MFA Assembly and to impose greater restriction on political reporting in the news media. A committee was appointed to reorganize the Assembly under the leadership of Capt. Vasco Lourenco, an outspoken opponent of Goncalves and his faction.

The Council issued a decree banning reports of events in military units or of political positions adopted by military units, factions or individuals. Publications could report only statements by Costa Gomes, the three armed forces commanders and Gen. Carvalho, and they could not interview any military officer not on the Supreme Council. The last ruling effectively denied Goncalves a hearing in the press.

The decree was protested by most Lisbon newspapers, including the Socialist paper A Luta, the Maoist publication Luta Popular and the Communist-oriented Diario de Lisboa. Luta Popular called for disobedience of "this fascist law" and published a report on a meeting of military police who were unwilling to serve in the embattled Portuguese colony of Angola.

Press reports were divided on the role of Costa Gomes in removing Goncalves from power. Some reports asserted Costa Gomes had been forced by moderates to abandon the ex-premier, while others said he had successfully maneuvered Goncalves out of the premiership by offering him the military command, knowing the armed forces would not accept him. Military sources quoted by the Washington Post Sept. 9 claimed Costa Gomes had strengthened his own position by easing out Goncalves yet denying full power to the moderate faction led by Maj. Melo Antunes.

New cabinet sworn. A cabinet dominated by moderate leftist civilians and military officers was sworn in Sept.

19, following three weeks of talks and disputes among top military officers and leaders of the three major civilian parties—the Socialists (PS), Communists (PC) and Popular Democrats (PPD).

The cabinet, headed by Vice Adm. Jose Pinheiro de Azevedo as premier, was composed of five military officers, four Socialists, two Popular Democrats, one Communist and three independents, two of whom were considered close to the Socialists. The civilian appointments roughly reflected the result of the elections for the Constituent Assembly in April, in which the Socialists won 37.8% of the votes, the Popular Democrats won 26.4% and the Communists, 12.5%.

Besides the premiership, military officers controlled four sensitive ministries in which some degree of military authority might be required: interior, labor, education and foreign affairs. The Socialists took over ministries concerned with the economy—finance, foreign trade, agriculture and transport—and a Socialist sympathizer, Antonio de Almeida Santos, assumed control of the information ministry, previously run by the Communists and their military and civilian allies.

The new cabinet:

Premier—Vice Adm. Jose Pinheiro de Azevedo; foreign affairs—Maj. Ernesto de Melo Antunes; finance—Francisco Salgado Zenha (PS); foreign trade—Jorge Campinos (PS); domestic trade—Joaquim Magalhaes Mota (PPD); agriculture—Antonio Lopes Cardoso (PS); transport—Walter Rosa (PS); information—Antonio de Almeida Santos (Ind.); social affairs—Jorge Sa Borges (PPD); public works—Alvaro Veiga de Oliveira (PC); industry—Marques do Carmo (Ind.); interior—Capt. Vasco Almeida Costa; labor—Capt. Tomas Rosa; justice—Joao Pinheiro Farinha (Ind.); education—Maj. Vitor Alves.

Virtually all the ministries had a politically varied mixture of secretaries of state (deputy ministers), although the social affairs ministry was controlled entirely by the Popular Democrats. The labor ministry, headed by air force Capt. Rosa, had a Socialist secretary for labor, a Communist secretary for employment and a Popular Democratic secretary for socioprofessional training. At the agriculture ministry, headed by the Socialist Lopes Cardoso, a Popular Democrat was in charge of agrarian development and a Communist of land redistribution.

The Communists supported the new

cabinet reluctantly, asserting they joined it only to help prevent a right-wing takeover in the government. The Portuguese Democratic Movement, a Communist ally, called the new cabinet "treacherous" and vowed to lead "social agitation" against it, it was reported Sept. 19. The Communist-dominated Steelworkers Union called on its 250,000 members to hold a one-hour protest strike against the government Sept. 24, it was reported Sept. 20.

Naming of the new cabinet had been delayed by bitter disputes between the Communists and Popular Democrats. The Communists had demanded the same number of cabinet posts as the Popular Democrats, and had refused to speak with PPD leaders, using the Socialists as intermediaries. The Socialists, led by former Foreign Minister Mario Soares, were considered to have gained the most political ground in the new government.

Program adopted—The cabinet was formed only after its prospective elements had negotiated the details of the program it was to follow.

The three civilian parties and the military leadership agreed on a moderate socialist program. The adopted plan, announced by Vice Adm. Pinheiro de Azevedo Sept. 14, pledged to support democratic and political "pluralism" in a number of areas heretofore dominated by the Communists, including the trade unions and the news media.

The program also pledged to encourage foreign investment in the economy; to strengthen agrarian reforms by helping small and medium-sized farmers; to aid small and medium-sized businesses and define the domains of public and private enterprise; to maintain Portuguese ties with the European Economic Community and the European Free Trade Association, and to open trade links with Eastern European and Third World countries in order to improve the balance of payments.

According to the program, government action would be based on socialism and democratic pluralism; the defense of democratic freedoms and the interests of the working class, especially the least privileged; completion of the decoloniza-

tion program, and reinforcement of government authority.

Previous "injustices" would be repaired and greater attention would be given to decentralization of the administration and satisfaction of the needs of Portugal's regions, the program stated. Singled out among the regions were the Azores and Madeira, the Atlantic islands where there was unrest among conservative residents wary of the leftist central government.

Adm. Pinheiro de Azevedo said the current nationalization program would continue, but reforms would be made in the nationalized sectors with great influence on the economy, especially the banks.

Legislation would also be introduced to deal with armed civilian groups, Pinheiro de Azevedo asserted.

Council drops left's backers. The Supreme Revolutionary Council, executive body of the ruling Armed Forces Movement (MFA), was reduced in membership from 24 to 18 Sept. 12. The move was seen as further reducing the influence of pro-Communist supporters of Gen. Vasco Goncalves, the ousted premier.

The new Council was composed of President Francisco da Costa Gomes, Premier Pinheiro de Azevedo, the three armed forces commanders, six representatives of the army, three each of the navy and air force, and the head of security, Gen. Otelo de Carvalho.

The new Council's members, elected by assemblies of the three armed services, included 10 strong anticommunists and four moderate anticommunists, according to a report Sept. 19. Costa Gomes was included among the moderate anticommunists despite his support for Gen. Goncalves before Goncalves' ouster.

In a related development, Brig. Gen. Eurico Corvacho, commander of the northern military region, was stripped of his command Sept. 13 and demoted to his permanent rank of major. Corvacho was the last supporter of Goncalves to lead a military region.

U.S., EEC grant emergency aid. The U.S. government and the European Economic Community granted Portugal $272 million in emergency economic aid in early October 1975 following the ouster of Goncalves.

Both grants were described openly as expressions of political support for the moderate socialists who appeared to take control of the provisional government and the Armed Forces Movement with Goncalves' removal. The grants were likened to aid being given to the Portuguese Socialist Party by social democratic parties in Western Europe and, according to reports, by the U.S. Central Intelligence Agency.

The EEC announced Oct. 7 that it was offering Portugal $187 million in emergency aid for investment projects in recognition of Lisbon's return to a "pluralistic democracy." The aid would be channeled by the European Investment Bank in the form of loans at preferential rates (6.5% instead of the usual 9.5%). The EEC also offered Portugal unspecified amounts of food and medicine for the hundreds of thousands of refugees returning from the war-torn African territory of Angola.

Portuguese officials discussed ways of using the aid with an EEC delegation in Lisbon Oct. 20–21. Special measures to aid the Angola refugees, many of whom were penniless, received top priority.

The U.S. State Department and the White House Oct. 10 announced an $85 million package of emergency aid to Portugal after Foreign Minister Ernesto de Melo Antunes conferred in Washington with President Ford and Secretary of State Henry Kissinger. Kissinger called the package a "first step" in "U.S. support for the political evolution in Portugal" and he expressed particular concern for the refugees fleeing Angola. The U.S. pledged to double its refugee airlift from Angola beginning Oct. 14—bringing the total number of U.S. chartered aircraft in the airlift to four—and the Ford Administration authorized the Export-Import Bank to finance the sale of a Boeing 747 to Portugal to assist in refugee flights.

The State Department said that during his meeting with Melo Antunes, Kissinger had "expressed his admiration for the foreign minister and other Portuguese

leaders in undertaking to restore democratic government to Portugal." Melo Antunes was a member of the so-called Group of Nine moderate socialist military leaders who appeared in control of the Supreme Revolutionary Council, the executive body of the Armed Forces Movement.

The Soviet newspaper Pravda had charged Aug. 27 that counterrevolutionary pressures were being exerted on the Portuguese government by Western European countries, the EEC and the North Atlantic Treaty Organization (NATO), and that "international monopolies" had instituted an "economic boycott" against Lisbon.

Among the monopolies cited by Pravda was International Telephone and Telegraph Corp. (ITT), which cut off all financial support of its Portuguese subsidiaries on grounds that it could no longer provide effective management, according to a report Sept. 6. ITT had informed the Portuguese government of its action in a letter dated Aug. 22, citing heavy losses caused by recent salary increases, a purge of management personnel and a lack of support from Portuguese banks and the government. ITT's local subsidiaries included a Sheraton hotel and an electronics factory with total assets of $100 million.

Portuguese President Gen. Francisco da Costa Gomes visited the Soviet Union Oct. 1–3, agreeing with Soviet officials to increase cooperation between Lisbon and Moscow on bilateral problems and on political and economic issues. He declared Oct. 1 that Portugal sought a "balanced diversification of foreign links."

Political aid given—Western European social democratic parties made new pledges of aid to the Portuguese Socialist Party, which played a key role in forcing Gen. Goncalves' removal. Socialist leader Mario Soares received pledges Sept. 5 at a meeting in London with British Prime Minister Harold Wilson, representing Britain's Labor Party; former West German Chancellor Willy Brandt, of West Germany's Social Democratic Party; Swedish Premier Olof Palme, representing his country's Social Democratic Party; Premier Joop den Uyl of the Netherlands, and French Socialist leader Francois Mitterrand. The group was supported by Austrian Chancellor Bruno Kreisky, who could not be present.

Brandt read a statement after the meeting denying that the group's "friendship and solidarity" with Portuguese Socialists constituted interference in Portugal's internal affairs. Portuguese law forbade foreign gifts to local political parties.

To get around the law, Portuguese Socialists had set up an "education fund" which could receive cash legitimately. In addition, foreign parties—notably Sweden's—legally contributed technical help, pamphlets and other aid in kind. However, Portuguese Socialists also received illegal cash payments, notably from the West German Social Democrats, who had contributed several million dollars in the last year and a half, according to the New York Times Aug. 29.

The Times reported Sept. 25 that the CIA also had sent millions of dollars to the Portuguese Socialists through Western European political parties and trade unions. The report was denied by Soares, but the Ford Administration refused to confirm or deny it. The Associated Press reported Sept. 25 that the CIA had sent $2 million to $10 million per month to the Portuguese Socialists since June.

Reports also continued of covert aid from the Soviet Union to the Portuguese Communist Party (PCP). Moscow had funneled $45 million to the PCP since the 1974 military coup, in one case "laundering" the money through the Transworld Marine Shipping Co., a Belgian-Soviet firm based in Antwerp, Belgium, according to sources cited by the Washington Post Aug. 24. (The Post report was denied by the Soviet news agency Tass Aug. 29 and by Transworld Marine Sept. 5.) British Prime Minister Wilson asserted Sept. 5 that Moscow was sending $100 million a year to the PCP.

Unrest & Violence, Leftist Uprising Crushed

The downfall of Vasco Goncalves was followed by a resurgence of unrest and political violence in which leftist military personnel played a leading role. These disturbances were climaxed by an unsuccessful uprising of military leftists in November 1975. The revolt was crushed by progovernment military forces.

Premier survives bombing. A bomb exploded at the navy's Seixas Palace outside Lisbon Sept. 21, causing property damage on the first floor but not harming Premier Pinheiro de Azevedo, who was sleeping on the third floor and was presumed to be the target of the attack.

No group took credit for the explosion, and authorities were divided over which armed organization on the extreme left or right might be responsible. A number of civilian commando groups were said to be well-armed, having received many of the 20,000 weapons that had vanished from military arsenals since the April 1974 military coup, it was reported Sept. 22. Military officers were presumed to have taken part in the arms smuggling.

One rightist group, the Democratic Movement for the Liberation of Portugal, was reportedly financed by wealthy Portuguese refugees in Paris and Rio de Janeiro and supported by ex-Gen. Antonio de Spinola, the ousted provisional president. Spinola, who was in Paris Sept. 3–13, said in an interview Sept. 11 that "the hour of liberation for Portugal is near" and that residents of northern Portugal might soon begin an "insurrection" against the "regime of treachery and lies" which had governed the country since his flight to Brazil in March.

The Supreme Revolutionary Council declared Sept. 12 that Spinola would be arrested if he ever returned to Portugal or any of its dependent territories. Spinola was "still considered incriminated in the counterrevolutionary coup" which preceded his flight, the Council asserted.

Military & civilian leftists active. Military personnel joined leftist civilians in denouncing what they called the government's shift to the right under the new premier. In the most serious protests, soldiers in Lisbon refused to evict extreme leftists from occupied radio and television stations, and troops in Oporto occupied a military transport regiment's barracks to demand the resignation of the regional army commander and reinstatement of several purged leftists.

Many of the protesters belonged to an extreme leftist group called United Soldiers Will Win (SUV), organized after the ouster of leftist ex-Premier Goncalves. The military leadership outlawed the SUV Sept. 25, and the next day created a new military security force to rival Copcon, the unit commanded by Gen. Otelo de Carvalho, who often sympathized with the extreme left.

(Carvalho had expressed approval Sept. 25 of the smuggling of more than 1,000 military weapons to an extreme leftist civilian group by Capt. Alvaro Fernandes, a Copcon officer who deserted and went underground. Carvalho said it would have been dangerous "if the arms had been given to the right, but since it was a leftist group I am satisfied they are in good hands.")

An estimated 3,500 soldiers, sailors and airmen joined several thousand civilians demonstrating against the government in Lisbon Sept. 25. After marching in the city's streets they moved to a military prison across the Tagus River from the capital and demanded the release of two soldiers arrested earlier for distributing leaflets urging others to join the demonstration. The governor of the prison refused to negotiate with the demonstrators, but Carvalho ordered the release of the imprisoned soldiers early Sept. 26.

Protests continued Sept. 26. Wounded war veterans seized tollbooths on the Lisbon Highway, allowing cars to go through without paying and demanding that the government give them adequate pensions. More than 10,000 leftist soldiers and civilians held a protest march in Lisbon Sept. 28. The Communist Party joined the protesters openly for the first time.

The situation worsened Sept. 29 when Premier Pinheiro de Azevedo ordered troops to occupy leftist-controlled radio and television stations to halt what he called a "provocative campaign of seditious attitudes" and restore "truly free, responsible and pluralistic information" to the mass media. The troops went to the stations but some openly sided with the broadcasters, refusing to evict them and allowing them to cut or omit a broadcast

by Pinheiro de Azevedo. Troops were withdrawn from most radio and television stations Oct. 1, but one station, the Catholic Radio Renascenca, remained occupied by rebel troops and leftist civilians until Oct. 15, when it was cleared and sealed by pro-government soldiers.

More than 20,000 Socialists and Popular Democrats demonstrated in favor of the government in Lisbon Sept. 30, hearing an appeal from Pinheiro de Azevedo for "discipline, discipline." Thousands of Socialists returned to the streets of the capital Oct. 1 to guard against what they called an imminent leftist coup. The Communist Party denounced the mobilization Oct. 2, charging that the Socialists were using warnings of a leftist coup in order to prepare their own "seditious uprising."

Military indiscipline continued Oct. 3 as 70 soldiers at an air base near Beja refused a transfer to the Azores which, they claimed, was ordered to punish them for participating in antigovernment demonstrations. Troops in Evora marched at the head of a civilian demonstration against the new military security force, which they likened to the PIDE, the secret police of the ousted fascist dictatorship.

An artillery regiment in Lisbon joined the protests Oct. 4, with soldiers issuing a communique denouncing the "incompetence of the government" and the government's alleged attempt to restore the "violent right-wing dictatorship under the cover of 'social democracy' or even of 'socialism.'" In Evora, members of the SUV denounced the ruling assemblies of the army and the Armed Forces Movement.

Premier Pinheiro de Azevedo denounced the extreme left, the Portuguese Democratic Movement and some elements of the Communist Party Oct. 5 for allegedly making it impossible for him to govern. President Francisco da Costa Gomes said Oct. 6 that it was "counterrevolutionary" for soldiers to support any political groups, "however progressive they may be."

Several hundred soldiers and armed civilians occupied the barracks of a military transport regiment in Oporto Oct. 6 after the regional army commander, Brig. Gen. Antonio Pires Veloso, ordered the regiment disbanded because its officers and men had vetoed the transfer of two extreme leftist officers and six soldiers. The rebels demanded that the transferred men and the regiment be reinstated and that Pires Veloso resign his command.

Civilian supporters and opponents of the rebel soldiers clashed in Oporto Oct. 7, leaving some 45 persons injured. They fought again Oct. 8, with more than 60 injuries, and Oct. 10, with another 60 injuries and more than 120 arrests. The rebels were backed by the Communist Party, which called their action a "magnificent riposte" to previous antileftist violence. They were denounced by the ruling Supreme Revolutionary Council, which asserted that "progressive political groups" had been "infiltrated by the extreme right in order to overthrow the sixth provisional government and permit the quick and easy establishment of a fascist-type regime."

The rebels ended their occupation of the barracks Oct. 14 after reaching a compromise agreement with Gen. Carlos Fabiao, the army staff chief. Under the agreement the transferred men would be reinstated, but their regiment would be moved to a new site and turned into a combat unit, and Gen. Pires Veloso would retain his command.

Violent unrest, however, continued in various parts of the country.

In an attempt to curb the growing unrest, President Costa Gomes Oct. 17 ordered an eight-day amnesty during which civilians could turn in any firearms they possessed illegally. Punishment for illegal arms possession thereafter would bring penalties of up to eight years in prison and $40,000 in fines. However, only a handful of arms were handed in by the end of the amnesty period Oct. 24. One extreme leftist group, the Revolutionary Brigades, publicly rejected the amnesty Oct. 19 and declared Oct. 23 that it was going underground to begin "a life-or-death struggle" against the government.

In opposition to violent leftist demonstrations, counterdemonstrations to support the government were held by the Socialist and Popular Democratic Parties and by the Social Democratic Center (CDS).

The demonstrations were accompanied by street clashes, bombings and charges of planned takeovers by various civilian and military factions. The armed forces were placed on alert Oct. 24–25 following a series of bombings by presumed rightists in and around Lisbon. Premier Pinheiro de Azevedo warned after the alert was lifted that civil war might break out.

Much of the unrest took place in the city of Oporto in the conservative north. Rebellious army officers there threatened new action against the government Oct. 17 after the regional commander, Brig. Gen. Antonio Pires Veloso, furloughed leaders of a recent mutiny by a transport regiment, pending the leaders' discharge from service. A bomb explosion in Oporto Oct. 25 destroyed part of the city's main Communist printing press, and explosions in the city Oct. 29 destroyed the automobiles of a civilian Communist and a leftist military officer.

Capt. Vasco Lourenco, a member of the Supreme Revolutionary Council and a reputed moderate, charged Oct. 19 that a right-wing military coup was being planned, while Francisco Sa Carneiro, leader of the Popular Democrats, asserted a leftist coup was at hand. A communique signed by the SUV Oct. 21 called for an "organized battle plan" against "the government of the bourgeoisie."

Communist leader Alvaro Cunhal called for increased leftist pressure on the government Oct. 19. Thousands of Communists and other leftists in Lisbon demonstrated against the cabinet Oct. 21 and 23, calling for the removal of Popular Democrat ministers and for the return of Gen. Vasco Goncalves, the ousted premier.

Several thousand leftist soldiers and civilians surrounded the Catholic radio station Radio Renascenca Oct. 22 as leftist employes broke the government seals on the building and reoccupied the station, resuming antigovernment broadcasts. Anticommunist workers took over the editorial offices of the Lisbon newspaper O Seculo Oct. 29, following a vote to oust the Communist management. Publication of the paper was effectively suspended because Communists remained in control of the presses.

The government, attempting to curb Communist influence in local administrations, announced the dismissal Oct. 21 of the civilian governors of the cities of Lisbon, Braga, Faro and Castelo Branco.

The governors, all linked to the Portuguese Democratic Movement, a Communist Party ally, were replaced by more moderate civilians. Extreme leftists occupied administrative buildings in Faro Oct. 27 to prevent the transfer of power, but they were evicted by anticommunists and infantry troops.

The government also replaced the commanders of the police and the Republican Guard Oct. 29 in order to strengthen both forces and increase their role in maintaining public order. Theft and crimes of violence had risen sharply in Portugal since the 1974 military coup, due partly to passivity by policemen who feared reprisals because of their identification with the ousted civilian dictatorship, it was reported Oct. 26.

Leftist air force officers asserted Oct. 29 that a rightist coup was being planned, noting that the air force was arming helicopters and spotter planes and moving warplanes, troops and munitions to a previously unused air base. Gen. Jose Morais e Silva confirmed the troop movements but asserted they were designed to protect the government from attacks by either the left or the right.

The government Oct. 30 arrested two air force officers associated with retired Gen. Antonio de Spinola, the exiled former provisional president, presumably for attempting to organize an insurrection. The two were Maj. Antonio Godinho and Lt. Benjamin de Abreu.

Rebellious soldiers sealed off the Lisbon arms depot Oct. 30, one day before the army began discharging 18% of its personnel because of the end of the Portuguese colonial wars in Africa. Leftist soldiers in some regiments had voted against the demobilization, but the government proceeded with it on schedule. The Communist Party warned Oct. 31 that rightist officers planned an uprising for Nov. 11, the day independence would be granted to the war-torn territory of Angola.

President Costa Gomes called urgent top-level meetings Nov. 3 after a leftist military group, the Committee of Revolutionary Vigilance of the Portuguese Armed Forces, predicted another rightist coup attempt during a nationwide military exercise planned for Nov. 7. Members of the SUV jeered Premier Pinheiro de Azevedo Nov. 4 at a rally in Faro organized by the Socialists and Popular Democrats and attended by some 10,000 supporters of the government.

Costa Gomes Nov. 6 called an unprecedented joint meeting of the cabinet and Supreme Revolutionary Council on ways to restore public order and obedience to the government. President Pinheiro de Azevedo had said Nov. 4 that he lacked "the authority or the capacity to govern," principally because of insubordination within the MFA.

Leftist revolt crushed. A revolt by leftist air force and other military units was crushed Nov. 25-26 as loyalist troops rallied against the rebels.

Three soldiers and six civilians were reported killed during the uprising, begun by air force paratroopers in Lisbon. More than 100 officers and non-commissioned officers were arrested and sent to a prison outside Oporto, and some 30 civilians were also reported seized, including leaders of Trotskyite groups, the Maoist MRPP and other extreme leftist organizations.

The rebellion was followed by a purge of radical leftists in the armed forces, begun Nov. 27, and the dismissal of the management and editorial staffs of eight government-owned newspapers, announced Nov. 28. Military authorities accused the newspapers of publishing "monolithic, distorted and tendentious information" and of running unnecessarily large operating deficits.

Among the military officers who were purged, according to reports Nov. 27, were Gen. Otelo de Carvalho, chief of the military security force Copcon, which was disbanded; Gen. Carlos Fabiao, army chief of staff, who was replaced by Gen. Antonio Ramalho Enaes; and Rear Adm. Antonio Rosa Coutinho. None of the three—all members of the Supreme Revolutionary Council of the Armed Forces Movement—were accused of participating directly in the abortive uprising.

Arrest warrants were also issued for Capt. Jose da Costa Martins, the former labor minister, and two leaders of the army's Fifth Regiment or propaganda department, it was reported Nov. 30.

The revolt began Nov. 25 when paratroopers seized the air force command and four air bases near Lisbon, and other rebel soldiers took control of the national radio and television stations. Loyal commandos led by Col. Jaime Neves recovered the air force command and two of the air bases Nov. 25, and took back a third base and the radio and television stations Nov. 26. The fourth air base, at Tancos, did not surrender until Nov. 28.

The rebels did not get expected support from either Gen. Carvalho or Communist party leaders, who had helped impel the recent leftist campaign against the government of Premier Jose Pinheiro de Azevedo. The Communists issued a statement Nov. 26 acknowledging serious errors by the rebels and calling for a political solution to Portugal's government crisis. "For reasons that must be reviewed later," the statement declared, "the revolutionary military, which has tried to resist purges of the left, has lost its position in spite of the courageous support of the working masses. The forces of the left have also committed a grave error in overestimating their own forces and trying any desperate act."

Nevertheless, the Socialists and other moderate leftists accused the Communists of being behind the revolt. Socialist leader Mario Soares said Nov. 30 that the crushing of the rebellion was a great defeat for Communist leader Alvaro Cunhal.

In the wake of the revolt Nov. 27, President Francisco da Costa Gomes said a military and civilian "coup of vast proportions" had been averted and he pledged to defend a multiparty democratic political system in Portugal. Costa Gomes had been widely criticized for refusing to take a side in the long conflict between moderate and extreme leftists in the armed forces and the government, according to press reports.

Cabinet on strike—Premier Pinheiro de Azevedo and his cabinet suspended activities No. 20 in a "strike" in protest against allegedly insufficient support from Costa Gomes and the Supreme Revolutionary Council in the face of radical leftist demonstrations against the cabinet's moderate socialist composition.

Pinheiro and his ministers demanded, among other things, that Gen. Carvalho be dismissed as commander of the Lisbon military region and chief of Copcon.

The Supreme Revolutionary Council denounced the cabinet strike Nov. 21. It dismissed Carvalho as head of the Lisbon military region, replacing him with Gen. Vasco Lourenco, a moderate leftist, but it retained Carvalho as Copcon chief, abolished a new security force established to rival Copcon, and directed Carvalho to proceed with the creation of a new political organization, the Popular Alliance, which would establish close links between the Armed Forces Movement and civilian workers' and neighborhood councils.

The Council's action was widely criticized. Leftist troops in Lisbon refused to accept Lourenco as their commander—prompting Costa Gomes to rescind Lourenco's appointment Nov. 22—and Socialists, Popular Democrats and other moderates denounced the projected Popular Assembly, which they saw as the nucleus of an extreme leftist dictatorship.

The government was paralyzed Nov. 23 as the cabinet continued to strike and military units in the conservative North demanded the replacement of leftist senior officers. Industrial workers in Lisbon staged a two-hour strike against the government Nov. 24, and members of United Soldiers Will Win (SUV), a radical military group, began legal action against the cabinet for abandoning its public functions.

Lourenco was confirmed as Lisbon military commander after the leftist revolt was crushed Nov. 27, and Premier Pinheiro de Azevedo announced the end of the cabinet strike Nov. 28. However, the civilian Constituent Assembly suspended its activities Nov. 25, citing military and civil unrest.

Large public demonstrations for and against the government had preceded the cabinet strike. In one rally, some 20,000 striking construction workers surrounded Premier Pinheiro de Azevedo's residence for 36 hours Nov. 12–13, demanding that the government grant 40% wage increases despite its economic austerity program. Pinheiro acceded to the demand Nov. 13 after Gen. Carvalho refused to order his

Copcon troops to disperse the demonstrators.

A rally in favor of the government by
some 30,000–40,000 persons in Lisbon
Nov. 9 had been interrupted by the
detonation of tear gas bombs and other
explosive devices by presumed extreme
leftists. Pinheiro de Azevedo, who was addressing the rally when it was disrupted,
later accused the radical left of trying to
lead Portugal "into the abyss of fascism."

In an earlier move against the left, the
government Nov. 7 had ordered paratroopers to blow up the transmitters of
Radio Renascenca, the Roman Catholic
radio station occupied by Communist employes. The action reportedly had the
consent of the Portuguese Church hierarchy.

Coup attempt brings personnel shifts.
The northern military commander who
had helped defeat the attempted left-wing
coup in November, Brig. Antonio Pires
Veloso, was appointed a member of the
Supreme Revolutionary Council Dec. 16
along with Major Vitor Alves, the minister
of education. Two left-wing generals believed sympathetic to the attempt—Otelo
de Carvalho and Carlos Fabiao—were demoted Dec. 19 to major and lieutenant
colonel, respectively.

Portuguese Empire Dissolves

*While Communists, other leftists and
moderates in Portugal were struggling for
control of mainland Portugal, the former
Portuguese colonies continued to follow
their often bloody road to independence.*

Mozambique wins independence. What
was Portuguese East Africa became the
independent People's Republic of Mozambique June 25, 1975. This followed 500
years of colonial rule culminating in a
10-year guerrilla war by which the indigenous Front for the Liberation of Mozambique (Frelimo) broke the Lisbon government's control over the territory.
Samora M. Machel, the Frelimo leader,

was installed as president, declaring his
intention to build "the first truly Marxist
state" on the continent.

Ceremonies in Lourenco Marques, the
nation's capital, included a street parade
and an inaugural address by Machel, who
said Mozambique would be run largely on
socialist principles. Most land and natural
resources would be state-owned, although
private property would be tolerated in
some instances, and farms would be
worked collectively. Frelimo was to lead
the new state, which would grant political
asylum to those who had been "perse-
cuted because of their struggle for peace,
democracy or national or social liberation." Candidates elected by the party
were to sit in a People's Assembly of
210 members. During the independence
festivities radio stations played "We Shall
Overcome" in Shangaan, the language of
a local tribe conquered and absorbed in
the 19th century by a Zulu general. In
South Africa the Shangaan were a major
tribe.

Machel, who had organized the initial
guerilla raids in Cabo Delgado in Sept.
1964, returned to Lourenco Marques for
the first time since then June 23 from his
headquarters in Tanzania.

At the airport, Machel was met by
Marcelino dos Santos, the Frelimo vice
president, and Prime Minister Joaquim
Chissano. Among the guests gathered to
welcome Machel were official representatives of Great Britain, China and the
Soviet Union. The U.S., West Germany,
Japan, France and Italy were not invited
to the celebration.

Mozambique was admitted to member-
ship in the Organization of African Unity
July 18 and to membership in the U.N.
General Assembly Sept. 16.

Sao Tome e Principe free. The two
small islands of Sao Tome and Principe,
150 miles off the west coast of Africa in
the Gulf of Guinea, became independent
July 12, 1975 after nearly 500 years of
Portuguese rule. The Democratic Republic of Sao Tome e Principe—with a
total area of 372 square miles, a population of 76,000 and a main crop of
cocoa—became the fourth independent

country to emerge from the decolonization of Portugal's African territories.

Manuel Pinto de Costa, an East Berlin-
trained economist who had headed the
Gabon-based Movement for the Liberation of Sao Tome e Principe, was proclaimed the country's first president,
having been unanimously elected head of
state July 10 by the movement's political
bureau.

The last Portuguese troops left the islands July 11, leaving most of their equipment behind for the new armed force of
150 local soldiers.

Sao Tome e Principe became independent under an agreement reached in
Algiers in 1974 by Antonio de Almeida
Santos, then Portugal's overseas territories minister, and Miguel Trouvoado,
a leader of the islands' liberation movement.

The new nation was admitted to membership in the Organization of African
Unity July 18, 1975 and in the U.N. General Assembly Sept. 16.

Cape Verde independent. Cape Verde
Islands became independent July 5, 1975
after 515 years of Portuguese rule over
the impoverished Atlantic archipelago,
400 miles east of the African horn.

Over 80% of the islands' 130,000 eligible voters had participated in the
election of Cape Verde's first National
Assembly June 30. All of the 56 members
elected represented the African Party for
the Independence of Guinea-Bissau and
the Cape Verde Islands (PAIGC), the
only political group that presented candidates. The PAIGC had fought for the independence of both territories and favored
the union of the islands with Guinea-
Bissau, independent since September
1974.

Meeting in the capital July 4, the newly-
elected National Assembly chose Aristides Pereira president and Maj. Pedro
Pires premier of the archipelago. Pereira
was secretary-general of the PAIGC and
Pires was the party's Cape Verde committee chairman. Both men were natives of
the islands.

(The U.S. Agency for International Development signed a $5 million assistance
agreement with the new government, it

was reported June 30. The archipelago,
now in its eighth year of drought, would
receive $2 million in food aid and $3
million in development aid.)

Cape Verde was admitted to member-
ship in the Organization of African Unity
July 18 and in the U.N. General Assembly
Sept. 16.

China refuses to take Macao. Western
diplomats in Washington told the New
York Times March 31, 1975 that Portugal's military leaders had attempted to
give the enclave of Macao back to China,
but Peking had said it did not wish to alter
the status of the territory.

The Portuguese Overseas Territories
Ministry denied the report April 1, asserting Portugal had held talks with China
about Macao but it had not asked Peking
to take over the colony.

Macao, a small enclave on the south
coast of China about 40 miles from Hong
Kong, had a virtually all-Chinese popu-
lation of 300,000. Although it belonged to
Portugal, it functioned in practice as a
Chinese dependency. The Peking govern-
ment had proclaimed Macao a "part of
Chinese territory" in 1972.

Rivals claim Timor rule. The Revolutionary Front for Independent East Timor
(Fretelin) unilaterally declared the Portuguese colonly independent Nov. 28, 1975
and renamed the area the People's Democratic Republic of East Timor. Fretelin's
action was countered Nov. 29 by four
rival political groups which claimed that
Timor was now part of Indonesia.

In marking the breakaway from
Lisbon, the flag of Portugal was lowered
in ceremonies held in the center of the
capital city of Dili and a new banner
representing the republic was raised.
Fretelin military commander Rogerio
Lobato said Portugal's "constant stall-
ing" on peace negotiations while Indonesia's forces continued military action
had contributed to the independence decision.

Francisco Xavier do Amoral was sworn
in as president of the republic Nov. 29.

Fretelin said 49 Afro-Asian countries
had pledged to back East Timor's right to

independence. Tanzania, Mozambique and Guinea-Bissau had also promised to campaign to have the next United Nations General Assembly recognize Fretelin as the sole legitimate representative of the East Timorese people, it was said.

Jakarta radio announced Nov. 29 that the Timor Democratic Union (UDT), the People's Democratic Association of Timor (Apodeti) and two other groups had branded Fretelin's declaration of independence a violation of an agreement between Indonesia and Portugal. Since there was no legal government exercising authority over the territory, "we declare that Portuguese Timor is part of the territory of the Republic of Indonesia," the four parties said. The pronouncement was contained in a statement signed by their leaders at Balibo, 40 miles southwest of Dili.

The UDT, Apodeti and the two other pro-Indonesian parties had called on Portugal Nov. 21 to set a specific date for talks to end the civil strife and to find a solution to determine the territory's political future. The proposal had followed a meeting in Rome Nov. 2–3 between Foreign Minister Malik and Portuguese Foreign Minister Ernesto Nelo Antunes, in which both men agreed to an early conference of all political groups on the island.

Portugal had conceded Aug. 21 that it had lost control of the situation in Timor. The admission came in a communique issued after a meeting of President Francisco da Costa Gomes, the heads of the armed forces, the foreign minister and a military mission from Timor. Portuguese officials on the island said "the situation is passing out of the control of the authorities" and appealed for international intervention to stop the fighting between Fretelin and UDT over the area's control and to remove the Portuguese and other nationals trapped by the war.

Several thousand persons had been evacuated from Timor to Australia and Macao, with the Portuguese nationals scheduled to go on to Lisbon. Among those to flee Aug. 27 were Gov. Lemos Pires and his staff.

Australian Prime Minister Gough Whitlam accused Portugal Sept. 21 of failing to take responsibility for ending the Timor fighting. He accused Lisbon of "just clearing out and dropping their bundle."

After more than two months of reported clashes between Fretelin and Indonesian forces in Portuguese Timor, Indonesian paratroopers and marines seized Dili Dec. 7 with virtually no resistance from Fretelin. Portugal immediately severed relations with Indonesia.

A Portuguese communique Dec. 7, announcing the decision to break relations with Indonesia, asserted that Jakarta's move had "brutally altered the process of decolonization" of the territory. Lisbon's failure to mount military counteraction, the statement said, was due to "a lack of means."

Portuguese Foreign Minister Ernesto de Melo Antunes, assailing Indonesia's move into East Timor as "armed aggression," declared Dec. 9 that Lisbon was still "the administrative power" there and demanded evacuation of Jakarta's forces.

An official Indonesian statement Dec. 7 said that Dili had been "liberated" that day "by the people's resistance spearheaded" by the forces of the four anti-Fretelin groups. The attacks against the capital, the statement said, "were this time assisted by Indonesian volunteers," said by Jakarta to number about 1,000 men.

Fretelin foreign affairs spokesman Jose Ramos Horta said Dec. 8 that at least 500 persons, mostly women and children, had been killed in the assault on Dili the previous day. He said most of the fatalities were caused by shelling from about 20 Indonesian warships offshore and by 2,000 Indonesian marines who shot their way into the capital.

While Dili was being taken, other pro-Indonesian forces seized the northern coastal town of Maubere and fanned out across the entire 50-mile coastal flank between the capital and the Indonesian border on the island, the Indonesian Antara news agency reported Dec. 8. Fretelin soldiers retreated to the hills south of Dili.

Indonesian Foreign Minister Adam Malik disclosed Dec. 18 that a provisional government had been established in East Timor by the Timorese Democratic Union (UDT), Apodeti, Kota and Trabalista parties.

The U.N. Security Council Dec. 22 approved by 15-0 a resolution calling on Indonesia to remove its military forces from Portuguese Timor. The document also urged adoption of measures giving the people of the territory the right to self-determination.

Malik asserted April 17, 1976 that peace had been restored in East Timor and that the provisional government was in control.

Angola: Independence & rival regimes. Angola's rival liberation movements proclaimed two distinct governments in the wartorn nation Nov. 11, 1975 as Portugal granted independence to its final African colony.

In ceremonies in Luanda Nov. 10, Vice Adm. Leonel Cardoso, the last Portuguese high commissioner in Angola, announced the transfer of sovereignty to "the Angolan people," indicating that Portugal was not yet recognizing the authority of any of the nationalist movements, still waging battle throughout Angola.

Shortly after midnight Nov. 11 the Popular Movement for the Liberation of Angola (MPLA) proclaimed its leader, Agostinho Neto, president of the People's Republic of Angola. The proclamation and subsequent celebrations were conducted in Luanda, the Angolan capital and stronghold of the MPLA which also controlled the band of territory across the middle of the nation.

Hours later in Nova Lisboa, the joint formation of the People's Democratic Republic of Angola was announced by the National Front for the Liberation of Angola (FNLA) and the National Union for the Total Independence of Angola (Unita). The two movements had agreed in Kinshasa, Zaire Nov. 10 to form a joint government headed by a 24-member National Revolutionary Council. Unita leader Jonas Savimbi presided over the ceremonies in Nova Lisboa, Angola's second largest city and Unita stronghold, which thereupon reverted to its indigenous name of Huambo, used before 1925.

FNLA leader Holden Roberto headed independence observances on behalf of the joint government in Ambriz, a Front stronghold 75 miles north of Luanda. Other ceremonies for the People's Democratic Republic of Angola were held in Carmona, another FNLA center, 170 miles northeast of the capital.

The Luanda government of the Soviet-backed MPLA was promptly recognized Nov. 11 by the former Portuguese colonies of Mozambique, Guinea-Bissau, Cape Verde and Sao Tome e Principe. Other nations recognizing the MPLA regime that day were: the U.S.S.R., the Congo Republic, Cuba, Guinea, Algeria, Brazil, Hungary, Poland, Rumania, Bulgaria, Czechoslovakia, East Germany, Mali, Mauritania and Mongolia.

The U.S. and other Western nations withheld recognition of either regime. In denying U.S. recognition, U.S. Secretary of State Henry A. Kissinger charged Nov. 11 that the MPLA was using Cuban as well as Soviet arms; he further stated that Havana's involvement in Angola was one of the reasons for Washington's delaying improvement in relations with Cuba.

(The U.S. consul, Thomas Kilhoran, and his staff left Angloa Nov. 3, advising all U.S. nationals to quit the territory as well.

(In another U.S. development, Central Intelligence Agency Director William E. Colby Nov. 6 defended the supply of covert U.S. aid to Angola, asserting that the U.S. interest there was one of general need to prevent a new country from falling under Soviet domination. His remarks, made to a closed session of the Senate Foreign Relations Committee in Washington, were cited by a senator present at the hearing.)

Among major developments of the year that preceded Angola's achievement of independence:

Referendum dropped—Portuguese Secretary of State for Foreign Affairs Fernando Falcoa had said Oct. 7, 1974 that a plan for a referendum in Angola in two years had been abandoned following the resignation Sept. 30 of Portuguese Provisional President Antonio de Spinola.

FNLA President Holden Roberto announced Oct. 12 that the FNLA had agreed to suspend hostilities in Angola, effective Oct. 15. The announcement followed two days of talks with Portuguese officials in Kinshasa, Zaire where FNLA headquarters were located. The FNLA was the last of Angola's three liberation movements to agree to a halt in fighting.

The FNLA, MPLA and Unita signed a political agreement in Mombasa, Kenya Jan. 5, 1975 as a step toward independence talks with Portugal. The MPLA and FNLA simultaneously signed a separate "peace" communique.

Pledging cooperation "in all spheres," the delegations agreed upon "a common political platform" on the formation of a transitional government, the role of armed forces in Angola and creation and installation of future institutions. With respect to Cabinda, the groups declared it "an integral and inalienable part of Angola," rejecting independence demands voiced by a secessionist group in the exclave.

Independence pact—After decolonization talks beginning in Alvor, Portugal Jan. 10, 1975, Portugal and the three major Angolan liberation movements—FNLA, MPLA and Unita—signed an agreement Jan. 15 under which Nov. 11 was set as the date of Angola's independence.

The independence accord was hailed by Portuguese President Francisco da Costa Gomes as "a fundamental step in the decolonization process generously conceived by the men of the armed forces in the clandestine nights that preceded the revolution of April 25," a reference to the military coup that toppled the regime of Marcello Caetano.

Under the terms of the agreement:

■ A transitional government, headed by a Portuguese high commissioner, would hold general elections for a constituent assembly before November. The assembly would elect a president who would formally accept sovereignty from the Portuguese.

■ A 12-ministry cabinet, carefully balanced with members of the three liberation movements and also representatives of Angola's white minority, would be created.

■ An armed forces plan was devised under which each movement would provide a contingent of 8,000 men to an Angolan national army; Portugal would match the total, furnishing 24,000 troops. All Portuguese forces were to leave Angola by February 1976.

■ A 10-member National Defense Council, headed by the high commissioner, would be responsible for defense and internal security and would oversee the military aspects of the agreement.

A transitional regime was sworn into office in Luanda Jan. 31 by Portuguese Minister for Overseas Territories Antonio de Almeida Santos.

Brig. Gen. Antonio da Silva Cardosa was installed as Portuguese high commissioner of Angola Jan. 28, replacing Adm. Antonio Rosa Coutinho who had been deemed "undesirable" by two of the territory's liberation movements.

Before long, however, fighting broke out again between the FNLA and MPLA.

(The MPLA, headed by Dr. Agostinho Neto, was a Marxist-oriented organization with strongest support among Angolan intellectuals and in the slums surrounding Luanda. The main group with which it was feuding, the FNLA, headed by Holden Roberto, was supported by the Bakongo tribe in north-western Angola. It drew substantial support, too, from the government of Zaire and was considered pro-western. The third movement, the National Union for the Independence of Angola [Unita], led by Dr. Jonas Savimbi, had been the smallest movement, but, in light of the continuing MPLA-FNLA conflict, was of growing political significance and strength. Its support was based chiefly in the central and eastern Angolan plateau, particularly among Umbundu-speaking tribal groups.)

Lisbon declares martial law—The Portuguese Defense Department May 15 issued a communique declaring Portuguese troops "totally responsible for security" in Angola, a decree tantamount to martial law. The announcement followed weeks of bloodshed and violence that left from 500 to 1,000 people dead in the fighting.

The May 15 declaration also directed the disarming of civilians in Angola, banned heavy weapons, called for an end to "private justice," ordered the "immediate expulsion of all foreigners in the service of the three liberation movements," and decreed that offenses committed "by any of the three movements" could be tried by ad hoc military tribunals.

Upon his return to Lisbon May 15 from a visit May 13–14 to Angola, Portuguese Foreign Minister Ernesto de Melo Antunes warned that there remained a danger of generalized war in Angola, which could prompt foreign intervention.

A peace accord was signed by FNLA leader Roberto, MPLA leader Neto and Unita leader Savimbi June 21 after six days of talks in Nakuru, Kenya, but fighting again erupted before long.

FNLA & Unita quit government. The FNLA and Unita withdrew from the transitional coalition government Aug. 9.

The FNLA and Unita withdrawals from the government left Angola virtually ungoverned, the FNLA having earlier begun boycotting cabinet meetings and other government functions having practically collapsed. Luanda radio Aug. 11 reported the situation in the strife-torn territory as "extremely confused" and, according to an Aug. 10 report, the capital was in particularly dire straits, with public services at a standstill, food shortages rampant and gasoline supplies nearly depleted.

Portugal Aug. 1 sent a high-level military delegation to Luanda to conduct a three-day inquiry into the situation in Angola. The mission comprised Army Commander-in-Chief Gen. Carlos Fabiao, Rear Adm. Antonio Rosa Coutinho, who was high commissioner in Angola until January 1975, and Maj. Jose de Canto e Castro.

Refugees flee southward, crowd cities— Refugees from the fighting throughout Angola were reported fleeing to cities in the south, which had until recently been considered safer than other regions, and crossing the border into South-West Africa as warfare intensified and conditions continued to deteriorate in the territory July 30–Aug. 11.

Refugees began pouring into South-West Africa (Namibia) in late July at the rate of 100–200 a week, it was reported July 30 and several thousands had crossed the border by Aug. 11. South-West African authorities established a tent village in Ovamboland, near the town of Oshakati, Aug. 4 to house 2,000 refugees. Officials there confiscated weapons from the fleeing settlers. South Africa, which administered South-West Africa, said Aug. 4 it would follow a flexible approach to the refugee problem and stated that it regarded the Angolans as transients en route to other destinations.

Nova Lisboa, like Luanda, had become a mecca for fleeing settlers seeking to leave the territory, with more than 22,000 refugees housed in unsanitary facilities, according to an Aug. 5 report.

Other cities beset with growing refugee problems included Lobito, to which 2,000 evacuees from Porto Amboim and Novo Redondo had been brought by Portuguese troops July 31, and Benguela, which, according to an Aug. 9 report, was housing 6,000 refugees.

Portuguese refugee airlift—Portugal Aug. 2 announced plans for an emergency airlift operation to evacuate all 250,000–300,000 Portuguese refugees from war-racked Angola before the territory acceded to independence Nov. 11. Airlift flights from Luanda to Lisbon began Aug. 4 and flights from Nova Lisboa, Angola's second largest city, began Aug. 10.

Lt. Col. Fernando Cardoso Amaral, head of Portugal's newly created relief agency, said Aug. 11 that Lisbon "can't abandon the Portuguese in Angola. It's our duty to get them out quickly."

(According to an Aug. 10 report, approximately one-third of the 450,000 white Portuguese settlers in Angola had already fled the territory by commercial airline flights or by land or sea, before the airlift began. The Washington Post reported Aug. 4 that, since 1961, as many as 1.5 million blacks had fled Angola as well.)

The U.S. State Department Sept. 2 offered two chartered planes to help in the evacuation of refugees from Angola following an "urgent appeal" Aug. 27 from Portuguese President Francisco da Costa Gomes. The flights began Sept. 7.

The $5 million cost of chartering the civilian aircraft by the Military Aircraft Command was paid for from disaster relief funds and was provided without conditions, a department spokesman said.

(The New York Times had reported Aug. 26 that Washington was seeking to link the granting of evacuation assistance to guarantees of political changes in the Lisbon government.)

France and Great Britain Aug. 28 had offered to provide one plane each to assist in the evacuation program. Switzerland continued to participate in the airlift.

Portuguese again in control—Portugal resumed administrative control of war-ravaged Angola Aug. 14, acting "in the absence of any functioning government" in the territory.

Announcing the Aug. 14 decision, Portugal's acting high commissioner in Angola, Gen. Fereira do Macedo, said the action was consistent with the provisions of the Alvor agreement, under which the four parties had agreed to an interim regime until independence. In taking administrative powers in the name of Portugal, Fereira do Macedo effectively dissolved the interim government. The remaining ministers, he said, would have to confine their activities to routine matters.

Portugal Aug. 29 "temporarily suspended" the Alvor agreement.

Adm. Leonel Cardoso was named high commissioner for Angola Aug. 28 and had, according to a Sept. 3 report, been vested with full governmental powers, including legislative powers. Absent ministers who had served in the transitional government were replaced by Lisbon with directors general in an effort to maintain official business and services.

Portuguese President Francisco da Costa Gomes Sept. 3 issued a stern warning to Angola's three rival liberation movements that Lisbon would declare a state of siege in the territory if they did not desist from "interfering with

Portuguese sovereignty before the proclamation of independence."

The High Commission in Luanda and the Lisbon Decolonization Committee announced that day that Portugal would maintain until the territory's independence the 24,000-man troop force level it presently had stationed in Angola, thus reversing the process of gradual withdrawal of army units from the interior to the coast.

Kissinger warns vs. intervention—U.S. Secretary of State Henry Kissinger Sept. 23 warned non-African nations against interfering in Angolan affairs, declaring, "We are most alarmed at the interference of extracontinental powers, who do not wish Africa well, and whose involvement is inconsistent with the promise of true independence." He made the statement in an address to representatives of African nations in New York.

Covert U.S. & other aid reported—Huge sums of money were reportedly being funneled into Angola by the U.S., China and the Soviet Union, according to Washington sources cited in a New York Times article by Leslie Gelb Sept. 24.

The covert financial operations by the U.S. Central Intelligence Agency were being conducted with the approval of President Gerald Ford and the knowledge, as prescribed by law, of several congressional committees, the Washington sources said.

CIA assistance had been responsible, the sources asserted, for the resurgence of FNLA leader Holden Roberto. Roberto had been sponsored and supported with U.S. money and arms between 1962 and 1969, but had been "deactivated" thereafter. Recent support and aid from the U.S. had enabled Roberto to challenge the Marxist MPLA, which was reported to be backed by pro-Communist elements in the Lisbon government.

The sources said the U.S. was maintaining its aid to the FNLA, despite the overwhelming ascendancey of the MPLA forces in Angola, in an effort to demonstrate its support for Zaire President Mobutu Sese Seko, who backed the FNLA. (Roberto was Mobutu's brother-in-law, and Mobutu was believed to be considering a takeover of the oil-rich Angolan enclave of Cabinda, if the Communists won control in Angola.)

China, too, was providing financial and military aid to the FNLA, according to the article.

Soviet aid was allegedly in excess of U.S. aid and reportedly had included several direct shipments of arms to the MPLA as well as transhipments through the Congo Republic and materiel delivered on Yugoslav and East German vessels. The arms supplied were said to have included AK-47 assault rifles, the standard weapon of Soviet bloc armies, and Degtyarev light machine guns.

Unidentified sources in Lusaka, Zambia claimed Oct. 23 that Cuban mercenaries were fighting alongside MPLA forces in Angola, the London Times reported. About 1,500 Cuban troops were alleged to be in Angola or en route from the Congo Republic where Cuban ships had reportedly docked in late September and early October.

Cuba refuels in Azores for Angola. Despite objections of the Portuguese government, Cuba was using the Azores Islands to refuel aircraft carrying soldiers and arms to Angola, the war-torn former Portuguese territory in Africa it was reported Jan. 18, 1976.

Portugal was officially neutral in the Angolan fighting, although some government sectors led by the foreign minister, Maj. Ernesto de Melo Antunes, supported the Popular Movement for the Liberation of Angola (MPLA), which was also backed by the Soviet Union and Cuba.

Cuban planes had refueled on Santa Maria Island in the Azores Dec. 20–30, 1975, but Portugal had subsequently barred Cuban stopovers there. The stopovers resumed Jan. 10 and continued Jan. 15 despite formal objections made by Portugal to the Cuban ambassador in Lisbon Jan. 13, according to reports.

The U.S. State Department said Jan. 19 that it had made strong protests against Cuban refueling in the Azores. The U.S. supported the MPLA's opponents, the National Front for the Liberation of Angola

and the National Union for the Total Independence of Angola.

Portuguese government sources in Lisbon said Jan. 28 that Cuba had ceased to use the Azores as a stopover for the flights. The Portuguese government had expressed its "displeasure" to the U.S. ambassador in Lisbon Jan. 23 over a state department announcement that the U.S. had been exerting pressure on Portugal to halt the Cuban refueling in the Atlantic islands.

A Canadian foreign ministry spokesman said Jan. 30 that Ottawa had barred Havana from using Gander International Airport in Newfoundland as a refueling point for its troop flights to Angola. The warning was sent to Cuba after Cuban aircraft twice had stopped at the airport en route to Angola, prompting a Jan. 23 protest from the U.S.

In another development Jan. 22, Portugal resumed its airlift to evacuate refugees from Angola. The refugees included thousands who had escaped to Zaire and South-West Africa, and several thousand more who were stranded at Sa da Bandeira in southern Angola, according to officials in Lisbon.

Meanwhile, the head of Portugal's refugee agency, Maj. Fernando Cardoso Amaral, said the nation could not absorb the 350,000 refugees already in Portugal unless their relatives and friends helped out. There were 20,000 refugees in Portuguese hotels or boarding houses who had no relatives or friends or who had been "put out in the street," Cardoso Amaral said.

Lisbon & others recognize MPLA regime. Portugal Feb. 22, 1976 recognized the government formed by the MPLA in Angola. This action was taken during an all-night cabinet meeting called after the Luanda regime Feb. 21 suspended the visas of those Angolans who had gone to Portugal and now wanted to return to Angola. The MPLA's action was seen as an expression of impatience with Lisbon over the delay in extending recognition.

The establishment of diplomatic relations was favored at the cabinet meeting by the majority Socialist Party, which had previously opposed recognition, and the Communist Party. The Popular Democratic Party, Portugal's second largest, maintained its opposition to the move.

Other Western nations extending recognition to the MPLA government included: Norway, Sweden, Switzerland and Canada Feb. 18; Austria Feb. 19; Finland Feb. 20; Mexico Feb. 21; Peru Feb. 23; and Spain Feb. 25. Japan established diplomatic relations Feb. 19, and Zaire, in a distinct policy reversal, did so Feb. 28.

Other African nations which recognized the MPLA government included: Liberia, Mauritania, Egypt and Morocco Feb. 13; Tunisia Feb. 14; Lesotho and Malawi Feb. 17; and Swaziland Feb. 23. Recognition was also extended by Kuwait and Pakistan Feb. 23 and by Malta Feb. 17.

In a related development, Zambia Feb. 18 refused to recognize the MPLA regime and reiterated its support for a political settlement amongst the rival Angolan movements.

Portuguese properties nationalized— President Agostinho Neto announced May 3 that Angola had adopted a law that allowed the confiscation of economic assets abandoned by Portuguese settlers when they fled.

The Financial Times of London reported that day that the so-called May Day law exempted Portuguese state-owned interests in Angola. Because Lisbon in March 1975 had nationalized most major industries, state-owned enterprises represented the greater part of Portuguese assets in the former colony.

Among 19 nationalizations reported May 6 were the takeovers of the Cuca brewery, the Textang textile group, three sugar companies, a cement plant and the Champalimaud group's steelworks. In each case, the government made specific charges to justify the confiscation. Cited were the flight of the Portuguese owners and technicans, their theft or misappropriation of company funds and/or the strategic importance of the industry to the national economy.

Angola severs ties with Portugal—The government of Angola May 19 severed diplomatic relations with Portugal and ordered Lisbon's representatives to leave the country immediately. Angola had closed its own offices in Portugal and had suspended all visas for Portuguese citizens April 26 during a series of complaints and generally deteriorating relations.

(Lisbon and Luanda had not exchanged ambassadors; diplomatic relations had been conducted through Portugal's charge d'affaires and through Angolan officials in the former mother country.)

Speaking in Lubango in southern Angola May 19, President Neto said that much of the blame for the strained relations lay with Angolan refugees in Portugal. Specific charges were contained in an April 26 diplomatic note to Lisbon. Cited were the April 22 bombing of Luanda's consulate in the northern Portuguese city of Oporto, the bombing of the Cuban embassy in Lisbon and Portuguese press coverage of a visit by a leader of the rival National Front for the Liberation of Angola (FNLA), the movement defeated by the MPLA in the Angolan civil war.

Power Struggle

Military Seek Continued Rule

Following the defeat of the leftist effort to seize power in November 1975, Portugal's military leaders suggested that the country needed several more years of military rule before it could be turned over to a civilian government. The proposal and its rejection by political party leaders set the stage for the next act in the power struggle that characterized Portugal's mid-1970s revolution.

New party accord planned. The Supreme Revolutionary Council Dec. 12, 1975 revealed its intention to renegotiate with the country's major political parties an agreement, reached in April, by which they accepted military rule for at least three years. It gave the parties until the end of the month to submit proposals.

Instead of being described in the usual way as "the motor" of the revolution, the armed forces were called the "final authority" in the nation's move to "democracy and socialism." The national radio said the new agreement would "reduce the degree of military intervention in politics." The council also promulgated a law asking for "cohesion and discipline" from the armed forces.

Military rule proposal scored. A proposal by the Supreme Revolutionary Council for continued military rule until 1980 was submitted to the five major political parties Jan. 13, 1976 and was denounced by three of the parties Jan. 18.

The Council's proposal had been drafted by five Council members under the leadership of Maj. Ernesto de Melo Antunes, the foreign minister and reputed leader of moderate socialists in the military. The parties had submitted suggestions for the new accord, but the Council had all but ignored them, according to party sources.

The Council's text would allow the election of a president by popular vote, but candidates would probably be limited to military officers since the president would head the Council and the armed forces, the Washington Post noted Jan. 18. The Council would remain responsible for its own organization, composition and functioning; it would have the right to veto legislation involving economic, financial and social policy, the limits of state, collective and private property, national defense, foreign policy and the regulation of political associations; and the right to dissolve the legislature if it consistently rejected the Council's recommendations.

A legislature would be elected April 25 if the armed forces and political parties agreed on a new pact in time for the Constituent Assembly to finish writing a new constitution. The campaign for the elections officially began Jan. 16.

The Council's draft was denounced Jan. 18 by Jorge Miranda, a leader of the centrist Popular Democratic Party (PPD), who charged the armed forces were assigning themselves more power than they now had. Mario Soares, the Socialist leader, asserted: "The new proposal is antidemocratic and consecrates military guardianship over our political life." Sources of the conservative Social Democratic Center (CDS) also critized the Council's draft.

(CDS leader Diogo Freitas do Amaral had denounced the provisional government Jan. 13, accusing it of endangering democracy and creating an "economic disaster." Freitas do Amaral criticized the PPD, Socialists and Communists for fighting among themselves and for being, as parties represented in the government, partly responsible for the economic crisis.)

Cabinet appointments. Premier Jose Pinheiro de Azevedo named Rui Machete of the Popular Democratic Party as social affairs minister Jan. 2, 1976. Agreement on other cabinet changes was reached Jan. 6 and announced that day by Pinheiro de Azevedo.

The Communist Party was to keep the post of secretary of state for agrarian organization but would replace Antonio Bica, the present occupant, with someone else. The post of secretary of state for the Treasury would continue to be held by Antonio Santos Silva, who had resigned from the Popular Democratic Party, and the PPD would be given the portfolio of secretary of finance in exchange. No secretary of tourism was to be appointed.

President Gen. Francisco da Costa Gomes swore in Jan. 6 Col. Jose Augusto Fernandes as head of the ministry of transport and communications and Walter Rosa, a Socialist, to run the ministry of industry and technology.

Spinola explains plans. Ex-President Antonio de Spinola said Jan. 3 in an interview with the Oporto newspaper Comercio do Porto that he would return to the country "peacefully only in the framework of the unification of efforts for the reconstruction of Portugal." He acknowledged leadership of the clandestine Democratic Movement for the Liberation of Portugal and said its goal was to create "the technical conditions for the functioning of democracy in Portugal" and not to seize power.

Carvalho seized in '75 plot. Former Gen. Otelo de Carvalho was arrested late Jan. 19 on charges of promoting the November 1975 leftist uprising.

Carvalho denied the charges, asserting he had not supported the revolt because he had "always been against any kind of adventures that open the way to the right wing." His arrest, he declared, was part of "an offensive of the right wing, which, little by little, will eliminate all obstacles that oppose it."

Also implicated in the revolt were the Communist Party, the Communist-dominated labor federation and several extreme leftist groups, according to a "preliminary" report by a military investigative commission, excerpts of which were broadcast by the national radio early Jan. 20. The Communists denounced the report Jan. 21, calling it right-wing propaganda.

The report said the Communists and their allies had organized the revolt in an attempt to regain the positions they had lost in the early fall of 1975, when moderate socialists took control of the Supreme Revolutionary Council and the provisional regime. Carvalho had helped prepare the revolt, according to the report, but he had not committed himself wholeheartedly to the operation once it began, thus contributing to its failure.

Carvalho was freed March 3.

Salazar aides freed—The government Jan. 21 released former air force commander Kaulza Oliveira de Arriaga and former Interior Minister Cesar Moreira

Baptista, the last two imprisoned aides of the late dictator Antonio Salazar.

The action signaled a marked change in policy by the provisional government since the abortive leftist coup attempt of November 1975, according to press reports. Many other supporters of Salazar had been released from prison since the abortive revolt, including ex-Adm. Henrique dos Santos Terneiro, Joaquim da Silva Cunha, the former defense minister; and Arnaldo Schultz and Alfredo dos Santos Junior, both former interior ministers, it was reported Jan. 23.

Violence

Shooting at prison. Three people were killed and 15 wounded Jan. 1, 1976 outside a prison in Oporto when paramilitary republican guards opened fire on a crowd in disputed circumstances. One of those wounded died later.

The incident took place while demonstrators were gathered near the prison gates to protest the continued detention of relatives held since the November 1975 attempted coup. News reports said several hundred demonstrators tried to rush the gates as they were opening to let out a prison vehicle and that guards fired into the air to warn them off. The protesters then began to stone the guards and, by some accounts, to return their fire, after which the guards shot into the crowd.

One of those killed was identified as Gunter Bruns, a West German student from Hamburg said to have been visiting a left-wing collective. Two of the others were Portuguese workers—Armenio Pereira da Silva and Celestino Rebelo Teixeira. Maria Teresa Metelo, the 70-year-old mother of Lieut. Col. Antonio Metelo, former deputy premier and one of those being held in the prison, was wounded, as was Metelo's 3-year-old daughter.

Although the London Times Jan. 2 said prisoners had been outside their cells receiving visits from relatives when the shooting took place, the civil governor's office issued a statement that day claiming

the inmates had opened their cells with the aid of prison employes and were getting ready to escape. The statement noted that the timing of events "allows one to presume the existence of a combined action." It absolved the guards of blame because they had acted "not only in legitimate defense but also to protect the security of the building."

The rector of the University of Oporto sent a message to President Gen. Francisco da Costa Gomes asking immediate punishment for those responsible for the shooting. A bomb was thrown from a passing car at the headquarters of the Republican Guard, causing minor damage to the entrance.

A statement released Jan. 3 by the armed forces general staff charged the demonstrators with having tried "to provoke" the guards with the object of "discrediting" prison authorities. It commented on the "aggressiveness" of the protesters and said "security forces were merely fulfilling their duty in defending the prison installations."

The Communist Party Jan. 3 denounced "the repressive acts" while appearing to disassociate itself from the attempt to enter the prison. The party communique warned against the dangers of "pseudo-revolutionary extreme-left provocation, artfully engineered by reactionaries" and "verbalistic radicalism or forms of struggle that do not suit the situation in which we are living." It called for unity within the Armed Forces Movement "so that it may continue as the military guarantee of our young democracy."

The Supreme Revolutionary Council declared Jan. 7 after an all-night meeting that it would draft laws to restrict the activities of foreigners, "many of whom are undesirable in their own countries." People were cautioned against being "used by political forces."

Communists under attack. Violence against Communists broke out in early January 1976.

Bomb attacks and anti-Communist violence took place around the country Jan. 7, beginning with an explosion in Provoa de Varzim near the home of Joaquim

Antonio Maria Moreira, a member of the Popular Democratic Movement. A bomb went off later that day in Oporto at the Arvore cooperative, from which the demonstration had been organized, and the Communist Party announced that "situations of coercion and reactionary violence" in Braga, Bragança, Guarda, Viseu and Leiria meant that its members and those of other leftist groups were "practically prevented from engaging in political activity."

At least 12 bombs exploded in the north Jan. 13–19, mostly at homes or businesses owned by Communists and other leftists. The blasts caused property damage but no casualties.

Four bombs exploded around Oporto early Jan. 13, damaging a bookshop, a dress shop and a parked automobile in the city and the residence of the Communist mayor in the suburb of Gondomar. A blast Jan. 15 damaged a cafe in Vila do Conde, 15 miles from Oporto, and explosions Jan. 19 damaged Communist headquarters in Viana do Castelo, the homes of leftists in Braganca and Santo Tirso, and four other sites.

Alvaro Cunhal, the Communist Party leader, asked Jan. 23 that the government take measures to end the recent wave of anti-Communist violence in the country. His action followed two bomb explosions earlier that day—one beneath the car of Jose Viana, a Communist who had publicly opposed the government, and the other at a youth center in Braga. He warned that the violence increased the threat of a right-wing coup and said the "free and democratic nature" of the elections planned for April 25 would be "gravely compromised." (Cunhal denounced Jan. 24 a decision made by the government the previous day to allow Portuguese living abroad to vote in the coming election. He said "falsifying" the result by changing the voting law would amount to a reactionary coup.)

Riot over wage freeze. A government-imposed wage freeze resulted in a riot in Lisbon in early 1976.

One person was shot dead and six were wounded Jan. 21 at Rossio Square in Lisbon when a riot broke out after leftist demonstrators, gathered to protest the wage freeze, tried to force a shop to close. Eyewitnesses said police and civilians exchanged gunfire when the crowd, which accused authorities of having pushed a pregnant woman, began throwing stones.

The Press

Newspapers reorganized. An administrative overhaul of Portugal's eight state-owned newspapers, whose management and editorial staffs were dismissed in November after the left-wing coup attempt, was completed Dec. 29, 1975 with the appearance of O Seculo, one of the nation's leading morning publications.

Both O Seculo and Diario de Noticias, the other principal morning newspaper, were expected to be more broadly pro-government than formerly. (The new editor of Diario de Noticias, Victor Cunha Rego, had once been a spokesman for the Socialist Party.)

A Supreme Revolutionary Council announcement of the reorganization Dec. 5 had said the move was being made to restore the "pluralism and objectivity" of the press. Newspapers were asked to conduct a "strict inquiry" into their financial situations to find ways of reducing an estimated $2 million weekly deficit paid for by the government.

In another move apparently intended to deprive the left of its control of the media, the government Dec. 3 nationalized television and nine of the country's private radio stations in order to promote "ideological pluralism." The only station not included in the take-over, Radio Renascenca, was given back to the Roman Catholic Church Dec. 29.

Republica ordered returned to owners. The Supreme Revolutionary Council ordered the Lisbon newspaper Republica returned to its Socialist owners Jan. 28, 1976, nine months after its offices were occupied by Communist and other radical printers.

The printers had first been ordered to

end the occupation in June 1975, but they had refused with the support of Gen. Otelo de Carvalho, then chief of security but since stripped of his post and rank.

Republica's editor in chief, Raul Rego, had founded a new paper, A Luta. He said Jan. 28 that the order to end the occupation was "a total victory—too bad it's six months late."

O Mundo starts publishing. The French monthly political review Le Monde Diplomatique launched a Portuguese edition, called O Mundo, selling out its first issue of 10,000 copies in Lisbon, it was reported Feb. 8. O Mundo's publication indicated a relaxation of press controls, according to the New York Times.

Economic Developments

Austerity program begun. The cabinet of Premier Jose Pinheiro de Azevedo made public Dec. 20, 1975 an austerity program designed to improve the country's economic situation.

Although few details of the program were released, news accounts said there would be increases of 20%–40% on "superficial and less essential" items, including automobiles. The cabinet announcement referred to a policy of "national reconstruction" supported by "voluntary and conscious acceptance of sacrifices" to avoid "greater privations and suffering in the future."

The cabinet said it planned to issue an internal loan of up to $741 million to cover an expected budgetary deficit for 1975. A foreign investment institute was to be established to provide "limits and guarantees" for investors.

Deficit budget for '76. The government Jan. 1, 1976 announced an austerity budget that showed projected expenditure for 1976 at 105 billion escudos (about $4.95 billion) with revenues estimated at $2.73 billion. Defense spending was greatly reduced.

According to a brief cabinet statement,

the main emphasis was to be on spending to create jobs, with large investments planned in public works, transport and communications. The military budget was to be cut from over $350 million in 1975 to about $78 million. Bus fares would increase one-third and television licenses were to go up 40%.

In a move to save energy, businesses were asked to turn off inside lights after working hours and outside ones by 10 P.M. Films and bullfights would end by 11:30 P.M.

A group of 13 labor unions issued a manifesto Jan. 6 opposing the increase in prices and urging workers to "resist the capitalist offensive." The unions complained that with every "day that goes by our wages are worth less."

After an all-night meeting the cabinet issued a statement Jan. 8 in which it said high food prices were "in large part not justified, although in some cases are inevitable." It said that maximum prices would be set for potatoes, meat, eggs, vegetables, fruit and fish and that wages would be pegged to the cost of essential items.

In a related development, the government confirmed Jan. 6 that it had recently sold four tons of gold on the international market, on an "exploratory" basis, valued at about $18 million. The country's gold reserves had been officially put at 800 tons.

Army manpower cut. Army Staff Chief Gen. Antonio Ramalho Eanes announced Jan. 23 that the army would reduce its manpower by 40% to 26,000 soldiers, reflecting Portugal's decreased defense needs following the liberation of its African territories.

The army had numbered 210,000 soldiers at the height of Lisbon's wars against liberation groups in the territories. Debts incurred in the purchase of military equipment during the wars insured that defense costs would continue to represent more than 20% of government expenditures despite the reduction in army personnel, the Financial Times of London reported Jan. 16.

Land Reform

Land seizures protested. Farmers in Rio Maior, 40 miles northeast of Lisbon, formed an association Dec. 14, 1975 and held a rally to protest the recent seizure of lands below the Tagus River by Communist-led groups. Army cavalry troops were used Oct. 27 to expel squatters and protect the holdings of a landowner at Azambuja in the central Ribatejo region.

Land reform curbed. Agriculture Minister Antonio Lopes Cardoso said Jan. 9, 1976 that the regime's program of land reform, which had drawn substantial opposition from farmers in recent months, would be limited and that some illegally occupied land would be returned to its rightful owners.

In his announcement, Lopes Cardoso said that farms of up to 75 acres would be left in the hands of their present owners and that 1.8 million of the 2.5 million acres seized for redistribution would be returned to their original owners because the land had been taken illegally. Future expropriations would take place only below the Tagus River in the southern districts of Setubal, Evora, Portalegre and Beja and parts of the central districts of Lisbon, Santarem and Castelo Branco. The new agrarian reform program was reported to have the support of the three parties in the government coalition—the Socialists, Popular Democrats and Communists.

At a Jan. 11 rally in Braga organized by the newly-formed Confederation of Portuguese Farmers, some 15,000 persons called on the government either to formulate within three weeks an agrarian reform policy in which farmers would have a voice or to prepare to face a tax revolt. Speakers denounced the "total incapacity" of the ministry of agriculture and branded Lopes Cardoso "a Communist infiltrated in the Socialist Party." They insisted on the end of all expropriation and the return of all occupied land. News

sources said the movement had the backing of the conservative Social Democratic Center and the Popular Monarchist Party.

Agrarian reform protests continue. Farmers led by the recently formed Confederation of Portuguese Farmers continued their protests against the agrarian reform law throughout January, demanding that the law be suspended, illegal land occupations be stopped and Lopes Cardoso be dismissed, and threatening to cut off Lisbon's food supplies if their demands were not met.

Leaders of the confederation met Jan. 30 with Premier Jose Pinheiro de Azevedo, who reportedly admitted that some of their grievances were justified but refused to suspend the agrarian reform law or fire Lopes Cardoso. The government issued a statement Jan. 31 defending the law but pledging to end "deviations" from it, specifically the illegal land occupations.

Some 16,000 farmers held rallies in five separate towns Feb. 1 to reiterate their demands. However, leaders of the confederation said they were "suspending all forms of struggle" until the Supreme Revolutionary Council of the Armed Forces Movement responded to the demands, thus abandoning an earlier threat to cut off the capital's food supplies if the demands were not met by Feb. 2.

The Revolutionary Council issued a statement Feb. 10 acknowledging that "errors" had been committed in the application of the agrarian reform law but asserting the mistakes were not the government's fault. Lopes Cardoso offered the farmers a compromise the same day, suggesting that expropriations for the rest of the current agricultural year be restricted to land not under cultivation. The minister had already offered a series of compromises, including one which would have excluded virtually the entire membership of the confederation—owners of small- and medium-sized properties in northern and central Portugal—from the agrarian reform program, according to the Financial Times of London. The farmers' refusal to accept the compromises had led to charges among leftists that their protests were part of a campaign to return Portugal to right-wing authoritarian rule, the Times reported.

International Relations

European loans. West Germany announced Feb. 4, 1976 that it would provide credits of $250 million to help strengthen the Portuguese economy. Switzerland and Norway pledged credits worth $50 million and $18 million the next day.

The loans reflected growing Western European support for Portugal since moderate socialists took control of the Armed Forces Movement and the provisional government from Communist-supported radical officers in August 1975. West German Foreign Minister Hans-Dietrich Genscher said Feb. 4, at the beginning of a two-day visit to Lisbon, that he was "pleased and deeply impressed" that the Portuguese people had prevented "with stubborn determination the installation of a new dictatorship."

West Germany earlier had promised Portugal $27 million in capital assistance, and the European Community (EC) had pledged $195 million in aid, press reports noted Feb. 5. Portuguese Foreign Minister Maj. Ernesto de Melo Antunes had toured Eastern and Western Europe recently in search of credits and trade agreements, visiting Hungary Jan. 12–14 and Czechoslovakia Jan. 14–16, and conferring with EC officials in Brussels Jan. 28. Portuguese External Trade Minister Jorge Campinos was in Belgrade Jan. 13 for the first meeting of a joint Yugoslav-Portuguese trade committee.

European Socialists meet in Oporto. The leaders of nine European Socialist and Social Democratic parties met March 13–14, 1976 in Oporto and endorsed a declaration that the primary threat to democracy in Portugal was no longer Communist subversion but a weakened economy. The conference was called by the Committee for the Friendship and Solidarity with Democracy and Socialism in Portugal, created in 1975 by the Socialist International to aid the Portuguese Socialist cause.

It was the third such meeting of European Socialists in 1976. Attending were four heads of state—Premiers Joop den Uyl of the Netherlands, Odvar Nordli of Norway and Olof Palme of Sweden, and Chancellor Bruno Kreisky of Austria—and five other national party leaders—Felipe Gonzalez of Spain, Francesco de Martino of Italy, Francois Mitterrand of France, Willy Brandt of West Germany and Mario Soares of the host country.

In their joint communique, the Socialist leaders pledged to impress upon their governments Portugal's need for economic aid. Mario Soares added an appeal to the European Community (EC) to ease its tariffs on his country's exports. He also asked the EC nations to extend to Portuguese immigrant workers the same social benefits accorded to their own citizens.

The meeting was denounced by both the Portuguese Communist Party and the liberal Popular Democrats as "intervention" in Portuguese affairs, it was reported March 15. The parties noted the proximity of the convocation of the conference to the national legislative elections scheduled for April 25, charging that the meeting was called to reinforce Socialist chances in the vote.

Autonomy Extended

Program for islands. The government said Dec. 13, 1976 that in accordance with "the just aspirations" of the people of Madeira and the Azores it was initiating a program to give the islands greater regional autonomy.

Until the Constituent Assembly could draft new constitutions for both places, "transitional" legislation would be enacted to bring about a "parallel" decentralization process. The decree set up the Madeira Agency for Regional Administration and Development, which was similar to one established earlier in the Azores.

Portuguese soldiers in the Azores had been put on the alert Oct. 16 following clashes the previous evening in Ponta Delgada, on Sao Miguel, with members of the separatist Azores Liberation Front (FLA).

The Front for the Liberation of the Madeira Archipelago (Flama) issued an ultimatum Sept. 11 calling on military commanders, politicians and bank managers to leave the island within a week or face "severe action" from Flama's "revolutionary brigades."

A public opinion poll in the Azores showed that only 18% of Azoreans favored the Lisbon government's plan to grant the islands autonomy with an elected assembly of deputies, it was reported Jan. 26, 1976.

Forty-five percent of those polled favored complete independence from Portugal, while 37% supported federal state status. The government's plan for autonomy was being written into Portugal's new constitution by the constituent assembly in Lisbon.

The government maintained that most Azoreans favored autonomy and that they had tolerated the FLA in 1975 because they were afraid of a Communist takeover in Lisbon, the New York Times reported Feb. 10. The FLA had recently increased its disruptive activities, according to the Times.

The separatists had sent an ultimatum at the end of December 1975 to the Azorean military commander, Gen. Altino Pinto de Magalhaes, telling him that soldiers were responsible for the killing of local cattle and threatening violent action if Pinto did not reveal the names of the guilty soldiers and punish them, the Times reported. On Jan. 28 the FLA organized a demonstration by several thousand persons at the airport to disrupt the arrival of the education minister, Maj. Vitor Alves, who flew in from Lisbon to inaugurate a university-level institute. The demonstrators, who waved the Azorean nationalist flag and sang the island's anthem, tried to hold Alves hostage but his plane rapidly took off for Lisbon.

Macao autonomy set. The Supreme Revolutionary Council approved a statute giving broad executive and legislative autonomy to Macao, the Portuguese enclave on the south China coast, it was announced Jan. 10, 1976.

Macao would continue to be ruled by a governor appointed in Lisbon, but it would be able to arrange foreign loans, make its own laws, appoint its own civil service and control its security force, according to Antonio Braz Teixeira, a jurist who helped draft the statute.

The governor would have wide executive powers and be assisted by a cabinet of up to five secretaries. There would be a consultative council including the secretaries, the chiefs of the civil and financial administrations and three persons representing the Chinese community, cultural interests and "moral" interests. The legislative assembly would have 17 members—six elected directly, six elected by interest groups and five appointed by the governor.

Macao functioned in practice as a dependency of China, from which it received food and water supplies. It served as an outlet for China's trade with the West, and as a free market for gold and a center for tourism and gambling. China claimed Macao as part of its territory, but neither Peking nor Macao's overwhelmingly Chinese population wanted the enclave to come under Chinese administration or become independent, according to press reports.

Constitution Adopted, Assembly Elected

New charter approved. The Constituent Assembly April 2, 1976 approved a radical new constitution, Portugal's first since the right-wing civilian dictatorship was overthrown in 1974. The charter was enacted April 25.

The document committed any future government to "socialist" policies that would enable "the working classes to exercise power democratically." It declared that education should promote a "classless society" and that political parties should participate in the "revolutionary process."

The constitution called for collective ownership of the principal means of production, land and natural resources, and it institutionalized the nationalizations of companies since the change of government in 1974. Guarantees were established for the right to strike and the rights of assembly and conscientious objection to serving in the armed forces. Censorship, torture and the death penalty were forbidden.

The constitution also committed Portugal to fight against all forms of imperialism, and it proclaimed the independence of East Timor although Portugal had not exercised power there for several months.

The new charter incorporated a pact between the military leadership and the major political parties which confirmed the change from a military-led revolution to a parliamentary democracy. The pact and the constitution itself would last until 1980, when the National Assembly would write a new charter.

Under the pact, signed in Lisbon Feb. 26, the armed forces' Revolutionary Council would relinquish its supreme powers and become an advisory body in all but defense matters. The council would be headed by the president, who could be a civilian or military officer, and would be composed of the armed forces' chief of staff and his deputy; the chiefs of staff of the army, navy and air force; the premier, if he was a military man; and eight officers delegated by the army, three by the navy and three by the air force.

The pact was promoted by moderate military officers and by the Socialist, Popular Democratic and Social Democratic Center (CDS) parties. It was opposed by the Communists and their supporters in the armed forces who believed the Revolutionary Council should remain in control of political decisionmaking.

The constitution itself was opposed by the Popular Democrats and the CDS. Both parties felt the charter's commitment to socialism would hamstring any future centrist or right-wing government.

Socialists win assembly elections. The Socialist Party won a plurality of the vote in elections for the National Assembly (parliament) April 25. They were the first free parliamentary elections in Portugal in half a century.

Final results of the balloting, announced April 27, gave the Socialists 34.97% of the vote to 24.03% for the centrist Popular Democratic Party (PPD), 15.91% for the conservative Social Democratic Center (CDS) and 14.56% for the Communist Party. The rest of the votes were divided among nine small parties, most of them on the extreme left.

The results entitled the Socialists to 107 representatives in the 265-seat assembly. The PPD won 73 seats, the CDS 42 and the Communists 40. One seat went to the leftist Popular Democratic Union, which won 1.69% of the assembly vote, and two other seats were undecided because of incomplete returns of overseas ballots.

The Socialists announced April 25 that they would form a minority government, and they resisted subsequent pressure for a coalition Cabinet from the Communists, the PPD and CDS. Socialist leader Mario Soares said April 30 that an alliance with any of the other parties would split the Socialist electorate.

The failure of any party to win a majority gave added importance to the presidential election scheduled for June 27. Under Portugal's new constitution, adopted by the Constituent Assembly April 2 and enacted April 25, the president was empowered to name the premier and his Cabinet, to veto legislation and to dissolve the National Assembly. He also would head the armed forces' Revolutionary Council (formerly the Supreme Revolutionary Council), which heretofore had held ultimate political power in Portugal.

The leading presidential contender was Gen. Antonio Ramalho Eanes, the army chief of staff, who confirmed his candidacy May 14. The other aspirants were Vice Adm. Jose Pinheiro de Azevedo, premier in the caretaker government, who confirmed his candidacy May 18; Octavio Pato, a member of the Communist Party's Central Committee, who also announced May 18; and Maria Vieira da Silva, a Trotskyist whose candidacy was reported May 12.

Gen. Ramalho was supported by the Socialists, the PPD and CDS. Mario Soares said May 12 that Ramalho alone could ensure the "cohesion and unity" of the armed forces as political power was returned to civilians. Soares said he had found support in the armed forces for a Socialist minority government, but he denied widespread reports that Ramalho had agreed to name such a government in exchange for Socialist endorsement of his presidential bid.

(Ramalho had urged Soares to run for president, but Soares had refused on grounds that he might be forced to yield leadership of his party to Agriculture Minister Antonio Lopes Cardoso, who headed the Socialist left wing, the Washington Post reported May 2. Ramalho had agreed to run only after the Socialists, the PPD and CDS agreed that as president he would not have to quit his army post.)

Pre-election violence—The vote for the National Assembly was preceded by widespread labor unrest and political violence in February, March and April.

The violence involved bombings, clashes between rival political groups and between police and demonstrators, and attacks on Communist Party headquarters in many cities and towns. At least six persons were killed and 44 injured in the strife.

The worst of the bombings occurred at the Cuban embassy in Lisbon April 22, killing two Cubans and injuring another four. A group calling itself the Portuguese Anticommunist Movement claimed responsibility for the attack April 23; the Cuban newspaper Granma April 24 blamed "fascist" Portuguese groups and the U.S. Central Intelligence Agency.

Other bombs were set off at the university in Oporto March 22; outside a CDS rally in Coimbra April 4; at Communist Party offices in Lisbon May 1, and under a radar tower at the Lisbon airport May 14. One person was killed and six injured in the Lisbon blast May 1.

In other violence: six persons were wounded when shooting broke out between Socialists and Communists at a Socialist rally in Benavila Feb. 22; two persons were wounded in a gun battle between Communists and Maoists in Lisbon March 27; and a farm worker was killed and 26 persons were injured during a night of rioting in Beja April 13–14. In addition, many persons were injured in the

"poster war" in which political militants, traveling armed teams fought for space for their campaign posters on city walls, it was reported April 20.

The labor unrest included strikes by leftist shopworkers in Lisbon Feb. 11, by oil refinery workers March 9 and by nurses throughout Portugal March 12–16.

Ramalho Eanes Elected President

Army chief wins 61.4% of vote. Gen. Antonio Ramalho Eanes, army chief of staff, was elected president of Portugal June 27, 1976 by a landslide victory.

Ramalho received 61.54% of the 4,885,-624 votes cast, according to final results announced June 28. His victory in Portugal's first free presidential election in half a century had been considered assured because of widespread support in the army and endorsements from the three largest political parties—the Socialists, Popular Democrats and Center Democrats.

The runner-up was Maj. Otelo de Carvalho, the former military governor of Lisbon, who received 16.52% of the vote. The other candidates were Premier José Pinheiro de Azevedo, with 14.36%, and Communist nominee Octavio Pato with 7.58%.

Pinheiro's campaign had been cut short June 23 when he suffered a severe heart attack while talking to newsmen in Oporto. His supporters asked the Supreme Court to postpone the election, but the court refused. Pinheiro's doctors said June 27 that he would recover but would be unable to participate in politics for six months.

(President Francisco da Costa Gomes June 24 named Interior Minister Vasco Almeida e Costa, a navy commander, to serve as interim premier.)

Ramalho Eanes pledged at a press conference June 28 to enforce "the laws of our young democracy" and "not tolerate parallel powers or any insurrectional activity contrary to the constitution." He specifically warned Communists and supporters of Carvalho against trying to undermine his regime.

A warning to secessionist movements in

Portugal's Atlantic archipelagos of Madeira and the Azores, accusing the movements of being antidemocratic, was issued by Ramalho. "These separatist groups will be easily neutralized with decisive action," he declared. (Regional elections in the islands June 27 gave a decisive victory to the Popular Democrats, who had supported broad autonomy for the islands and had been linked to the separatist movements.)

Ramalho said he would not order the rearrest of Carvalho, whose house arrest had been lifted in May to allow him to run for the presidency. Ramalho said the courts would decide whether to punish Carvalho further for his role in the abortive revolt by leftist military officers in November 1975.

Carvalho said June 27 that he and his "People's Power" movement would remain active politically despite their election defeat. The movement was considered a threat to the Communist Party, which it outpolled not only nationally but in the Communist strongholds of Beja, Evora and Portalegre in southern Portugal.

The presidential campaign was marked by sporadic violence and by bitter personal attacks among the candidates. One person was killed and 13 were injured June 17 when Communists clashed with supporters of Ramalho in Evora. The one death occurred when soldiers fired into a leftist crowd that was attacking Ramalho's automobile. Sixteen persons were injured June 5 when a bomb exploded in a Lisbon building that housed headquarters of the Portugal-Mozambique Friendship Association.

During the campaign both Carvalho and Pinheiro de Azevedo emphasized that Ramalho had not played a leading role in the April 1974 military coup, and implied that he might return the country to a rightwing dictatorship. Carvalho charged June 21 that Ramalho was a stalking-horse for ex-President Antonio de Spinola and that a Ramalho-led government would intensify class antagonisms, leading to violence.

Ramalho remained aloof, ignoring the charges and pledging to support national independence and democracy. However, many of his supporters shared his opponents' fear that Ramalho might impose an authoritarian government, according to the New York Times June 13. "We hope he is a democrat," said one Socialist quoted by the Times.

Ramalho's personal political beliefs were unclear. He had been army staff chief since November 1975, when he led troops in crushing an attempted leftist coup. Since then, Ramalho had purged leftist officers and assumed tighter control of the army, according to the Washington Post May 2. He had made no clear political statements, but had told a few sources that he was a "democratic socialist," the Post reported.

The candidacies of both Premier Pinheiro and Octavio Pato reportedly were responses by leftists to what they perceived as Ramalho's political conservatism. Pinheiro, who was considered more radical and popular than Ramalho, said May 18: "What is important for the president is his past, his personality, his capacity to get things done, his popularity." Pato pledged the same day to "inspire the confidence of the working masses."

Carvalho also attacked Pinheiro de Azevedo and his government. At a press conference May 29, two days after announcing his candidacy, Carvalho charged that the government had "allowed the return of the bosses and freed the agents of the old political police." He also denounced the U.S., "which interferes at all times in our domestic politics," and social democracy, "which doesn't defend anything but an advanced capitalist society."

Announcing his candidacy May 27, Carvalho stressed his role as an organizer of the 1974 coup. "I took the responsibility for causing the overthrow of the fascist regime which was oppressing the Portuguese people," he asserted. He also indicated that despite the parliamentary government established by the new constitution, he supported an alliance between the Portuguese people and the armed forces based on regional and local workers' and neighborhood councils.

Carvalho called for the "development and consolidation of the popular-power organizations, which must gradually take over day-by-day control." He also pledged to fight for national unity and independence and for solidarity with the world's oppressed people.

Ramalho Eanes campaigned on a moderate socialist platform, the Paris newspaper Le Monde reported June 4. He supported a vigorous public and nationalized sector of the economy but also recognized the role of private enterprise in "stimulating competition," Le Monde said. He vowed to protect small and medium-sized industries and to pursue an agrarian reform without "excesses."

Analyzing recent Portuguese political history, Ramalho, according to Le Monde, called the 1974 coup the "process of liberation which has made possible the revolutionary conquests of our people." In an indirect attack on Carvalho, he called the November 1975 leftist revolt "the end of 'putschism' and anarchy which would have returned us inevitably to misery and dictatorship," Le Monde said.

Carvalho implied May 27 that the revolt had been provoked by Ramalho and the officers who crushed it. "History will denounce November 25 as an enormous machination designed to deviate the revolutionary process from the line of purity imposed upon it by the working classes and generous and progressive military men," he said.

Index

143